Okanagan Univ / College Library

01898428

K

Accommodating Protest

HQ 1793 .Z9 C356 1991
Accommodating protest
Macleod, Arlene Elowe

189842

DATE DUE

MAR 2 1 1995	
APR - 4 1995	
APR 1 9 1995	
FEB 2 2 2001	
FEB 1 8 2002	
OCT - 9 2002	

BRODART

D1052602

OKANAGAN UNIVERSITY COLLEGE
LIBRARY
BRITISH COLUMBIA

Accommodating Protest

Working Women, the New Veiling, and Change in Cairo

ARLENE ELOWE MACLEOD

Columbia University Press
NEW YORK

Columbia University Press
New York   Chichester, West Sussex
Copyright © 1991 Columbia University Press
All rights reserved

Library of Congress Cataloging-in-Publication Data
Macleod, Arlene Elowe.
    Accommodating protest : working women, the new veiling, and change
in Cairo / Arlene Elowe Macleod.
        p.   cm.
    Includes bibliographical references (p.   ).
    Includes index.
    ISBN 0-231-07280-5
    ISBN 0-231-07281-3 (pbk.)
    1. Women, Muslim—Egypt—Cairo—Social conditions. 2. Women,
Muslim—Employment—Egypt—Cairo. 3. Working class women—Egypt—
Cairo. 4. Women, Muslim—Egypt—Cairo—Conduct of life. 5. Veils—
Social aspects—Egypt—Cairo. I. Title.
HQ1793.29.C35M33   1991
305.42′0962′16—dc20   90-2435
                                                                              CIP

∞

Casebound editions of Columbia University Press books are
printed on permanent and durable acid-free paper.

Printed in the United States of America

c 10 9 8 7 6 5 4 3 2 1
p 10 9 8 7 6 5 4 3 2 1

TO MY GRANDMOTHERS,

Clara Phinney Eaton
and
Warena Banny Elowe

CONTENTS

Contents

NOTE ON TRANSLITERATION

A simplified version of the system used by the International Journal of Middle East Studies has been used to render Arabic words. The j, for instance in *hajj* or *hijab*, has been rendered as a hard g to follow spoken Egyptian usage. Some names and places commonly known in their English forms have been retained, for example, Nasser. Common loanwords, as found in Webster's Third New International Dictionary, are also used in their English forms.

PREFACE

The situation of lower-middle-class women in Cairo who leave the home to work and at the same time advocate and adopt the new veil, the *higab*, is puzzling. Are these women supporting a return to traditional patterns of women's inequality by reviving this powerful symbol of women's subordination? Are they helping to reproduce the power relations which have constrained them in the past, despite the chance for change opened by the new experience of working outside the home?

This paradox of women seeming to support their own subordination, and even to reproduce it under new conditions, is part of the generally perplexing story of women's participation in the interactions of tradition and modernity, and the related renegotiations of power. The new veils present an especially dramatic picture of women's confusing struggles in a changing Cairo, yet such revivals of tradition are hardly limited to Cairo or even to the cities of the developing world. By examining the motivations and reasoning of lower-middle-class women through their own words, and observing the subcultural social and economic context that frames their decisions, I hope to tell the specific and very interesting story of working women and the new veils in lower-middle-class Cairo.

Indeed, it turns out to be a quite different story than first appears, for I argue that these women are involved in a struggle to create a new way to be a woman in a changing Cairo.

In this book, women's symbolic action of veiling is examined and found to be not reactionary behavior, but part of an ambiguous political struggle that I have called "accommodating protest." This characterization of women's style of political struggle helps account for the ambiguous pattern that emerges when one looks at the situation of women, who seem to both struggle in a conscious and active way against their inequality, yet who also seem to accept, and even support their own subordination. While this is a study of women in the encounters of change in Cairo, and while I emphasize the importance of locating women's struggles in the specific interactions of the gender, class, and global inequities of this subcultural setting, I think the results are suggestive for understanding women's contradictory role in relations of power elsewhere as well. The idea of accommodating protest captures the style of women's struggle in the ongoing negotiations of power and so provides a better foundation for basing our understanding of how "political space" is negotiated and inequalities either reproduced or fundamentally altered during times of social change and political opportunity.

The dramatic and controversial symbolism of the new veils thus offers the chance to explore the complicated interactions of tradition and modernity from women's perspective and ultimately provides the chance to capture the complex and often ambivalent ways in which women react to their inequality and try to struggle against it.

THE CASE STUDY

The arguments advanced in this book are based on a careful exploration of the experience of lower-middle-class women in Cairo, Egypt. As a major city in the developing world, Cairo offers a compelling place to attempt to capture the experience of the transition to modernity from women's perspective and to explore the part women play in perpetuating and altering relations of power. My initial impressions, as I flew over the city one night in September 1983, were a complicated mixture of elation at finally arriving in the field, awe at the spread of lights in the desert delineating the city's boundaries, and confusion as the taxi sped through the dark and nearly deserted streets; the glimpses of life I could see in occasional alleyways forced me to question my carefully contrived plans for entry into this society and wonder if I would ever complete this project. The Cairo I eventually came to know is an intense, exciting, and insistent presence, contributing to the actions of the women I was to meet in multiple ways.

The women I focused on, women of the lower-middle-class, are an especially interesting group; beneficiaries of government policies in economics and education, their expectations of mobility have been raised in recent years, but the benefits they have been encouraged to anticipate have slowed and even reversed in the last decade. These families exemplify well the optimistic hopes and the pessimistic realities of life in urban areas of the developing world. In addition, despite their importance, the middle-class has been relatively neglected in recent Egyptian and Middle Eastern studies; ethnographers have tended to focus on lower-class groups, whether traditional urbanites or villagers, and political scientists, on elites and state-level politics.[1] Yet the middle-class is a very important group, exemplifying the contradictions of modernizing life, and embodying the interesting tensions of transitional figures in the complicated movements of change.

The women of these families are particularly intriguing, adding the dimension of gender to class and global interactions. They find themselves in a predicament, caught between lower-class traditional standards which they only partially wish to abandon and upper-class Westernized standards they only partially wish to emulate; they live enmeshed in the confusing choices of modernizing Cairo. Their subcultural setting forms a dilemma for these women, and they seek a solution through the symbol of the *higab*.

The descriptions of women's lives in the pages that follow are based on detailed exploration of women's experience gained through field research conducted primarily through informal interviews and observation in traditional quarters of the city and in the government offices. The research involves a close association with 28 households, informal interviewing of about 85 women, including 58 working women, and additional, more systematic interviewing of 25 of the younger working women.[2] Further, I have been able to follow these families and women over a period of about five years;

the initial research was conducted from September 1983 to December 1984, and additions to the study were completed in February 1986, and in June and July 1988.

The small-scaled case study has many advantages for exploring the questions of power and change that I hoped to investigate. Since I primarily wished to understand perceptions and interactions from women's perspective, a methodology allowing women's own words to emerge was clearly necessary. Larger-scaled surveys, despite their advantages, have the great disadvantage of allowing only a limited form of information to emerge—conversations are structured in question-and-answer format decided in advance by the researcher, answers are altered by the power-laden setting of an interview, and discussion is necessarily more superficial. In crossing the boundaries of class and culture, these problems can be magnified. Perhaps a case study of some 85 women in a city of 12 million people has its limits in terms of narrowly defined standards of proof, but it allows exploration into women's own interpretations of the constraints and choices they face daily in a way not possible in large-scale surveys or formal interviewing sessions, and allows us to gain a different and deeper insight into the tensions and contradictions of women's position.[3]

I have attempted to provide the fine-grained information and the textured quality of women's experience which is only possible by sitting with, talking with, and living with these women on a day-to-day basis for many months. For example, I have been able to observe differences in expressed attitudes and actual behavior, or between attitudes offered at one time and in one context and those expressed at another time and place. The chance to observe as much as possible the everyday interactions of women in the family and in the workplace is invaluable for the questions I hoped to answer. I also had the extended opportunity to observe the reactions of these women to me, to the questions I was asking, and to my identity as a Western graduate student, wife, and, eventually, professor and mother. Especially as I made the transition from childless wife to mother in the course of the field research, women's interactions with me altered as well. I was able to gain new insight from this process.

The actual research consisted of informal interviewing and observing, in women's homes and mine, at women's workplaces, and while commuting or shopping in the city. Through informal contacts I met several women, who introduced me to their families, neighbors, and coworkers. In this way an ever expanding group of families entered into the context of this study, for the great hospitality of women and their families meant that insistent invitations were extended constantly. Eventually, however, the requirements of hospitality meant that I had to put a cap on the number of households, for it was impossible to make the expected and necessary visits to each home on a frequent basis. Women insisted that I visit with them often (a visit lasting anywhere from an hour to an entire day or overnight into the next), at least three times a week (daily was even better), and became upset and offended when I was not able to do so. In addition, I had decided not to focus on a particular neighborhood, since these women generally followed visiting patterns that traversed the city, and indeed they often did not know their neighbors at all.[4] This resulted in my spending considerable time commuting from house to house, or with women to and from work, cutting into the ability to visit many families in one day. Ultimately, I think this led to better quality information, since I developed the habit of spending whole days with women in their homes instead of stopping in and out, and as a result I came to be treated as an honorary "sister" in the homes of women I came to know especially well, and at least not as an honored guest in the others.

Eventually, I selected twenty-five of the younger women from the larger sample to concentrate on in a later stage of the research, with more systematic questioning, focused on work, the veil, and family-work interaction. I continued my visits with all the families but added these questioning sessions to the routine. This worked very well in some cases, sparking family discussions or leading to involved conversations about women's feelings; in other cases women were bored with this more obviously directed approach and cooperated only with my entreaties or promises of return favors. Yet, these two forms of information gathering worked well together, allowing women to help structure the questions initially and permitting more systematic questioning to occur after I had been able to observe what mattered most to women and their families.

Words and behavior, descriptions of events, furnishing of homes, interactions I observed, and anything that struck me as important were recorded in the form of field notes as soon as possible after the conversations took place; use of a tape recorder would, I felt, have restricted women's answers and changed the atmosphere, eliciting what women thought they should say, rather than what they really felt. I also tried to elicit information from a variety of sources by talking with women, with their mothers and sisters, with male family members, with neighbors and with colleagues at work. Over time, the contradictions that emerged between one person's account and another's and between attitudes and actual behavior proved to be at least as interesting as the more coherent, and perhaps less spontaneous, articulations I received initially.

The families I came to know in Cairo can be divided into households of two kinds, based on position in the life cycle, a distinction that becomes important as the impact of social change affects these households in different ways. First, there are the older families with parents in their forties and fifties and children ranging in age from their early teens to their mid-thirties. These families generally live in central and traditional areas in Cairo, such as Sayyida Zeinab or Old Cairo. Families in these more established households began renting their flats when the parents married some twenty or thirty years ago. Due to rent control, their monthly payments are generally low, averaging about £E 5–7. These are large families, usually counting five to ten living children. The unmarried children continue to live at home and often some of the grandchildren live there as well, for at least part of the week. The mothers are usually uneducated and work only in the home, leaving the rooms only occasionally to shop or visit. The fathers generally hold jobs as laborers on construction sites or as mechanics or drivers; several are absent, working off in the Gulf states. Current household incomes vary widely, depending on how many children are still at home and contributing to the family budget. Generally, these families are better off now than they were in the past, despite price increases, because the children are grown up and an economic asset at this point in the family lifecycle.

The second type of family is younger, with the parents in their twenties or early thirties. These are recently married couples, or couples with young children. Most live in newer areas of the city, less conveniently located and requiring long commutes to their work downtown—areas such as Dar al-Salam, Imbaba, and Helwan. Because of the terrific housing shortages, they often had to wait two or three years to find flats and they pay much higher rents for homes which are very similar or only slightly larger than those of their parents. These rents average about £E 40 a month. In these households both husband and wife are literate and have usually finished secondary school or continued on to a higher institute or college. The men work either as mechanics, drivers, or repairmen or for the government bureaucracy in low-level positions. As suits their occupations, they have abandoned the "lower-class" *galla-biyya* for Western pants and shirts. The women work in clerical jobs, generally for the government. Their combined household income averaged about £E 100–150 a month in 1984. These families, despite the advantage of two salaries, are struggling to maintain their position; rents consume an enormous part of their earnings and children will be an added expense rather than economic asset for years to come.

Although I began my research with the intention of understanding the impact of change on women's lives, women began to restructure the direction and details of my research as soon as it began. My initial, rather mechanistic idea of picking three areas of change and describing women's perspective, gave way to a concentration on the much more interesting and complex tensions that the women themselves constantly discussed. Ultimately I believe I have ended up with an account true to them, and to our interaction. In such studies, the identity of the researcher clearly has an impact on the results obtained, and I was easily able to observe some of the ways my identity affected the information and interactions of the field process. First, I am a political scientist, not an anthropologist, and so my focus falls on understanding power, albeit in a widened sense benefiting from feminist research and studies of everyday, non-elite forms of power negotiation. Also, I am a woman, which allowed me access to the women's world, yet limited me in some ways as well. While I found I could cross the gendered social boundaries to interact with men because of my foreign and class standing, I found the information I gained in this way to be less open. Also, women tended to feel that this crossing of boundaries was inappropriate, and it was clear that becoming integrated into their world required rejecting some of the opportunities of a Western woman. Therefore, I chose with increasing frequency to interact within their world, avoiding the men's room at family gatherings and trying to avoid male attempts to monopolize conversation in mixed groups. This had the result of making women welcome me in a more open way. This opening process was encouraged by the fact that I am also part Arab. My father comes from Iraq, while my mother comes from Maine. This proved to be important to women as a way to welcome me into their community, as a kind of honorary insider. Since I had grown up in America they could excuse my lapses, and indeed it was their responsibility to teach me about my own culture, which worked very well for my research needs as well. Indeed, they could call on either my Arab or my American identity as suited them; in some contexts the prestige of an "American friend" was very important, while in others the closeness of "she's an Arab like us" was convenient. Because I was married and my husband accompanied me to Cairo for most of the research period, I did not have the problem of explaining what I was doing alone in a distant city. Indeed, women assumed, although I made great efforts to honestly describe my research project and the process of writing a dissertation and eventually a book, that I was in Cairo because my husband was working.[5] Finally, when I could ultimately return to Cairo with pictures of my one-year-old baby, I achieved a fuller recognition, as women could relate to my role and feelings as mother far better than as professor and researcher. These aspects of my own identity, and changes in my own life, shape the kinds of interactions and information that I could encounter in Cairo and therefore the story I have to tell in the pages that follow.

To tell the interesting story of Cairo's lower-middle-class experience with the novel move from household to workplace and the dramatic gesture of the new veiling which women use to symbolize their accommodating protest, requires a careful recounting of women's words, behavior, and interpretations of their own actions and opportunities. I have tried to be accurate in this task of relating women's experience in their own terms. To discuss, on the basis of this case study, the larger question of women's involvement in relations of power and to characterize women's style of political struggle requires different procedures. It becomes necessary to step back from the phenomenological perspective and reflect on the meaning of women's words and actions.[6] This involves a kind of reading of the cultural text, and the creation of a unified whole, which illuminates the question one is asking. In this endeavor, I have, for example, used sources and information not available to these women, such as knowledge of the world economy or the procedures of the state, or the cross-cultural perspective of my own background, or theories of women and power. Ultimately, reflecting in a theoretical way on the meaning of women's actions is necessarily an act of interpretation. Of course, I have tried to make it clear where women's interpretations and my own converge and where they differ. The point is that allowing women to speak on their own is crucial and necessary; yet, it is also important to face the reality that even description involves interpretation. I have attempted, by interweaving these two levels of material, to allow the strength of the case study to emerge, its ability both to project the immediate and the unique, as well as cause us to reflect on larger questions and problems.

ACKNOWLEDGMENTS

From the women of Cairo who are the subjects of this study, I learned a great deal, about their society and also my own. Their names have been altered in this account and they remain anonymous; however, I wish to thank them for letting me enter their world on a temporary basis and for teaching me everything I recount in these pages about their lives. Their humor, hospitality, and courage made my time with them unique, and their patience with my constant questions, imperfect Arabic, and persistent presence made this study possible. Their willingness to let me see their society through their eyes is the source for this study, and they have my deep respect and gratitude.

I would also like to express my gratitude to the American Research Center in Egypt, who administered the grant funded by the United States Information Agency, which made my field research in Cairo in 1983–1984 possible, and who provided a haven in downtown Cairo. The directors, Robert Wenke and Nannette Pyne, were extremely helpful and their advice to a novice in Cairo was most appreciated. In addition, I want to thank Bates College for providing the funds to continue my field research in the summer of 1988, and for a sabbatical leave in the fall of 1989 which allowed me the time to complete the manuscript.

I would also like to thank many others who read, commented, and questioned, and who have helped shape both the field research and the ideas finally expressed in these pages. I especially want to thank James Scott, who gave me detailed, thoughtful, and thought-provoking comments through the various versions of this work, and generously shared his insight into power relations and popular struggles.

I would also like to express my appreciation to Frederic Shorter, Barbara Ibrahim, Cynthia Myntti, Homa Hoodfar, Diane Singerman, Ragui Assaad, Huda Zurayk, Leslie Anderson, Barney Rubin, Adolf Reed, David Apter, and Jean Elshtain for their thoughts on all or part of the manuscript in its various incarnations, and for their encouragement and practical suggestions during the process of field research.

For help in Cairo and in Maine with the tasks of checking sources, verifying translations, producing the manuscript, and providing child care to make the writing possible, I am very grateful to Wafa Ayaad, Lynn Clifford, Carol Eaton Elowe, Edmond Nasir Elowe, Claire MacLeod, Jennifer MacLeod, Jaleen Milligan, Pauline and Allen Kerry, Bruce V. MacLeod and the University of Southern Maine Childcare Center. Lastly, I would like to thank Kate Wittenberg of Columbia University Press for her enthusiasm for this project.

Researching and writing this book has often taken time away from my family, and it is impossible to acknowledge how much their love and support has given me. I am very happy to thank Morgan, both for giving me new insight into many of the choices of family and work which now shape women's identity, and for prodding me on with the question, "Are you done working yet, Mommy?." And, especially, I want to thank Bruce, for sorting out involved arguments, for practical help, and for continuous encouragement, even in a Cairo summer; his patience and occasional impatience have helped to make this project, finally, a reality.

Accommodating Protest

ONE

Women, Power Relations, and Change in Cairo

Aida sits on the cotton-covered sofa, her bright dress overpowering the faded shades of the old pillows, and her lively voice fills the still, hot corners of the tiny room as she tells her story. Aida is twenty-four, and she lives with her family in a traditional quarter in central Cairo. The household includes her parents, who are both children of migrants from the countryside, and two younger siblings. Three older sisters have already married and established homes of their own in the outlying areas of the city, for affordable apartments are no longer available in their neighborhood. Aida's family straddles the border between the lower and the lower-middle-class, a border formed not only by income level but also by size of apartment and, most important, by occupation. Her family is especially lucky as their home is fairly large; it has a living area where meals are taken and guests entertained, and two tiny bedrooms circled with low cotton couches where everyone sleeps and household goods are stored. There is also a tiny kitchen- bathroom area with cold running water, a small sink, a butogaz stove, shelves for pots and pans, and behind a screen, a toilet.

Aida's father is a migrant laborer who works as a driver in the Gulf states and has been away for many years; her mother is illiterate and a *sitt al-bayt*, a housewife, who has never worked outside the home. The children, however, work in clerical jobs with the government, raising the family status to lower middle class, despite their small incomes of about £E 45 a month.[1] Aida also works as a clerk in the large government bureaucracy; she and her sisters, who hold similar jobs, represent the first generation of working women in her family.

Some time ago, Aida broke off her formal engagement to a man from her neighborhood; their conflict centered on her fiance's refusal to allow Aida to continue working after their marriage. Yet Aida definitely wants to continue in her job; her reasons center on the income she can earn, with the resulting ability to help purchase needed goods for her family and insure security for herself. She also enjoys the chance to meet people and socialize, and she wants to keep herself busy and occupied. She pondered the breakup, a somewhat scandalous move in her neighborhood, most carefully, but in the end decided that her job was extremely important to her, important enough to rid herself of this suitor and cast about for another. About six months later, she was again engaged, this time to a friend of her brother-in-law, who agreed that she could continue working after the wedding, a plan they worked out in a series of pre-engagement conversations held in her home. In addition, this suitor, who worked as a mechanic in a large factory, also held one-sixth share of a local taxi, which could provide always needed extra cash for the family income. Weighing her options, Aida said, "He seems a good man, and we will be able to live here in the neighborhood where I can still walk to my mother's house. His mother will live downstairs—well, we will see how that goes! Anyway, he is handsome don't you think? And he will let me keep working. Of course, it cannot interfere with cleaning the house and preparing meals, and then, God willing, there will be the children. But still I can keep going to my job."

One day, in a family gathering at her home, while discussing her ideas for the marriage celebration and her future as a married woman, Aida revealed her intention to become a *muhaggaba*, a covered woman. She planned, at some indefinite date after becoming a wife, to change her colorful western outfits for a long, modest dress and a headscarf wrapping over her hair and shoulders. Her fiance was surprised and not very pleased. "Why wear these clothes? They are ugly and not necessary. These are modern times!" Voices rose as Aida's announcement was debated by all; the controversy that swirled about the small room only ended as people tired late in the evening and tabled the discussion for another day. Despite these conflicting views, a little over a year after her wedding, after giving birth to a son, Aida made the decision and did indeed put on these covering garments, called the *higab*, the new veil.

Aida's story initially draws our interest because it confronts us with a puzzling connection; why would a woman like Aida—educated, dedicated to working, modernized—voluntarily return to a traditional symbol like the veil? Why would she initiate and encourage what seems to be a return to a traditional and inferior status? The *higab* poses, in a dramatic way, the problem of understanding women's puzzling participation in the modernization process, the clash of tradition and modernity that envelops much of the contemporary world. It also poses, again in a public and powerful way, the problem of understanding women's contradictory and even paradoxical participation in relations of power.

WORKING WOMEN AND THE NEW VEILING IN CAIRO

Aida's story is not at all unusual; indeed, her beliefs and behavior are quite typical of the thoughts and actions of many lower-middle-class working women in Cairo today. These women are the first in their families to work outside the home, an important and sometimes confusing change in women's experience. Holding positions as clerical workers in the government bureaucracy, they staff the overcrowded government offices. Most come from families only one or two generations away from village life and they have benefited from Nasser's reforms of the 1960s providing for relatively free and compulsory education, making schooling a possibility for families on the upper margins of the lower-class, and especially for the daughters of such families. The Nasser era reforms guaranteed hiring of graduates of secondary schools and were designed to encourage social mobility through education and work in the government bureaucracy. For women, they offered equal opportunity in education and in hiring as well as equal pay and benefits. The result was an influx of young men and women who finished their education because of this guarantee of secure income and relatively high status employment. For women in particular these jobs were a chance to add to family income without degrading individual or family status. These jobs provide little money, perhaps less than women might earn in some other jobs, but add a steady amount to straightened budgets, as well as insuring a raised level of family prestige and social status.[2] For women, secondary school or higher institute degrees not only insure them their positions in the government bureaucracy, but these positions also signal their entrance into the lowest echelons of the middle classes.

These women work primarily as lower-level clerks, recording appointments, running copy machines, signing and stamping lengthy forms, or typing letters and documents. Upper-class women in Cairo have participated in the labor force for some years now, attaining considerable success in many professional areas, but for lower-middle-class families, these young women are a sometimes unsettling novelty. They hold positions of relatively high status compared to less-educated urban women who must work in the factories, as domestics, or as street peddlers. These women are a good example of reasonably successful working women in the urban developing world, and they have high expectations for raising their status further in the future. They are willing to work hard and endure considerable tension to pursue their new-found ability to venture out of the household, and to earn the funds for necessary household goods to ensure or even raise their middle-class status.

Recently, many of these working women have started to wear the veil, the *higab*.[3] They replace their Western outfits of colorful and silky skirts and blouses with long, loose-fitting dresses and headscarves which wrap around their hair and neck to fall over their shoulders. They call themselves the *muhaggabat*, the covered women. This new veiling has become an increasingly common picture, not only in Egypt, but also in many parts of the Middle East and indeed in the larger Muslim world.

Voluntary support of the new veiling, by educated, working women, part of the modernizing middle classes, presents a paradox, for why would women who are already on the path to modernized life choose to resurrect a symbol which seems to portray and encourage their subordination?

Resorting to destructive stereotypes of the backward Middle East, or the inequities of Islam toward women, or the naturally conservative woman enmeshed in false consciousness is not likely to help in reaching any real understanding of women's behavior. Recent studies have fortunately expanded our vision of women's lives in the Middle East, correcting the distorted picture of the past by emphasizing the variety of women's lives in different class contexts, and different political and economic settings, yet the veil seems to be such an evocative symbol that it tends to revive old stereotypes. Nonetheless, the style of women's dress, the degree of coverage, the requirement of seclusion, or the ability to leave the household for economic, educational, or other reasons are all matters subject to local interpretations and exhibit virtually the full range of possible variation from considerable freedom to strict seclusion. This important variation across the boundaries of village and urban contexts, lower- or upper-class settings, and different historical periods demonstrates that ahistorical and undifferentiated references to Middle Eastern, Islamic, or female behavior simply cannot be substantiated.[4]

Rather than relying on such dubious sources and inferring women's contemporary position, we need to explore what this decision to wear covering dress actually means to the women who do it in this unique subcultural setting. Do they see working and veiling as a contradiction? How important is the new veiling to them? What do they feel the symbolic action of veiling expresses, or resolves? To consider the paradox of working women's voluntary veiling in lower-middle-class Cairo requires delving into a deeper understanding of women's own motivations and the context which frames their actions. Local differences shape women's lives so that a village in the Nile Delta, a Bedouin community in the desert near Alexandria, and an urban *hara* (neighborhood alley) in Cairo, for example, present quite different pictures of women's options and powers. The stereotypes of idle women lounging in the harim never had much reality, except perhaps for some very wealthy women in a few urban areas. The actual situation of women's condition is a much more complex and interesting story shaped by economics, local interests, ethnic differences, the exigencies of village or urban life, and the clash of cultures, all factors that interpenetrate and interact with gender beliefs in an evolving context. Class relations and global dependency form a web of power relations which intersect with local gender beliefs to structure the kinds of decisions women will be faced with and the kinds of choices they may be able to initiate. Investigation of the concrete, historical, and contextual background to women's symbolic gesture is extremely important for understanding the meaning and the political potential of women's puzzling behavior.

CONTROVERSIES OVER WOMEN AND CHANGE IN THE MIDDLE EAST

To begin thinking about working women who choose to adopt the new veil in lower-middle-class Cairo, the unique aspects of Egyptian life and women's place within it must be put in the larger context of power relations and change throughout the Middle East. In this endeavor three significant areas of women's inequality should be emphasized. The first, the position of these women as members of a community located in the developing world leads to relations that might be called global inequality. The second, class, focuses on women's status as members of the lower-middle-stratum in Cairo society. The third centers on the gender issue, on specifically sex-linked relations of inequality. Clearly, these relations of power do not influence women of lower-middle-class Cairo in the same ways or with the same impact. Global affairs are distant and certainly only vaguely understood by these women, while personal male and female inequities are immediate and the focus of great concern. Yet, the fact of Cairo's position in the world political economy, for instance, affects the prospects and decisions of these women, just as the inequality of duties in the home has an impact as well. How class interacts with gender is very important indeed, for many of the problems Cairo's women experience are problems of poverty and not purely of gender inequity. Yet, class status affects lower-middle-class women differently than it does lower-middle-class men, who are themselves subject to many class and gender-related pressures. Further, while all these inequalities are analytically separate, they do not act distinctly in society or in their effect on women. Examining the way these relations of power intersect in this particular subcultural setting is the key to understanding the experience of this group of women.

Cairo's women share many crucial beliefs and forms of behavior with other Middle Eastern women, yet they are also distinguished from their counterparts in other countries by the specific and unique history of Egypt, and by the contemporary position of their country in the global political and economic structure. Further, Cairo's women inhabit an urban environment, in a dynamic and changing major city with a rich and complex cultural history. Their lives are inevitably different from the lives of women in Egyptian villages or rural areas in other parts of the Middle East.

As a country with a long and proud history, Egypt holds a special place in the Arab world as a center of cultural and political life.[5] Unlike some other Middle Eastern countries, Egypt has a strong sense of national identity, derived from its unique history as a political, economic, and cultural community dating from Pharaonic times. Egyptians also identify themselves as Arabs, and seek to emphasize ties with the rest of the Arab world, yet they remain Egyptians first, a crucial element in Egypt's political history in recent decades. Emerging from the colonial era with its culture relatively intact compared to other North African countries, Egypt entered the postcolonial period as an increasingly important strategic center in the Middle East. This importance means that Egypt has been the focus of considerable international interest; in recent years, the interest of the West has come in the form of large sums of foreign aid pouring into the country, creating a sometimes uneasy political and economic alliance. The Camp David accord, while tying Egypt to the United States and insuring significant aid funds, has alienated Egypt from its traditional place as a leader in the Arab world. This loss has offered the political opposition a chance to argue the regime's lack of leadership and moral decay. Increasing opposition to government policies, and especially the opposition of Islamic groups, creates a tense political situation and tends to bring issues of women's status and family roles into the political arena.[6]

Even as Egypt seeks to renew its ties to the Arab world and regain its position of leadership, the political situation is aggravated by economic difficulties; Egypt's foreign debt is very high, and its economy suffers from a dependence on remittances and tourism, both of which have fallen in recent years.[7] While its birth rate has also fallen, population growth has still created an excess of young workers who have crowded the educational institutions in the hope of gaining government jobs. Temporary migration offers many workers a chance for relatively high paying employment and brings foreign currency into the country, but it also leaves an unskilled workforce at home. Further, Egyptians return from periods of work in the oil-rich countries with an envious resentment of the treatment they have received and the disparity in resources they have observed. Finally, the growth of bureaucracy, the result of attempts to encourage education and provide employment, has exceeded all bounds, creating an unproductive workforce and a substantial drain on government resources, already hampered by the necessity of continuing food subsidy payments. The government has slowed its hiring of graduates, and unemployment is bound to exert a negative influence on women's opportunities in the workplace in the coming years.

Women in Egypt participated in feminist activity long before women in other areas of the Middle East, and are viewed as leaders for women in other countries. In fact, Egypt has a long history of activity promoting women's rights, beginning with feminist efforts in the last half of the nineteenth century, and continuing with the efforts of early feminist leaders through the years of growing nationalism and change in the first part of this century; the name of Huda Shaarawi, the founder of the Egyptian Feminist Union, is well known.[8] More recently, reforms in the early 1960s providing for compulsory and free education and allowing women into the workforce in both factories and the government bureaucracy have produced changes in women's lives. Legislation on women and work covers women's right to work, equal pay for equal work, and the chance to be hired by the government bureaucracy on an equal basis with men. Further labor laws protect women through setting limits on night work and providing for maternity leaves and for the establishment of child care centers in large workplaces.[9] Finally, change in the Personal Status Laws, accomplished in 1985 after years of controversy, is designed to protect women's rights in cases of marriage and divorce.[10]

Yet, while Egypt was an early leader in encouraging women's rights, it now lags behind other Arab nations such as Tunisia in providing legal support for women.[11] Indeed, in the new political climate, women are seeking to hold onto gains they have already made as questions of women's rights in the workforce and in the family are reviewed in an atmosphere of intense controversy. At the same time, women have become a more formidable and organized force in the last few years, especially with the creation of the new Arab Women's Solidarity Association, geared toward the expansion of women's opportunities.[12]

These disputes over women's status in Egypt, as in the rest of the Middle East, are firmly enmeshed in debates over future political, economic, and cultural direction. While most of these exchanges range around the question of women's future role in a modernized Middle East, the question of what the modern state, economic firm, educational institution, or family life ought to be can call forth many quite varied interpretations. Further, the controversy is influenced by historical, economic, and political factors such as the specific history of colonialism in each country, which has shaped class boundaries, affected political institutions, and penetrated and altered cultural norms to very different degrees. The current economic health of each nation also factors into the debate, not only in the division of oil-rich versus oil-poor countries, but also in the degree of development of productive industry, the extent of unemployment, the manner of integration into the world economy, and the amount of debt. The degree of political conflict also affects women's situation as peace, war, or extended conflict shape women's options for work, political activity and leadership. More recently, the success of religious activists in entering politics has shaped the debates over women's status.

Two examples can highlight how these differences shape the current debates over women's status and place the case of Egyptian women in context. Algiers and Istanbul, like Cairo, are important urban centers for their countries' political, economic, and cultural life, in which the coexistence of various classes and ways of life creates a dynamic environment of alternatives and opportunity, but also of special stresses and tensions which impinge on women's lives and influence the debates over women's future.[13]

In Algiers, one's first impression is of the lack of women in public places; the city seems to be populated only by young men. Women appear only occasionally in public, often in the *haik*, a form of veiled dress, and accompanied by men. In a country where many women still live secluded in the home, relatively few women leave the household for the workplace, and those who do tend to be young and single middle-class women who are working on a temporary basis until marriage. Algeria is a country with a recent colonial past and a history of bloody revolution, both factors which shape the current debates over women's situation. The culture of the country was seriously permeated by the French, and this has led both to an ongoing disruption of Algerian culture and to a rejection of the West.[14] This leads to a rejection of Western ideas on women's position and Western feminism stressing women's placement into the labor force or their participation in public life. Although Algerian women were serious fighters in the revolution, the gains they made were not expanded after independence. Instead, the stress on authentic culture emphasizes an ideology of family where women's place is in the home. In practice, this leads to a reinforcement of women's seclusion and restriction from public life. This entrenchment has been aggravated in recent years by economic difficulties, arising in part from the drop of oil prices and a very high population growth, leading to a serious problem of unemployed youth. The growth of a Muslim alternative has lent ideological coherence to this restriction on women's public activities, further emphasizing women's role in the family. And finally, the disruptions of modernization have disturbed the patterns of family life; people often migrate into Algiers from rural villages and women, who led freer lives in the company of relatives in a village setting, must live more secluded lives in the company of strangers in the housing developments surrounding Algiers.

In Istanbul, in contrast, women are highly visible on the streets and in the offices. The European dress and professional achievements of elite women signal a different frame of reference shaping the ongoing debates over women's position.[15] Turkey has preferred in recent years to stress its ties to Europe rather than to the Middle East, and has a history of sixty years of government-initiated modernization programs. Included in these programs are legal reforms transforming the position of women and allowing women into the workforce, into public positions of authority, and into the formal political realm. In Istanbul, elite women do hold such positions in the hospitals, universities, and law offices; however, corresponding changes in social customs and attitudes have been far slower to alter even in this sector of society. For women confined to low-ranking bureaucratic jobs, or to factory or informal labor, transformations in women's position have rarely been debated, and never implemented. With the economic problems of unemployment, returning migrant labor, and increasing inflation, state-led development programs are being questioned. The issue of women's proper role has resurfaced in this context and the political opposition, including Islamic groups, has seized this issue to raise a host of challenges to the state. Women's role is consequently politicized, despite the protection of legal initiatives.

In both these cases women's status forms the focal point for a range of arguments concerning the proper path for modernizing societies to tred; women's future position will be shaped by these controversies in the tumultuous environment of a dependent and rapidly changing society. In Cairo, just as in Algiers or Istanbul, women's position has clearly altered in recent decades. Here, women fill the streets and the offices of the crowded city center. Wearing Western dress, traditional clothes, or the new veils, women wander in the traditional markets or the stylish downtown areas with ease, and ride the crowded buses or walk to work in the packed streets. Yet here too debates over women's proper place continue, shaped, as in Algiers or Istanbul, by political and economic factors. Should women be in the workforce at all? What should women's role and rights be within the family? Should Egyptian women seek to emulate Western women, return to a traditional past identity, or try to create a new alternative? Clearly there is no one Middle Eastern experience that is uniform for women or that could answer women's questions in an identical way in such different contexts. Even less are women's problems the same as the issues women face in the West. This fact emphasizes the need for case studies that trace the particular restraints and opportunities for women in a specific social context; Cairo's lower middle class is an especially interesting group, little studied to date, for these women embody the clash of tradition and modernity, the controversies and contradictions that arise as women seek to define a new identity in a changing world.

WOMEN IN THE CLASH OF TRADITION AND MODERNITY

Middle Eastern societies have been rocked by change, and to show a society under change and describe what is happening to women in this context can be a bewildering task. Trying to understand what living change means for women is an especially important problem, for only by comprehending the way change is directed and determined can the opportunities and openings that it creates be encouraged to grow. The unprecedented alterations in women's status in recent years have created a feeling of optimism among women, and yet these alterations sometimes seem accompanied by the incredible persistence of inequalities as well. In this process, the puzzles of lower-middle-class Cairo are not completely unique. Turning in the direction of traditional symbols, customs, images, and behavior forms an important countertrend in a modernizing world. In India, for example, the incidence of *sati* by middle-class women is reportedly increasing.[16] In China, the revival of traditional saints and shrines in rural villages is also gathering strength.[17] And in the West, the support for traditional patterns and traditional notions of women's place has certainly reappeared with force. These revivals of tradition must be examined more closely to

11

understand their meaning in the context of power relations which frame and encourage their appearance.

The new veiling is an example of such a revival of tradition, played out in the specific context of Islamic and Middle Eastern symbols and signs. To understand this impulse to restore traditional culture, we need to focus on these women in the grip of change, both to portray the turmoil women are experiencing and to comprehend the way the linked potentials of greater opportunity and increasing restriction interact in concrete settings with the intermingling of tradition and modernity.

Of course, the classic frame for understanding such social change in the Middle East dates from Daniel Lerner's famous study of 1958, *The Passing of Traditional Society*. Lerner describes the dynamics of change in the developing world through the frame of an evolutionary transition, from a traditional past to a glowing and modern future. Everywhere, he argues, tradition is giving way inexorably to modernity, which involves the eradication of many human ills, including blatant inequality and the subordination of women.[18] Yet to return to a more distant era, Rousseau, writing in eighteenth century France in a time when change was also being embraced as the chance to rationalize and humanize the world, claimed an inverse connection between development and equality: "inequality, being almost null in the state of nature, draws its force and growth from the development of our faculties and the progress of the human mind.[19] Rousseau questioned the unexamined assumption that development is linked in any necessary way to positive political outcomes and indeed warned that change brings new and more problematic inequalities rather than simple progress. His distant warnings have a familiar ring to our ears, as they have been repeated and amplified in recent years in the debate over development theory. No longer is modernization seen as a smooth or inevitable path; no longer is development perceived as linear progress; and no longer is positive social change seen solely as secularization, democratization, and the creation of Western-style political institutions. For women particularly, development has been criticized as a process that may actually worsen their status rather than necessarily creating a situation of increasing equality or opportunity.[20] Modernization does not inevitably liberate women but rather challenges them by removing traditional sources of influence, sometimes replacing them with male prerogatives. Thus modernization alone does not automatically insure positive political outcomes; certainly the road to modern life, despite its considerable successes, whether productive factories, widened education, or increased food supplies, does not lead to the automatic solution of many social ills, including the significant one of gender inequality.[21]

Building on the mounting criticism of development theory and on a Marxist foundation, dependency theory sought to reformulate the understanding of how tradition and modernity interrelate.[22] It focused in general on the ways the world economic system served to keep certain countries in positions of peripheral and underdeveloped status, and it argued that this unfortunate trend occurs as a result of modernization—institutionalized underdevelopment, not progress. This approach has one great virtue over the development account, the focus on understanding the relations of power which underlie all social change and are part of the process of moving from tradition to modernity. The transition, in other words, from a traditional society with certain traditional forms of inequality to a modern society, without such inequalities, is posited as a struggle, rather than an inevitable conclusion. This allows the crucial question of the struggle of dispossessed groups during the process of modernization to emerge; as economies alter, openings are created, political spaces where social relations are necessarily restructured and renegotiated. Marx called this process of continuous change and the resulting continuous negotiation of power the problem of the reproduction of social relations.[23]

Despite this important advance, the dependency approach has its own problems, primarily that it virtually ignores, or at least downplays, the conscious choices of subordinate subjects. By focusing on how structures and institutions interact, the implicit assumption emerges that the outcome of struggles is decided and determined by structures, and not by human actors. The issues of how people view change, and what people say they are struggling for are ranked as relatively insignificant. In fact, the whole question of consciousness becomes a rather substantial and troublesome problem. For subordinate groups often manifest interests and desires which do not seem to push in emancipatory directions. Within this framework, such articulations are interpreted as evidence that people are both mystified about the real nature of the social relations in which they live and unwitting participants in aiding the needs of the capitalist system and the ruling classes in maintaining momentum and perpetuating inequality. The question of consciousness, in other words, is framed as the problem of false consciousness, allowing the expressed desires of subordinates to be disregarded.[24]

Further, once again the more specific problem of women within change is not well understood. In part because of the overwhelming emphasis on class and class inequalities, the intricate relationship between patriarchy and capitalism and the intertwining of class and gender inequalities which assumes great importance as economies alter during the process of development is too often ignored. The question of class and gender, and their complex interaction, remains a puzzle, with gender relations subsumed under class and the complicated and often contradictory class position of women left more or less unaddressed.[25]

For understanding women in lower-middle-class Cairo, the difficulties with these approaches amount to crucial obstacles. For it is important to emphasize at the outset that the *higab* should not be considered a re-veiling but a new veiling. The dress these women choose to wear differs from traditional outfits in style, materials, and name. Indeed, the new veiling movement should not be read as an example of women maintaining or reactivating traditional ways, but instead as the active appropriation of a cultural symbol for new purposes. Women's "reversion" to the veil should not be viewed as reactionary, but recognized as a new form of social action—a new veiling.

The modernization approach toward understanding change simply cannot accommodate this form of social and cultural action; a form located neither in the traditional nor the modern vocabulary. Relying too heavily on the underlying idea of tradition as something negative, yet hardy, with a surprising tendency to survive and persist, coupled with the portrayal of women as the prime defenders of this outmoded tradition, the modernization approach commonly reduces women to irrational, backward and conservative preservers of a inequitable past. Similarly, the dependency model, which rests on the Marxist idea that the superstructure is determined by economic alterations, cannot account for situations such as the new veiling. For it appears that the superstructure, or ideological understanding, has not followed automatically along in the wake of economic transition. After all, working and leaving the area of the home provide an·opening, both physical and political, an opportunity for women, altering set patterns and routines, unsettling traditional identities, and thereby creating political space for the potential renegotiation of gender inequalities, for the discarding of old patterns and the creation of new and widened options for all women. Yet instead, the reverse seems to have occurred; apparently, women's consciousness has not arisen as they have entered the workplace. The economy has opened a political space but in no way insured, inevitably decided, or determined how women would interpret and act upon this opportunity. Consequently, in both these accounts women's behavior remains an "irrational" mystery blocking the onward march of progressive change.

The problem centers on the way that the everyday struggles of subordinate subjects are glossed over in such accounts, ignoring significant personal conflict and social struggle. This glossing becomes important for it aggravates misunderstanding by feeding into reactionary myths about women and about Middle Eastern women in particular. Further, it inaccurately masks the reality of the political struggles that women face during times of transformation.

As a result, we need to use a new approach to understand women's actions in Cairo today. In this task we can turn once again to Rousseau. In the *Discourse on the Origins of Inequality Among Men,* Rousseau argues that as tradition gives way to modernity, tremendous individual, social, and cultural costs accumulate. For Rousseau, the major problem lies in the growth of new forms of power and new and more difficult kinds of inequality.[26] He counsels that modernization can create new ills, new problems, and much more difficult, subtle, and powerful forms of domination. Indeed he argues that change should be seen not as progress but as the growth of new forms of struggle over resources and control and that these new forms lead to increasing domination, not to greater freedom.[27] Development experts, arguing about the problems of universal development programs, anthropologists observing women who argue against the standardization of Western forms of gender inequality, and political theorists of power such as Michel Foucault, who argues that modern forms of power lack a center, an "eye" which can be identified or targeted,[28] and are therefore much more difficult to overcome, seem to corroborate Rousseau's disheartening vision.

In the past, theorists of change have relied too heavily on terms such as break, gap, lag, and transition to disguise a lack of understanding of the actual dynamics of the moment of social and political change. Lost in this theoretical void is a grasp of the power relations that shape the outcome of the transition from tradition to

15

modernity, and especially of the concrete actions and concerns of subordinate groups in relations of power, the concrete struggles and negotiations which end at times in the reproduction of power relations and occasionally in real change in the terms of inequality. Aida's new form of dress, the significance of her symbolic act, and the struggles that arise in times of transition remain inexplicable within such accounts.

In his book *All That Is Solid Melts Into Air,* Marshall Berman attempts to portray the nature of such struggles; defining modernism "as a struggle to make ourselves at home in a constantly changing world,"[29] Berman focuses on the contradictions and conflicts which make the confrontation of tradition and modernity so powerful and the experience for people caught in its turmoil so intense, creative, and potentially revolutionary. Through a historical examination of the modernization process in Petersburg, in pre-revolutionary Russia, Berman portrays the conflicts, confusions, and pressures which change inevitably brings. He argues that these tensions are deepened in the developing world today by reference to an already modernized, powerful, and dominant Western culture. The difference in a search for modernity which is shaped by relations with an already modernized West, the confusing combination of envy and rejection, must be emphasized, he maintains; he calls this kind of change the "modernism of underdevelopment."

The tribulations of societies experiencing this form of change are familiar; on the nightly newscasts we are overwhelmed with images of the loss of traditional identity and the struggle to realize an authentic future. Most of this process is conveyed on the national and international level; scenes of the confrontations and disintegration in Lebanon are a tragic and familiar example. This book will take a more intimate perspective and focus on the experience of women in the midst of such dramatic social change. Personal trials and family interactions, everyday routines, responsibilities and pleasures, beliefs, interpretations, and hopes are the center in this study, allowing the unique and particular evolution of modernity in lower-middle-class Cairo to emerge. Women's experience with rapid change in Cairo is shaped by the search for an authentic identity coherent with traditional culture yet consistent with women's goals of increased opportunity, a search for modernism that builds on, rather than rejects, traditional culture and the traditional sources of women's power.

WOMEN AND THE NEGOTIATION OF POWER

From the Western vantage point, women in the Middle East have been pitied as the victims of a difficult and oppressive cultural milieu, usually mechanically equated with the Islamic religion. They are perceived as downtrodden, repressed, and severely constrained victims, and the ultimate symbol of their oppression is the veil.[30] Yet, as anyone who has known Middle Eastern women quickly realizes, this picture is impossible to reconcile with the assertive behavior and influential position of women in many Middle Eastern settings. In Cairo, for instance, women manage the household budgets, conduct marriage arrangements, and coordinate extensive and very important economic and social networks. They display a degree of assertive and confident behavior which is rare among Western women. Clearly these women can not be categorized as passive victims, and their often cutting and humorous backstage portrayals of men and male behavior signal that these women should also not be compressed into the role of completely deferential and consenting partners. The literature on Middle Eastern women in recent years has offered a proliferation of examples of women's informal powers, bargaining tactics, and hidden strategies—all the means through which women may exercise considerable influence on their families and the greater society.[31] One observer of Mediterranean peasant communities even suggests that real power resides with women and that men must be satisfied with simply the "myth of male domination."[32]

Although this focus on the variety of women's sources of power is welcome, it remains true that women in many cultures also serve as staunch supporters of customs and relations which constrain and limit women's lives. The oppressive orders and restrictions through which mothers-in-law control young wives in many traditional cultures, the supervision of older women in binding their daughters' feet in pre-revolutionary China, women's support of female circumcision in Africa and North Africa, and the popularity of restrictions on women's rights of choice among American women are all examples of women perpetuating the subordination of their own sex and thereby helping to reinforce the foundations of gender inequality.

This kind of complicity and accommodation, coupled with the

17

idea of women's informal powers, needs further examination. Which picture accurately portrays women's part in power relations? Why do women sometimes acquiesce to authority, and when do they seek to circumvent its dictates? What kinds of resistance are available to women, and how do women's actions sometimes reinforce and at other times refute the existing relations of power? Working women in Cairo who choose to wear the new veils illustrate well the contradictory parts women may play in encouraging either social reproduction or social change, offering the chance to examine this puzzling problem of women's ambiguous roles in relations of power.

Though not concerned with gender relations, the work of the Italian Marxist Antonio Gramsci can be very useful in this endeavor. Gramsci's brilliant reflections in his *Prison Notebooks* on class relations and class struggle, written in the context of the growth of fascism and new forms of popular support for relations of inequality, revise our understanding of how power relations actually operate. His major innovation, for our purposes, is the development of the idea of hegemony, a complex notion which he uses as a description of the way relations of power work, both during ordinary times and times of transition and change.[33] Gramsci emphasizes the point that all power issues from a relationship, an interaction between two parties. Power is conceived as a dialectical interaction in which both dominant and subordinate parties have active roles to play; in other words, power relations necessarily involve two implicated, although not equal, partners. His realization recalls Rousseau's famous line: "All ran to meet their chains."[34] With the idea of hegemony, Gramsci explores the interplay of coercion and consent which forms the dynamic of relations of power.

Further, the hegemonic interaction or power relationship is most successful, he argues, when force is not even required and full consent of the subordinate party is achieved. Hegemony, therefore, describes the process of the intellectual or moral leadership of dominants, rather than the exercise of force, the framing of the ideas and vision of subordinates which ensures the acceptance of inequalities. But even this leadership, and the consent it creates, does not ensure a passive subordinate within the power relationship; it requires instead an ongoing struggle, an ongoing process of negotiation, concessions, and underlying threats. Therefore, power is portrayed not as a possession of dominant groups, nor as the execution of force; it is instead the ongoing creation of a tie, a bond, a relationship which encourages the complicity and consent of the subordinate partner.

By focusing attention on the struggle that underlies the appearance of permanence in power relations and situations of inequality, Gramsci's account forces us to reconsider the nature of power relations. The false picture of stability conjured up by the persistence of inequality covers up a series of negotiations in which subordinates, including women, contest and try to expand the boundaries of their experience, yet also consent and accept their situation. Power, in other words, involves a relationship in which women, even as the subordinate players, take an active role. Women may appear as passive victims, unable to muster any opposition to the forces allied against them; or as consenting partners, acquiescent and apparently satisfied with their deferent role; or even as active participants, supporting and sustaining their own inequality; yet women also, when the times are ripe, seize the opportunity to participate in an ongoing series of negotiations, manipulations, and strategies directed toward gaining control and opportunity. Whenever changing circumstances open a political space for the possible renegotiation of existing relations, this contradictory process of hegemonic politics is at work.[35]

Gramsci's reformulation of the functioning of power into the idea of hegemonic interaction emphasizes the certainty of political struggle, yet he also forces us to consider the uncertainty of the outcome for subordinate groups.[36] His focus on the political moment and the political space when the linked potentials of reproduction and real change in relations of power are both possibilities is clearly very important as it allows us escape the mechanistic finality of historical models which equate change with progress and which ignore the role of human subjects and their choices. Viewing power as a hegemonic relationship permits us to capture the human struggle that underlies the larger social movements of change; the everyday resistances and sometimes the extraordinary protests of subordinate actors can be brought into view, as can the more problematic behavior of acceptance, complicity, consent and accommodation.

This dimension of Gramsci's use of hegemony is particularly interesting for understanding women's lives in Cairo today. Their world is shaped by the dramatic confrontation of tradition with Western values—the transition to some form of modernity. This ongoing transition, which commenced in the last century, continues to involve a tremendous upheaval for the entire society, including these women and their families. Identity, status, and future roles are all open to possible alterations and the hegemonic struggle to shape these changes invades every aspect of their lives. The problem is that we need to know a great deal more about how such struggles actually take place; we lack precise knowledge of the dynamics of the hegemonic relation itself, and especially of the part played by specific subordinate actors during moments of change. And, as Michel Foucault reminds us:

> Power is not to be taken to be a phenomenon of one individual's consolidated and homogeneous domination over others, or that of one group or class over others. What, by contrast, should always be kept in mind is that power... must be analyzed as something that circulates. ... It is never localized here or there, never in anybody's hands, never appropriated as a commodity or piece of wealth. ... And not only do individuals circulate between its threads; they are always in the position of simultaneously undergoing and exercising this power. They are not only its inert or consenting target; they are always also the elements of its articulation. In other words, individuals are the vehicles of power.[37]

Foucault's realization that subordinate as well as dominant individuals form the locus of intersecting forces of power and that subordinate individuals are in many ways involved and implicated in the continual recreation of power strongly suggests the need to explore the complicated and contradictory ways subordinates pursue their ends in times of change.

Toward that end, this book has two purposes. The first is to tell the important and intriguing story of lower-middle-class women in Cairo in the turmoil of change. Many women are leaving traditional modes and identities behind as they are pushed into the new role of worker by changes in the domestic and global political economy. Their experience of this change offers a most interesting story in itself. The chance to explore the controversial and ambivalent reaction of the new veiling requires discovering what these women view as injustices or inequalities in their situation, what they believe might be worth altering and perhaps worth struggling for, and what they feel is worth retaining. Through an in-depth look at lower-middle-class women in the context of their everyday experience a picture can be drawn of the subtle interactions which color the clash of tradition and modernity from the perspective of the involved subjects.

A second goal is to use the paradox of voluntary veiling by working women to achieve a better understanding of women's part in power relations during times of change, when reproduction or real alterations in relations of inequality are both potential outcomes. To that end, this book explores the dimensions of political space and the subjects who operate in and push beyond its boundaries in the defined arena of lower-middle-class Cairo. The attempt to chart relations of power during what Bourdieu calls "the progressive differentiation of a society" under change[38] necessarily involves a close and concrete mapping of the experience of the subordinate actors whose struggles continually revise the boundaries of unequal social relations. Through such an exploration, some perspective can be gained on the contradictory part women play, both sustaining and resisting, in the negotiations of power.

TWO

Lower-Middle-Class Women in Cairo: The Subcultural Context of Subordinate Subjects

TWO WOMEN OF LOWER-MIDDLE-CLASS CAIRO

Hoda. Hoda sits behind a large wooden desk with an open ledger pushed off to the side. Around her in chairs and seated on the desk are several other young women; they are all laughing and talking, sipping glasses of strong, sweet tea. Hoda is twenty-five and unmarried, and she works as a bookkeeper in this large government office building. She keeps the accounts for the building cafeteria and each person who buys a sandwich or soft drink comes in to pay, making the room crowded, noisy and cheerful.

The room is quite large, with doors opening onto the dusty courtyard, making the space cooler in summer but very chilly on cold winter days. Two posters, slightly askew, showing winter scenes of pine trees in Switzerland, adorn the mustard-colored walls. Ten people, six of whom are women, work at the desks arranged in a large U-shape along the sides of the room. Usually, the central area is crowded with men and women laughing and chatting while they pay for their food or eat their sandwiches and drink their tea. Hoda would prefer a more "proper" ·office, such as the one where her friend Fatma works. There, four or five women sit at two desks in a small and relatively private room. Their work load is comparatively light since they are responsible only for occasional typing for a department supervisor down the hall; they spend most of the time chatting over cups of tea or bottles of Schweppes orange to pass the time from nine to two when they can go home.

Hoda leaves the office at two as well and usually walks with Fatma or another friend to a busy street nearby where they catch one of the enormously overcrowded buses which teeter along in the traffic, slowing only slightly at the bus stop while a few people jump off and many more try to climb on. Passengers already on the bus are helpful, reaching out hands for the new riders to grab and dragging them up and into the press of people jammed against one another. Sometimes Hoda simply decides to walk after waiting for five or six buses, which all arrive too crowded for even this arduous procedure. Then she and Fatma begin the long stroll home. As they are both wearing high-heeled shoes, walking on the uneven street, through the piles of sand and rocks waiting to be converted into sidewalks and curbstones, is not easy. They link arms to avoid some of the stares and attention of men passing by and continue until they reach the side street leading to the traditional quarter of Cairo which is their home. Here the paved streets lined with honking and maneuvering cars give way to narrow dirt lanes lined with small shops selling lentils, macaroni, or spices in large baskets. Piles of plastic pails in brilliant reds and blues sit on one corner; across the street is a small hand cart where a man is carefully piling his oranges in a tall pyramid. Sometimes the street is nearly blocked by the wooden tables and chairs of a coffeeshop, filled with men drinking tea, smoking water pipes, and commenting on the world passing by.

Now Fatma and Hoda separate and Hoda continues down a narrower street. The houses have the shutters thrown open as women watch their children playing ball below. A few sheep calmly chew their alfalfa and some chickens scratch around in the dust. Hoda's home is on the end of the *hara*, the alley, and she lives on the second floor with her parents and three sisters; two older brothers are already married and live in other parts of the city. The flat has two main rooms, one serving as the seating area for guests by day and as a bedroom at night. The other also has cushion-covered benches which serve as beds at night and in the day functions as the eating area and general sitting room for the family. A final small space is partitioned off into kitchen and bathroom; there is cold running water at a tiny sink surrounded by wooden shelves loaded with pots and pans, dishes and glasses for tea. Behind a screen there is a hose rigged up as a shower and a traditional toilet. Hoda dreams of living in a bigger flat some day, with more rooms and modern plumbing, perhaps in a quieter area.

Meanwhile, the money that she earns at her job, now that she has graduated with a *diplome tigara*, a degree from a higher institute in business and commerce, helps the family budget a little. But most is saved toward her trousseau of household goods which will one day furnish a flat of her own. She is saving to buy a refrigerator now and expects to be able to purchase one in another year. She also spends her earnings on clothes. She is always carefully dressed in modest but colorful skirts and blouses, her long hair set and styled. She hopes to meet her future husband soon, perhaps at the office, since she would like to marry a *muwazzaf*, or government employee, like herself.

Karima. Karima met her husband, Assam, at her workplace, a government office building. They were introduced by colleagues and talked for a few minutes over some tea. Shortly after that first meeting, Assam dropped by her office and asked to call at her home. She agreed, depending on her family's approval, and the following week he visited her home, where they talked and he met her parents; not long after, they decided to become engaged and soon held the formal engagement party. Friends, colleagues, and family helped celebrate the engagement with special fruit drinks and sweet cakes, and everyone was dressed in their finest clothes for the festive occasion. Two years after the engagement celebration, Karima and Assam were married, after finding an apartment in an outlying area of the city, furnishing it, and preparing for another large celebration. Again, friends and family gathered for the celebration. The bride was dressed in a white wedding gown with flowers and a net veil over her head, and the groom wore a Western suit. Guests appeared in their best clothes, bright colors and sparkling materials, and the many children ran from one adult to the next, excited with all the activity. Bride and groom sat on a throne of gold chairs decked with flowers while the guests sat and chatted in rows of chairs arranged to face the new couple. Refreshments of cool drinks and sweets were passed about for guests to consume as the innumerable requisite photographs were taken of the new couple posing with family members of both sides.

Karima and Assam are very happy together and have two children, ages three and one. Karima says this is enough since she hopes to provide her children with the advantages of education and the cost of living is always rising. She is less happy with their flat, which is small and dark and usually cold and damp. They live on a narrow dirt street lined with four story apartment buildings and the occasional bread shop or orange stand. Goats and a *gamusa* (water buffalo) stand calmly in the dust chewing on alfalfa. Her childhood home was on a similar street, but in the center of Cairo. There, windows were always flung open and people called out: "Hello, how are you, how is your family?" as you passed by. Here the shutters are closed tight. Most people have moved to this area in the last few years, as buildings are hastily erected by the wealthy landlords. Neighbors are suspicious of people with origins in different quarters of the city, or different villages in the countryside, ranging from the Delta to upper Egypt. Much of the easy friendliness of Cairo's center has evaporated in this outlying area. Karima's street is filled with recent migrants from the countryside who have come to Cairo to work in factories as they can no longer make a living on the land. Her own family, and her husband's as well, migrated into Cairo in her grandparents' time. This makes her a comparatively long-lived resident of Cairo, a distinction she is careful to draw when explaining local customs or discussing her discomfort in this part of the city and her desire to move. Still, the rents are affordable at approximately £E 12 a month and apartments are available, which is no longer true back in her childhood home.

But Karima is ambitious for her family, and she has been to look at other flats and talked with the landlords putting up the buildings. She has her eye on a building in the same area but on a newer and neater street. The building is scheduled for completion in six months and she could reserve a home now by paying £E 5000, half as key money and half as an advance on the £E 50 monthly rent. Since her husband works at two jobs, beginning at nine A.M. and finishing at eight P.M., the money from his work and hers combined amounts to a monthly budget of about £E 150, making this rent a possibility but a severe strain. The key money will be raised by *gama'iyya*, an informal savings cooperative, with a set of close relatives and friends, male and female. This provides the funds fairly quickly but requires a lengthy and expensive repayment period. Other young couples solve this problem by sending the fiancé to the Gulf states to work for two to four years to earn the

25

sum in a bulk, lessening the strain on a growing family and growing expenses later.

Meanwhile, their current first-floor apartment is small but sufficient. There is the usual entry hall with a large table taking up most of the space, a crowded parlor for guests with gold-painted chairs and a rug over the packed dirt floor, a bedroom, almost completely filled by a large bed and an armoire, and, off the entryway, a tiny kitchen-bathroom with a cold water tap.

Actually, Karima and Assam are not really in the flat very much. They leave the house early for the commute into the city. Karima takes an employee bus which is segregated by sex and which gives everyone an assigned seat, a huge improvement over the mobbed public bus system. At the workplace, she makes appointments for a supervisor, keeping his records in a small appointment book which she consults at the start of each workday. She works in an office of about ten by ten feet, furnished with two large desks and a number of rather rickety wooden chairs. One desk is occupied by a manager who holds meetings with people throughout the day as they sit grouped around his desk drinking tea and eating sugary cookies. The other is shared by three women who all perform secretarial jobs. Karima explains that their work overlaps so it is easy for them to cover for each other while one goes off to run an errand, to do the shopping for all three, or to pray. The atmosphere is friendly and jovial, with lots of joking and laughter, people crowding in and out of the cramped space, and quantities of sweet tea consumed. Someone is always dropping by to visit for a half-hour chat.

Karima holds a college degree in the arts making her better educated than her office mates, who have only finished high school. She would like a better job, with more interesting and challenging work and certainly with better pay. But such jobs are scarce and very difficult for families from this socioeconomic level to acquire, as they lack both the necessary connections and the language skills. Also, she is so busy outside work that it is difficult to contemplate the thought of looking for other work, even if she knew how to begin.

After two, Karima walks to her mother's house, which is about half an hour away, with all the shortcuts through winding paths amidst shouting children playing soccer and bored-looking sheep chewing endlessly as they stand in the mud. Her children live here with her mother who cares for them. She could use the childcare facilities provided at her work, but she does not trust them. Stories about lack of cleanliness, poor care and little love are commonly traded among the women. So most prefer to leave children with mothers or perhaps with non-working younger sisters or cousins. Generally, the children will return to live with their parents once they start school. Karima spends the afternoon at her mother's house playing with her son and daughter and talking with her younger sister who is still at home finishing school and has recently become engaged. The rest of the six children are already married and living in various parts of the city. With only three adults and two children in the house, the two tiny rooms seem much more spacious than ever before.

Asma, the younger sister, helps play with the children while she studies and waits for her fiancé to arrive for his daily afternoon visit. She wears Western dress with carefully matched shoes, bags, and jewelry, all in bright shades of reds and yellows. Karima used to wear similar clothes but switched a few months after the birth of her son to a kind of modified Islamic dress. She generally wears Western-style clothes, but cut loose and quite long with wrist-length sleeves and high necks. On her head she wraps a gauzy scarf carefully to cover her hair, neck, and shoulders, pinning it with a glittering barrette. Only in her own home does she take this head-scarf off, showing her long, curly brown hair. She wears kohl on her eyes but no lipstick to work; again this is carefully applied only at home.

Karima's long day continues when she rides the train home sometime after six, stops to pick up some vegetables and stops again for some bread on her way, and finally arrives at her own door. Inside, she quickly starts the vegetables stewing and puts the macaroni on, preparing herself and her house for her husband's arrival home. He comes in tired and hungry, eats and turns on the television while Karima makes the tea.

THE SUBCULTURAL SETTING OF
SUBORDINATE SUBJECTS

These two women, Hoda and Karima, are representative of the lower-middle-class women who are the subjects of this study of power relations under change in Cairo. Their stories portray the essential elements which shape the lives of single and of married working women. A knowledge of the particular stratum of society in which they live, with its unique living areas, customs, economic realities, and ideologies, is crucial for understanding the experiences these women face and the context in which they make their decisions as they try to make sense of the changes in Cairo society and negotiate a better future for themselves and their families.

To call this unique cultural setting a subculture serves to emphasize two points, first, that the lower-middle-class context is different and not merely part of a generalized dominant culture. Their environment cannot be reduced to stereotypes of Arab, or even Egyptian, behavior, much less repetitions of Islamic ideals. Yet this idea of a subculture also emphasizes the point that this class context is in many ways integrated into the larger societal portrait. In other words, while this group has its own unique culture, the prefix sub captures the related point of a subordinate culture, whose subjects participate in a variety of relationships with and within the larger society, including the important association of power.[1]

The descriptions that follow, brief sketches of the city of Cairo, local politics, class relations, family structures, religious beliefs, and gender constructs, lay out the rough outlines of the subculture of Cairo's lower-middle-class women. These descriptions can serve as an orientation to their unique context and as an introduction to their experience.

CAIRO

Cairo, an enormous, frustrating, and fascinating city with a long and illustrious past as a center of Middle Eastern culture, is currently home to some eleven million people.[2] In 1900 the city housed about half a million people; by 1970 this number had climbed to six million, far exceeding the two million which it is estimated the city can reasonably accommodate, and during the 1970s a migration rate of about 100,000 people per year arriving from the countryside coupled with natural increases propelled the number still higher.[3] The result is a city plagued by crowding, housing shortages, inadequate water and electric supplies, packed public transportation, unbelievable traffic, and nonstop noise.

Yet, Cairo is justifiably famous for its remarkably patient, good-natured and friendly population in the midst of turmoil, economic troubles, and an array of problems common to what *Time* and

Newsweek dub the "nightmare cities" of the developing world. The numerous reconstruction projects now initiated, including an expanded metro system, new telephone lines, highway overpasses, and sidewalk and housing construction, all promise some relief in the future. Meanwhile, however, they contribute to the general level of dust, noise, and inconvenience. Tahrir, the central square of the city, once a green park circled by palm-lined roads has been a massive construction site for years as the central metro system was slowly installed, but now it is gradually returning to a semblance of order, with bus stations relegated to one side of the square and pedestrians carefully routed along designated paths. On most streets, however, cars, cabs, buses, donkey carts, and bicycles all compete with pedestrians as everyone tries to find a path across the interlocked traffic. Most people dart quickly from one safe point to another—a mixture of well-dressed businessmen, government workers heading to the office, and peasant women with boxes of melons on their heads and children on their hips—all fighting their way to their particular destination. Cairo's traffic is not just an annoyance; it is an ever-present fact of this city's life.

Yet, this traffic influences people differently. The wealthy rarely walk anywhere, preferring to drive even extremely short distances in their personal automobiles. The people of the lower-middle and lower classes, on the other hand, do not own cars and indeed can seldom afford even the relatively inexpensive taxi fares. In addition, they are generally unable to live close to where they work. Long commutes by bus, minibus, or train are the rule and they can be arduous.[4]

Fortunately these inconveniences are only a part of Cairo as a city. The older quarters are a fascinating mixture of beautiful, if crumbling, architecture and narrow lanes of four- or five-story buildings full of flats housing much of Cairo's population, including many of the women in this study.[5] On the whole, people are proud of their ancient Egyptian heritage—the pyramids, Sakhara, Luxor, and Aswan; frequent short television programs on this ancient heritage ensure that everyone is aware of Egypt's long history as a center of civilization. But beautiful old mosques and *madrasas* (schools) rise in the most unlikely spots of the city as well, often unknown to the immediate inhabitants as part of their historical or artistic heritage. These buildings lend architectural grace and charm to the city, although many are falling gradually into ruin.

The Nile, of course, winds its way through the center of the city.

The streets lining the river are packed with cars but the sidewalk is shaded by lush trees. Cooled by the breeze off the water, the river banks form a haven, especially on warm spring and summer days, for people out for an afternoon stroll, for street vendors and their families camped on a spot of grass, for villagers far from home crouched around a fire making tea, for couples in search of privacy and a view. Most Cairenes point out the tall buildings, intricate architecture, and even the decorative pyramids of oranges and grapefruit piled high in the fruit stands with pride, and they compare their city's safety and general level of cheerfulness under adversity favorably with the portraits of violent and anonymous Western cities they see on imported television shows and Chicago gangster films. Despite the city's many difficulties, aggravated by rising population and deteriorating services, most people remain confident that Cairo's warm and sunny weather, friendly and welcoming population, and rich cultural heritage make this an enviable place to live.

Cairo is subdivided into local areas, each with a unique history and character.[6] The center of the city encompasses a diversity of districts including Garden City, a modern quarter built by the British and once filled with villas surrounded by shady trees and colorful bursts of bougainvillea. Glimpses of this past can still be encountered, but now the gardens have largely given way to high rises filled with expensive flats and business offices.

If one crosses busy Qasr al-Aini, however, and walks past the railroad tracks, one encounters a different world. Sayyida Zeinab's center is the shrine, a favorite place for women seeking spiritual help in matters of marriage or children. Tarred main streets give way to unpaved alleys lined with four-story mustard-color buildings full of flats. People lean from their windows and children laugh and shout at their games in the streets. On the corners vendors arrange their fruits in decorative stacks—a watermelon topped by an orange, topped with a lemon—ready for purchase. The smells of fruit mingle with spices from the next shop; further on a carcass hangs dripping from a hook in front of the butcher's door. Baskets heaped with lentils and macaroni crowd the next tiny shop. This is one of Cairo's more traditional areas, filled with men gossiping in the coffeehouses and women carefully shopping, examining the vegetables and housewares. History and traditional ways are alive in this part of the city; people who can no longer find a flat in the now overcrowded buildings recognize this vitality and wish they too could live in an area where life runs a familiar path rather than in the outlying districts where young couples must now venture to find any housing.[7] Those areas are seen as cold and new, lacking the strong sense of neighborhood bonds that characterize the older quarters. Garden City is nearly a foreign world to the people who live in these traditional sectors of the city, the people of this study. They inhabit a world utterly different from that of the wealthy or even the upper-middle classes; and they are geographically and culturally divided by way of life, beliefs, and behavior, not only by income.

Cairo is a city containing immense contrasts; old ways and Westernizations walk hand in hand, even as they compete and conflict.[8] Pajama-clad children playing in the streets clutch plastic racing cars or Santa Claus balloons. Young men dressed in Italian chic escort sisters or wives wearing full-length and long-sleeved dresses, their heads wrapped in gauzy scarves. A plump village woman wearing a long black dress cautiously weaves her way between honking and impatient drivers with a huge television balanced on her head. The city itself is a vital and vibrant presence, a dramatic setting for the clash of old and new that influences the lives of all its denizens.

LOCAL POLITICS

For the lower-middle-class families of this study, the historical progression of Egyptian politics and economic changes as well as interactions with the international political economy shape the social options available today. The socialist reforms of the Nasser era in the early 1960s were very important for these families; they are the beneficiaries of the policies of land reform, free education, and job opportunities for all in the government bureaucracy.[9] At the same time, their expectations were raised by the optimistic outlook this government also promoted; the ideals of social mobility and rising standards of living were extremely attractive and motivated people to pursue education and the dream of a middle-class life. Therefore, people of the lower-middle-class tend to look back on this era as a good time for their families, an age when the concerns and needs of people of their economic standing were appreciated and accommodated within government policies. "Nasser, he was a very good man. A real leader! He knew the people, and never drew away from them. He wanted to make the lives of the ordinary people easier." Many homes still have pictures of Nasser hanging on the wall along with portraits of the head of the household, and people talk about his life and work with great pride and obvious affection.

The same people view the Sadat era, with its policies of the *infitah* (the Open Door), and the Camp David accord with Israel, with far less favor.[10] One effect of the *infitah* has been the creation of a dual, public and private, economy, which has affected this group in adverse ways. Since lower-middle-class people are in effect restricted to the public sector, where jobs are secure but of low prestige and remuneration, and can only look from afar with envy and resentment at the rise of new and wealthy participants in the private sector, these families have become disenchanted with the policies of the Sadat government. They comment that Sadat himself was insensitive to the needs of the people, that he refused to realize the plight of many, and that he preferred to spend his time on international junkets and spending sprees at the cost of the Egyptian people, rather than diligently pursuing the problems at home. His policies toward Israel seem less crucial than the domestic economy in this portrait; most are relatively indifferent to the politics of accommodation, or indeed regard peace as considerable improvement over the need and expense of constant military aggression. However, many are saddened by the break with other Arab countries and feel that Egypt's rightful position as leader of the Arab world was compromised by Sadat for the uncertain gain of American ties. Welcoming the foreign aid from American coffers which has accompanied this political move, yet feeling ambivalent about its origins, most take a wait-and-see attitude. However, the feeling that Sadat neglected them, ignored his duty to provide for the Egyptian people, preferring the international limelight to the difficult and intransigent problems his economic policies had created in his own backyard, causes these families to see the Sadat era as one of increasing hardship. Active enthusiasm for government's role in their lives changed to dismay, discouragement, and anger during his era of leadership.

Mubarak is characterized as a well-intentioned, but perhaps not terribly competent successor to his more charismatic and influential predecessors.[11] Most people maintain that he is trying very hard to solve the problems of Egyptian life, but they also say these problems seem too difficult and intransigent for any one person to resolve. The qualities of dramatic leadership they crave are not found in this president, yet they seem to feel that he is, on the whole, a good man with a very tough job to handle. They are willing to give him a chance and are pleased and quite proud about his successes in cleaning up the city, lessening traffic problems, and getting the metro rolling. But most remain unsatisfied, feeling that the government is not responding in a comprehensive or effective manner to the severe economic crisis their class is now experiencing.

National politics, however, is a realm that most of these families regard as outside the concerns and activities of their daily lives; in fact, it is a difficult and dangerous arena they prefer to avoid. Generally, they do not participate in formal ways in the political world and regard political matters as outside their forms of expertise and control. Yet, while larger political contests are outside their view, this does not mean that they see their lives as completely victimized or that they portray themselves as passive in the attempt to deal with political problems of control of resources, distribution, or access to opportunity. Although many complain about the insensitivity and corruption of political leaders and the manipulations of the superpowers, they tend to regard themselves as competent in solving many of the more immediate and pressing problems they experience, problems that are less global, but no less political. Their means for solving these problems lie outside the more formal political channels, in the realm of family and neighborhood networks.[12] Through these informal networks, people obtain jobs, arrange marriages, distribute scarce goods, and pursue contacts who can help them acquire whatever they need or desire. These networks are a key element of the political realm, even in the upper echelons, and for people of the lower middle class these forms of family politics are the most immediate and effective way of pursuing their goals.

Yet, the global position of Egypt in world political and economic structures obviously impinges on these people's lives, shaping their options from the distant offices of foreign governments and multinational corporations. This world of international interaction falls far outside the realm of local control or even awareness. Yet, the reaction to Egypt's situation of dependency, whenever political events or economic problems bring the issue into the limelight, is one of somewhat puzzled discontent and increasing anger. Especially as localized forms of politics become less effective and even unable to provide well-paying jobs, good apartments at reasonable rents, or household appliances at affordable prices, this discontent could develop into a potent political force. Thus far at least, most of these families remain critics of the economy but strong supporters of stability over the chaos of protest or any form of revolutionary change. The future is less certain.

CLASS RELATIONS

Other factors contribute to the setting in which lower-middle-class women's decisions are made. One is the division of class, a distinctive but complicated dividing line in Cairo society. Clothes, for instance, provide an easily visible mark distinguishing economic groups.[13] Members of the upper classes generally wear fashionable Western dress, often purchased or imported from Paris or Rome; the middle classes dress in well worn and often handmade clothes, styled in more modest and less extreme Western fashions; lower-class men wear the traditional Egyptian *gallabiyya*, a long, wide gown of cotton material, and lower-class women wear bright dresses covered by black overgarments and gauzy headscarves. Yet, while dress symbolizes these distinct class divisions, overgeneralization can be deceptive. The same *gallabiyya* in fine cotton or wool may signal a very wealthy but religious or traditional man. Similarly, while areas of the city are easily identified as generally wealthy or poor, people will often choose to continue living in an old neighborhood rather than move to modern sections of the city, even though they succeed in business or inherit wealth. The crucial point relevant in this context is that Cairene society is divided by class and people have a strong sense both of hierarchy and of their place in this social and economic ranking system.

One observer, Saad Eddin Ibrahim, attempts to use a more objective set of standards to distinguish the strata of Cairo society; he divides it into six categories with the following estimates of the population falling into each sector:[14]

The lowest stratum—the destitute:	11.2%
The low stratum—the poor:	10.3%
The low-middle stratum—the border line:	26.5%
The middle stratum—The upwardly mobile:	36.1%

The upper-middle stratum—the secure:	15.3%
The upper-stratum—the rich:	1.0%

The families of this study straddle the border between the low and low-middle strata, and achieving secure lower-middle-class status is the desire of all these families. What does this desired status actually mean in Cairo society? Ibrahim uses income, occupation, education, and durable goods (lifestyle) to construct his classification system.[15] He describes the destitute as families with a single unskilled and illiterate breadwinner who live in one-room apartments with very little in the way of household goods.

The poor are those with a head of household who is generally a semi-skilled or clerical worker and often at least partially literate. They live in a flat of one or two rooms and can afford to let their children stay in school, perhaps even to college. These people live immediately below the poverty line, but they often do not describe themselves as the poor despite their clear need for better living conditions.[16]

The lower middle class is a borderline group living on the upper edge of the poverty line. They live in flats with two rooms, they own appliances such as a radio, butogaz stove, and television set. The head of the household may be a skilled worker or clerical worker for the government. These people identify with the middle class, but their income rises just above the poverty level.[17] Consequently, they are hard pressed to achieve their goals and expectations. And with the difficult economic conditions in Cairo, including high inflation, these families are finding it increasingly difficult even to maintain their position.

The middle-middle-class, the group immediately above the families of this study and consequently the group to be emulated, is distinguished by the size of their flats, usually three or four rooms. Their occupation, generally as young professionals, senior clerical workers, or private sector workers, further distinguishes them and provides the means for the more expensive rents and household furnishings.[18]

Finally, the upper-middle-class are those whose gains are secure; they live in three to five rooms, have completed college and have gained jobs as established professionals.[19] They, and the rich families who rise above them, have substantial incomes and live in large and lavish apartments; they generally work in the private sector or hold high government positions.

Grouped around the dividing line of the poor and the lower middle class, the families of this study focus on their lower middle class goals. The least well off have only one semi-skilled earner who brings in about £E 50 monthly; they live in two rooms and they have a television, cooking stove and refrigerator but no other appliances. The most prosperous live in four rooms; the man of the house works in a private firm earning some £E 100 a month and the wife "does not need to work."[20] But the great majority of these families fall in the range between these two extremes.

A typical home is located in a traditional urban quarter or a new industrial suburb of the city on a narrow, unpaved street lined with mustard-colored buildings full of flats and families. Stairways are dark and dusty, but once the threshold is crossed the flats are clean and cheerfully arranged. There may be two or even three very small rooms plus a tiny kitchen-bathroom area which is usually wet due to the leaking plumbing which plagues the entire city. This limited living space was home to some ten to fourteen people in the families in which the women of this study grew up; perhaps as a result, most younger couples plan smaller families.

In addition, these are families who have been settled in the city for one or two generations; their parents or grandparents came from villages in the Delta or Upper Egypt. These women identify themselves as Cairo residents of long standing, even though they are not true long-term residents, and distinguish themselves from more recent migrants whom they describe as uneducated and backward—as "*fellahin*" (peasants).

The particular stratum in which these people live is a strong component of their sense of identity; they all call themselves "people of the middle level." But in fact, the ability to shift into the lower middle class rests primarily on the woman of the household working in a formal salaried job, effectively doubling household income. Therefore, older families, further along in the life cycle, in which the mother generally stays home as housewife fall into the poor category, while younger families in which the wife typically works are able to climb to lower-middle-class status on the foundation of a combined income.

Important as the objective criteria are, in addition, the fact that these younger families perceive themselves, and talk about themselves, as members of the lower-middle-class is crucial. This phenomenological perspective contributes strongly to their class identification and therefore to decisions they make regarding where to live, the household goods to buy, the clothes to wear, or the level of education to give their children. Yet, it should be kept in mind that this class status is quite fragile and only recently accomplished and that it depends heavily on women's entrance into the workforce.[21]

FAMILY

Relations with family members are certainly the strongest links in women's lives. In Cairo, the importance of family in all arenas can hardly be overestimated. Some version of the extended family remains the ideal among all classes, and living in the same building or neighborhood with brothers, sisters, mothers or cousins is still considered the best situation.[22] Yet, because of the housing shortage in Cairo, this ideal can seldom be realized as couples marry and seek apartments today. Children search for, but often cannot find, flats in the vicinity of their parents and their childhood home. So, they are forced to find housing in more distant neighborhoods, and make long and arduous trips when they wish to visit family members.

This often means a loosening of bonds within the family as it may be impossible to visit all family members regularly. For instance, Nadia goes every Friday to see her sister who lives in the Pyramids area, and they spend the day sewing together and talking; she has two other sisters but since they live in Shubra and Imbaba, more distant from her home, she tends to see them only on special holidays. The effort to maintain family ties is important, but it has become necessary to be more selective and cultivate some ties over others. To solve these problems, two brothers or two sisters will often set up households in the same outlying district; for example, Husnayya and Nadia are both saving for the key money for apartments located in the same building in Shubra. They plan to set up households side by side so that they may care for each other's children, share household appliances, and maintain strong family bonds. The ideal situation of extended family living together remains very strong despite the pressures working against it.

Older children generally live at home until marriage, with the exception of some young men who temporarily migrate to other Arab countries looking for better paying jobs. Young men and certainly young women never take a flat out on their own, for both economic and social reasons. Even widowed or divorced women often return to their parents or ask someone in to live with them. To be alone is not only considered detrimental for one's reputation; people rarely enjoy it. Jihan, for instance, is a married woman in her early thirties with two small children. Her husband's job requires him to be away one week every month. For this week she always moves with the children into her aunt's home which is a full hour away from her own flat and no closer to her work. But, she explained, she could not stay alone; it would not be right and she would be uncomfortable and afraid.

The majority of social occasions also center on the family. Friday remains the day for visiting, despite the required long treks across the city, and celebrations such as weddings or holidays are always family affairs. The women of this study define themselves in terms of their place in the family and their actions are guided by a sense of being part of this whole rather than discrete individuals. Family provides a sense of place, a congenial setting, and a social network for financial and personal support. People often mention that life in the West, with its emphasis on individual needs and pursuits, looks very lonely and self- centered. The structure and ideology of family remain crucial for the networks of resources they continue to provide and for a sense of identity.

RELIGION

The rituals of religious practice are easily perceived in Cairo; mosques dot the city at frequent intervals, men pray on straw mats on the sidewalks on Fridays, and chanting from the minarets fills the air five times a day. As in any society, personal commitment no doubt varies widely, but the ritualized behavior and beliefs of Islam form a foundation for society in a way perhaps difficult to understand in secularized, commercialized America.

However, the Islam that shapes people's lives cannot be drawn directly from the ideals stated in the *Qur'an*, and deciphering what religion means to lower-middle-class people is a complex task. In reality, local variations of interpretation combine with customs to alter ideals into a diverse set of religious practices and beliefs.[23] Islam in lower-middle-class Cairo corresponds to classic Islamic ideals but adapts them to fit particular needs. For instance, while the verses of the *Qur'an* are considered the foundation of religious truth, most people do not read these verses themselves and are often rather confused about their exact content. Many who are unable to read tend to rely on the interpretations they hear at the local mosque, or on what a particularly religious family member or neighbor says. Even those who are educated often find this literature difficult or less interesting than newspapers, television, or radio, also sources of religious knowledge through special programming. In this manner, certain aspects of religious tradition and history are emphasized, adapting a rich tradition to fit more immediate needs. Depending on who is doing the interpreting—whether the state, the Egyptian religious hierarchy, members of the Muslim Brotherhood, or one's neighbor down the street—these interpretations may vary considerably and may also diverge from classic doctrine or practices in other Muslim countries.

Further, the Islam of men and that of women varies.[24] Women in Cairo, for example, generally pray at home rather than at the mosque.[25] While men attend mosque meetings on Fridays, women usually pray by moving to a separate corner of the room at home and covering their heads with a scarf after the ritual cleansing with water. Women also appeal to their own special saints, particularly in matters of marriage problems and family crises, by going to the saint's shrine and performing special rituals to entreat their aid. For example, women spend hours at the shrine of Sayyida Zeinab when they feel "sad, or lonely, or need to make a decision and wonder what way to go," or they come with other women who help in the ritual march around the saint's tomb, considered an aid for childless women. *Zar* ceremonies, while popular in Cairo, tend to be regarded as "lower-class" and are therefore avoided by these women, concerned with establishing their lower-middle-class standing. But special methods of appeal, including appeal to saints or refuge in forms of spirit possession, not sanctioned by the more legalistic classical doctrine, are part of women's village heritage, and appear at times in lower-middle-class Cairo.[26]

In general, the Islam of the lower-middle-class is the strong and unquestioned cultural foundation of their lives. Unlike wealthier groups, lower-middle-class people have not adopted many of the Western habits or customs which would lead them to violate traditional religious tenets. The five pillars of Islam, for instance, are considered important and proper, although they are not always consistently observed. Nearly all people pray on Fridays, and some pray throughout the week, often in special rooms provided at their workplace. The Ramadan fast is carefully observed, and even pregnant women, who are excused, eat very little. A trip to Mecca is a goal held by nearly all, but it requires careful saving. Women today often accompany their husbands and perform the pilgrimage themselves. Giving alms is done for women by their husbands, leaving their income exempt. Occasionally, men violate the ban on drinking alcohol, but these breakdowns of tradition are circumspect and never occur in the home in front of women or guests. Drinking beer or whisky is not the mark of a good family man, and women are careful to ask around, when considering future mates, about the habits of their prospective fiancés. Religion is the foundation and the justification for actions in all areas of life, whether these customs and actions are really specifically Islamic or actually local traditional custom. Islam, in a sense, is the language in which all social encounters are conducted; but this language has its own local dialect and its own interpreters, who may emphasize those aspects of the doctrine they find most convenient and useful.

Finally, Islam is not an ahistorical category, but an evolving set of beliefs and institutions as well. The current upsurge of interest in fundamentalist Islam throughout the Middle East has deep roots in Egyptian history of the last century. Evidence of this resurgence is readily apparent in Cairo and the subject of political controversy and cultural concern among all social groups.[27] In the families of this study, there is certainly a corresponding resurgence of interest in religious life. Men, especially, may debate religious matters and sometimes follow the arguments in the newspapers by prominent religious thinkers or writers. Women, in general, are less involved and less interested; they tend to regard this religious interest as a public and political matter, one out of their realm of real interest, the family.

Yet, there is a general feeling expressed often among this group which centers on the belief that life is inexplicably getting worse; politicians seem unable to arrest this process, and many people wonder why the economic situation has degenerated so far in recent years. The Islamists provide a ready answer insisting that a return to the traditional values that uphold Islamic culture is necessary for times to get better. This common feeling that life is hard and needs answers beyond the confusion and commercialism of the everyday grind, is accompanied by some increased interest in praying and perhaps performing the pilgrimage. Beyond that, most of these families remain uninvolved. Fundamentalist groups are typically regarded as political organizations, better avoided. Often, the militants are characterized as "crazy people," and many emphatically point out that Islam does not countenance violence. Politics, not religion, is seen as the concern of such groups, and therefore people separate what they consider political activities and organizations from religious matters.[28] But religion, or rather a return to an interest in cultural roots in the hope for a better future, is a strong sentiment in this subcultural group.

GENDER RELATIONS

A final issue shaping women's lives in lower-middle-class Cairo concerns matters of gender, including ideology, personal relations, and structural constraints. The Western stereotype of relations between men and women in the Islamic world as the interaction of sheer power and abject obedience is quite inaccurate. Women are not passive victims, and they quite actively argue their case and seek to widen their opportunities when the chance is offered. Yet, this activity is a form of influence or manipulation within constraints which differs from the powers exercised by dominant groups.[29] Characterizing the exact nature of these complex and subtle relations, however, is difficult and the task of exploring the changing form of women's power and protest is the goal of this study; here it is sufficient to note that women certainly seek an active role and expanding options, yet within the boundaries of cultural guidelines.

In lower-middle-class Cairo, gender roles are clearly delineated and supported by a strong set of beliefs about female nature and proper behavior. Men and women alike regard the male-female relation as one of complementarity; men and women have different natures which lead them to different roles, duties, interests, and positions. Men are led, because of their nature, to work outside the home and women, again because of their nature, are suited for activities in the household, including both the financial aspects of household management and the emotional factors of care and love. Negotiation of particular problems and decisions takes place within this general ideological context.

Further, it is important to mention that in Cairo, and certainly within this particular social stratum, women spend much of their time with other women. For example, when both men and women are being entertained at a party it is still most common for the men to cluster in one room and the women in the other. The concept of the *harim*, understood in the West purely as the placing of women away from the real and important public world of men, ignores the fact that men are actually excluded from the women's world as well—an important exclusion when one reflects on the power of gossip in a culture shaped by concepts of family honor and shame. The women's world is crucial in Cairo where men are often out of the home, or even away working in another country for long periods of time.

While Egypt has a long history of feminist activity and legal initiatives which protect women at work, women's position in lower-middle-class Cairo is still dependent on social custom, the limits of poverty, and difficult decisions on proper identity or behavior. Women's organizations, designed to support and encourage reforms in access to education, vocational training, and literacy and staffed primarily by upper-class women have an important history in Cairo. Many volunteer organizations focus on charity programs and have a long and successful record of helping women in the city and surrounding rural areas.[30] Specifically feminist organizations or activities are much more rare and limited almost exclusively to upper-class women involved in the effort to understand their new role as professionals in a society where most women continue to focus on the home. The newly formed Arab Women's Solidarity Association, for instance, pursues the goals of increasing women's participation, instituting social justice, promoting the development of women, and improving work conditions.[31] Yet, penetration to the women of the lower middle or lower classes is imperfect and extremely limited to date. Feminist ideals, whether of the Western or the Middle Eastern version, have hardly affected this sector of society at all, and organizations of lower-middle-class women to promote such ideas are virtually non-existent.

LOWER-MIDDLE-CLASS WOMEN IN CAIRO

These themes of the dominant culture—family, religion, class, politics, women's place—pattern the lives of the women of this study, shaping the possible choices they can make. But women, it must be remembered, are not simply pawns in this process. They also help to form and maintain these patterns, just as they try to alter them.

Women, as members of a subordinate subculture, are participants in a set of relations of power, compromise, influence, accommodation and struggle. While viewing women as active participants is hardly new, it needs, nonetheless, to be stressed, for too many theoretical approaches toward understanding women's role in times of change still ultimately emphasize the causal effects of outside forces and ignore the variety of women's responses, the context of women's decision-making, and the actual experience of change, constraints, and choices in which women are immersed.[32] Indeed, women are well integrated and even implicated in the social structures and power relations of their society.

The subculture is the setting where this integration and implication take place. It is the medium through which its members learn to interpret and ultimately act upon aspects of the social system. This setting involves economic, structural and ideological dimensions which are in constant movement, metamorphosizing with the needs of its members as they act in response to their own interests and react to those of the dominant culture. Although the subculture is integrated into the dominant culture, it remains a somewhat separate entity with its own needs, interests, institutions, and relations.

With dramatic social change, such as the economic change of women going outside the home to work for the first time, there is space for creating alternatives, more potential for counter-ideological and counter-institutional directions. It is this space that becomes crucial in the fight women face to alter unequal social relations. Their struggle within the subcultural context of constraints and opportunities is central to the chance to actually affect such relations and to the question of the ultimate reproduction of the inequalities of global position, class, and gender that restrict women, or for advances toward real change. It is to this issue of space and struggle that we can now turn, by looking first at the dramatic change these lower-middle-class women are experiencing.

THREE

Women At Work Outside the Home: The Experience of Change

Nadiya and her mother, Um Nabil, sit side by side on the elaborately carved, golden-painted, red-velvet-covered sofa of the guest parlor. "In the past, in the days of my mother and my grandmother, women 'sat' in the home; now we leave the house and go out to work in any job." Nadiya's answer to the question, How does your life vary from your mother's? differs markedly from Um Nabil's quite puzzled response: "My mother, God have mercy upon her, 'sat' in the house, the same as me. We cook the food, we wash the clothes, we make the tea, we care for our children." As more women responded to my question, this demarkation between the responses of younger and older women became more pronounced. Um Nabil and her contemporaries, women in their forties and fifties, saw their lives reduplicating the patterns of their mothers and grandmothers. But for Nadiya and the other younger women of this study, going out of the home to work figured prominently and consistently in their conversation; these young women perceive paid employment outside the household as a dramatic and important change distinguishing them from older female relatives and older patterns of women's experience. For lower-middle-class families, women's work patterns typically trace these generational lines.

Looking, at two women, Fatma and Samira, for instance, venturing out of the home to work immediately appears as a significant difference in the lives of these daughters and their mothers, breaking the inherited chain of a reproduced female role as *sitt al-bayt* (housewife). Fatma's mother, Um Mahmoud, was raised in a village in the Delta. Her family, relatively well off, owned some land planted with orange and tangerine trees and a house boasting a front parlor furnished with cotton-covered sofas for special guests. In the last few years further improvements have been made; the village now has electricity and the family owns a television, which functions somewhat uneasily on the uneven current. They also have the village's only inside spigot for running water; it pours a thin stream of cold water into a large plastic pail for washing dishes or drinking. Yet otherwise the cycle of everyday events and tasks remains essentially the same as in the days of Um Mahmoud's mother's childhood.

Their house is built of mud brick polished to smoothness and whitewashed inside. The floors are pounded dirt which must be swept clean of debris daily with cornhusk brooms. One room, employed as a storehouse for food and produce, is filled with plastic tubs containing cheeses, *turshi* (pickled vegetables) and preserved lemons prepared by the women themselves. In the central room, a cooking fire burns in the middle of the floor, providing heat and a handy means to boil water for the constant drinking of tea. Stairs lead up to the flat roof where fruit and straw are drying in the sun. As a girl, Um Mahmoud helped her mother with the housework, the cooking, cleaning, laundry, water carrying, and childcare. She also helped care for the animals, feeding the goat and water buffalo, and picked oranges and tangerines at harvest time.

Since marrying and moving to the city, Fatma's mother continues her work as a housewife, supervising the household and raising ducks, pigeons, and chickens in a small and dusty courtyard off the living room area. She leaves the home and neighborhood only rarely, usually to visit relatives in other parts of the city or in her native village. Fatma's father, a clerk in a government office, proudly points out that his wife has never needed to find work outside the household. And Um Mahmoud, for her part, considers her life a relatively happy and successful one. She has a good husband, eight healthy children, and reasonable economic security. She views the patterns of her life as reflections of the patterns of her mother's and grandmother's. And even though Um Mahmoud left her village for Cairo to marry and changed her immediate environment dramatically, she sees her life as essentially the same as that of former generations of women in her family. Her life replicates their duties and pleasures, their everyday routines and everyday struggles, transplanted into a new setting.

Her daughter Fatma, on the other hand, after finishing her college studies in social work and waiting about two and a half years for an assignment, was granted a job in the government bureaucracy and she goes off to the office six days a week. So do all of her sisters. The lives of Um Mahmoud's daughters break a lengthy chain of traditional female identity and activity.

Um Ahmed, Samira's mother, like Fatma's, does not work outside the home in any formal capacity. She was born and raised in an old, traditional quarter of Cairo whose residents are proud of their lengthy heritage in the city, and her married home lies only a short walk from her childhood neighborhood. Her husband works as supervisor on a construction team and generally makes a good income in recent years because of the building boom and lack of skilled laborers, most of whom have migrated to work in other Arab countries. Their five living children, except for the youngest daughter, are grown and married. Um Ahmed seldom ventures beyond the narrow alley which is her home, barring a Friday visit to her sister or special festivities like a wedding or engagement celebration. Asma, her youngest, or children from the neighborhood, are sent out on errands to buy the daily loaves of flat bread or sweets to serve a friend who has stopped in. Um Ahmed does the family cooking, most of the cleaning, and supervises the household finances and organization. Her youngest daughter helps with most of these tasks, snapping beans, for instance, while she reads her textbook and prepares her lessons for school the next day. Also, Um Ahmed cares for the small children of her married daughters while they work at the office or do run their household errands.

In addition to these household tasks, she spends considerable time maintaining the network of family members and friends which provides economic and emotional support for her family. For example, Um Ahmed is known as an honest and capable manager among her neighbors and relatives, so she has assumed the role of financial organizer, overseeing a variety of cooperative financial groups known as *gama'iyya*. These co-ops are crucial for families of

46

this economic level and provide the funds for important engagement and marriage ceremonies, key money payments for apartments, and cash for furnishings or appliances. Her position at the center of these arrangements gives her considerable economic power, which is a great resource for her family. Certainly Um Ahmed, like Um Mahmoud, recognizes her value to the smooth operation of the household and sees her role at the center of family organization as very useful. Her life runs essentially the same path as that of her mother and grandmother, a life focused on the importance of family.

However, Um Mahmoud's daughters, including Samira and her older sister Mona, work as secretaries in the government bureaucracy. They leave their small children with their mother during the week, visiting in the afternoons after work and picking them up on Thursday nights, before the Friday holiday. The lives of Fatma, Samira, and their mothers are typical of the rest of the households in this study; as one older woman stated, "Before, people wanted women to stay at home, now everyone goes out to work; it is what all the young women do today." Women like Fatma and Samira see a large gulf between the everyday tasks and pleasures which shape their mother's lives and those which frame their own. While these perceptions of a divide are powerful and important for these mothers and daughters, the image they convey of a lengthy and unbroken thread suddenly snapping, separating traditional mothers from modern working daughters, shows a partial and somewhat distorted picture. Actually both mothers, as these examples demonstrate, are involved in economic activity which provides significant resources for their families. Um Mahmoud provides food through her raising of poultry and Um Ahmed social security through her management of financial networks. Yet, neither woman would call these activities "employment," although both certainly recognize that significant work, effort and time are involved. For instance, when asked if she works, Um Mahmoud answers indignantly, "Of course I work, can't you see all the duties I have here in the home! I am working all day long, from sun up to sun down." Despite this recognition of the value of the labor in the home, neither of these older women would emphasize her part as a breadwinner for the household, although each contributes a considerable amount to the family finances. The reality of women's economic input, in other words, is not explicitly drawn out; instead, women tend to cover up the exact amounts they bring to family finances.

This suits women's need to maintain control over resources by masking the actual amount and range available, and it suits men as well, allowing them to exaggerate their role as sole breadwinner for the family.

Both women and men, though for different reasons, focus on women's image and identity as wife and mother, rather than their actual activities, thereby disguising women's productive capacities. Seen as wives and mothers, not as workers, these older women and their daughters perceive the change of paid employment as a crucial transformation in women's lives. It is this household-centered identity of women, important to both men and women, that is challenged by women's increased presence in Cairo's formal labor force. We need to explore their employment experience in more depth to understand how this change in the pattern of women's lives is perceived by these lower-middle-class women and to understand the controversies it generates in their lives.

WOMEN AND WORK IN CAIRO

First, lower-middle-class perceptions about women and work must be placed in context through discussion of the different strata of contemporary Egyptian society. In fact, the idea that working outside the home is an unprecedented situation for women emerges as a particular rather than general truth, fitting this specific class of women's very recent family histories, but neither universally nor uniformly accurate for all of Egyptian society.

Discussions of traditional patterns of women's work often assume an unvarying situation of women restricted to the home and uninvolved in economic activities. Actually, as recent historical studies have demonstrated, women's economic participation varied considerably in different time periods, across different geographical divisions, and over different class settings.[1] For instance, in the last century, many lower- and middle-class urban women became involved in joint businesses with their husbands or worked independently in the context of female labor guilds.[2] Urban women were often employed as food traders, dressmakers, factory laborers, or midwives, and women's options in the informal service economy expanded rapidly and were especially important in the second half of the nineteenth century.[3]

By the 1880s, female advocates of increased rights for women, and male advocates, such as Qasim Amin, linking improvement in women's condition with a liberal version of nationalism, stressed women's need for education, opening the way for further increases in women's paid employment in the modern context.[4] Even such a brief glimpse into the recent historical experience of Egyptian women suggests crucial variation in women's working situation, reinforcing the idea that the traditional economic role of women has evolved and changed over time and is not a set or ideologically determined pattern. Even the role of quite wealthy women involved considerable managerial effort and expertise which contributed to the financial resources of the household; the notion of the idle women of the *harim* is essentially a myth.[5] A great deal of variety in economic activities has been the historical reality, and the category of "tradition" encompasses a large range of possible economic participation by women.

Even more significant is the diversity of obligations and opportunities for women workers across the strata of contemporary Egyptian society. While the focus of this study centers on women who leave the household for paid employment, it is not, of course, true that all young women in Egypt work outside the home, a fact easily ascertained from the female labor activity rates which remain exceedingly low in Egypt, as in other Muslim countries. For instance, in 1979, only 10.4 percent of Egyptian women were recorded as economically active.[6] However, all such figures must be considered with extreme caution.[7] In general, severe undercounting of working women is the rule, and furthermore, these numbers virtually ignore all the informal avenues of employment which are so important for much of Cairo's population, male and especially female. There is also evidence that women's participation in paid formal employment has been increasing quite rapidly, in part due to the advances in educational opportunity for women in the last two decades. For instance, while Egyptian women held only 3.3 percent of positions in industry in 1961, by 1976 they formed 13 percent of the industrial labor force.[8] And while women held only 4.5 percent of clerical positions in 1960, by 1976 they held 27.4 percent of these jobs.[9] In fact, the demand for work seems now to be outpacing the supply of available jobs, pushing poorer, less educated women who want paid jobs into unemployment and lower-middle-class women into underemployment in the Cairo bureaucracy.[10]

To understand the position of the lower-middle-class women of this study and their specific and unique working experience, some crucial divisions of Cairo's society must be kept in mind. One is the difference in lifestyle and expectations between rural and urban women. Traditionally, rural women have performed the majority of household tasks and also have gone out to work in the fields, sometimes performing specialized tasks and sometimes laboring alongside men.[11] The exact extent to which women participate in such labor is not entirely clear; available data are scanty, unreliable, and slanted toward severe undercounting. One observer suggests that up to two-thirds of women's working day is used on agricultural rather than strictly household tasks.[12] A drive through the Egyptian countryside certainly provides immediate evidence that women help in agricultural labor; women can be seen feeding camels by the side of the road, picking fruit and vegetables, or watering crops.[13] Urban women often visit relatives back in their family's village of origin, if it is not too far from Cairo. When I went along on these visits, we often helped to harvest oranges and tangerines, working a long day in the hot sun. The harvesters were generally groups of women, who joked as they picked fruit, tended the children playing amongst the trees, and cooked tea over small fires, returning home only in the late afternoon to serve the main meal to the men in their families.

When these village women move into Cairo, as they and their families have in enormous numbers, they find a new environment. No longer do they inhabit a community where they are related to many of their neighbors and well known to the rest. Instead they crowd into urban quarters with many people who come from other villages and who may practice different customs. Agricultural work becomes limited to growing poultry or cultivating very small plots of vegetables. Since these women generally have little or no formal education, urban jobs considered respectable are hard to locate.[14] These recent migrant women and their families make up some of the bottom rungs of the income ladder in Cairo and both recent migrants and long-time residents of Cairo's poorest areas share in an informal labor market.[15] Women often embroider or sew, raise poultry, or sell vegetables on street corners. They may also help their husbands sell snacks on the street or peddle other wares. Such women participate in the gathering of economic resources in ways that cross the boundaries of standard definitions of employment, working in informal service jobs somewhere between household and workplace. They also may find more regular jobs, often in service occupations, such as becoming a cook, maid, or nanny for upper-class families, but such work can be difficult to find and even more difficult to keep as women do not have the necessary skills or knowledge to support this different class lifestyle. For example, women may not know how to clean vegetables according to upper-middle-class standards of hygiene, or how to prepare certain meals using ingredients too expensive for their own purchase and use at home.

Women with some education, generally those who are the children of these recent migrants to the city, can find work in the factories on the outskirts of the city. Such jobs for women were popular in the 1920s and 1930s with the establishment of textile factories, but these opportunities dwindled with mechanization and the resulting replacement of female with male workers, and declined further with the general economic slide in Egypt in the 1940s.[16] By 1952 women's activity in formal labor outside of agricultural work was at an all time low.[17] Yet today, many women commute by streetcar and bus to the factories daily to labor in assembly lines where they are valued as workers for their supposedly nimble fingers and skill with delicate tasks. Factory work is difficult labor, with long hours and little hope of advancement or increases in pay.[18] But it is popular with women of limited education for its steady income, the chance to socialize with other women, and the chance to save for otherwise unattainable household goods.

Women of the middle class are distinguished from lower social groups by the completion of at least a high school and increasingly, a higher institute or even university education. Nasser's social reforms, which provided for free education for children of both sexes, have had great impact on the urban middle classes. Rural and poor families have not often been able to afford the cost of books, tutors, uniforms, and the loss of the child's income, but for the slightly better off schooling has become, in the last two decades, a possibility.[19] For women particularly, education has developed into a valued opportunity. Since, until recently, the completion of schooling insured a government job, women who obtained a degree had access to relatively respectable work and a secure, if small, income.[20] Middle-class women also have the option of pursuing secretarial jobs in private companies, which in both salary and prestige offer significantly more. Some even gain access to the high-prestige university departments of engineering or particularly, medicine and can plan on future jobs in the professions.

51

At the top of the social scale, upper-middle-class and upper-class women, with the benefit of good education at the better universities or higher degrees combined with Western-influenced ideas about women's rights, are able to fulfill the claim women voice that in Cairo "Women are in every job." In fact, they often excel at jobs which in the West are regarded as male preserves. They own their own companies, work as doctors, teach at the universities, and often travel abroad to complete their education or to work.[21] Discussions of women's work in the Middle East have progressed far beyond the old stereotypes of idle women in the *harim* as more people recognize the responsibility and skills required for running an extended household, for managing family income and resources, and for reaching the recent achievements of upper-class women in professional fields.

Both the poverty and the necessity for degrading labor in the lower classes and the accomplishments of women in the upper-classes shape the perceptions and position of middle-class women. Yet within the middle class are additional, most important, distinctions. The women of this study come from the lowest layers of Cairo's middle classes and they distinguish themselves, in conversation and behavior, from those groups immediately below and above.[22] In fact, although the wide divisions of society traced above provide background for discussing lower-middle-class women, much more significant are the most immediate social and economic divisions which shape these women's real and perceived options.

Lower-middle-class women distinguish their families from those of the "poor," the *"fellahin,"* the "rough, hard" and uncultured masses who are not "modern" or "civilized." Poor women, they comment, are ignorant and uneducated, thus they cannot find suitable jobs. In contrast, lower-middle-class women are educated and work in offices. They stress their "modern" and "civilized" way of life which, they claim, separates them from the urban poor and certainly from the rural peasants.[23] For example, women point out their length of tenure in the city as evidence of their modernity and sophistication; families whose parents are migrants from the countryside are regarded as backward when compared to those whose grandparents were the actual migrants. "Backward" beliefs or behavior, such as arguing that women are not allowed to work, or wearing a very complete version of the *higab*, or thinking that women must always be accompanied by a male in walking about the city, are all cited as evidence of a too recent background of village life.

In turn, lower-middle-class women are firmly divided from the middle and upper ranks of the middle class by the distinction between public and private firms and jobs. Private companies require better education, degrees, and skills and they pay several times the salary of government jobs. However, these jobs are seldom open to lower-middle-class women except those of exceptional initiative or connections. Many women dream of obtaining these jobs but have no clear idea how to go about finding them and indeed can seldom compete with better educated and more sophisticated women from the upper ranks of the middle class. One young woman, for instance, who was trying to obtain a job in a private travel agency tried pulling in family members as go-betweens, calling on neighbors who knew the shop owner to intercede, and wandering in the street outside the office, attractively dressed, for several days trying to gain the owner's attention. She did not succeed and was forced to abandon this quest by female family members, who said she was making a fool of herself. "They will not hire you!" they claimed, "you do not speak French and English, you do not have the money for proper clothes, you do not belong to their social circles."

For members of this class, small differences in social background loom large as they try to differentiate themselves from the lower class, which they have barely left behind, and identify themselves with the middle or upper-middle class, to which they scarcely belong. These immediate social distinctions, from those just below and just above, relations of differentiation and of identification with their immediate reference groups, are most important for understanding the nature of lower-middle-class women's experience with moving outside the home to work.[24]

LOWER-MIDDLE-CLASS WOMEN'S WORK EXPERIENCE

For lower-middle-class women, as the stories of Fatma, Samira, and their mothers demonstrate, the change they see as central is the move from the household into the offices of the government bureaucracy. This change, which has dramatically altered the pattern of their lives, they perceive as "both good and bad": "This going outside the home and working has changed all our lives but some of the changes are a mistake and cause many problems in our families and in our society. We must keep the good parts and fix the problems." All the women see paid employment as a major change which differentiates their lives from those of women of their mother's generation, but after weighing the benefits and the costs many remain undecided about which way the scale ultimately tips.

This ambiguity is, of course, unsettling for these women, and particularly since they had extremely high expectations of what the benefits of leaving the home to work would bring. Their families often sacrificed considerably to enable these daughters to stay in school, forgoing their possible contributions to family income over their teenage years and paying the not insignificant costs associated with their schooling. In fact, young girls will often continue in school even after their brothers drop out to work in mechanics, construction, or factory labor. It is common for these young women to be better educated than their brothers and sometimes better educated than their husbands. In one family, for instance, the sisters were all attending school—high school, a higher institute in secretarial studies, and university studies in social work. However, their two brothers were both employed in apprenticeships as mechanics in a garage in their neighborhood. Neither brother had finished high school and neither considered this a problem, for mechanics can earn more than government employees and they need not wait for years for government jobs which may not be forthcoming. A woman's need for a respectable and secure income and the chance to marry up in the class hierarchy is best met by gaining this educational insurance of job security; but a man's need for higher paying jobs are better met outside the government bureaucracy.

As more and more women enter Cairo's formal labor force the problems and prospects of these lower-middle-class *muwazzafin* will become even more important.[25] By 1976, one-third of the entire female labor force involved women working in these government clerical jobs, and this figure rises slightly when considering younger women; again in 1976 for instance, 37.5 percent of working women 25–30 years old were employed in such clerical positions.[26] These women are a highly visible and crucial subgroup in numbers, but their political significance extends even further. Their experience with working will set the pattern for other lower-class women entering the formal labor force. In assessing what this pattern will be, we must be very cautious in our assumptions about what these women expect or want from these jobs. As an example, while lower-middle-class women come from families striving to rise firmly and finally out of the lowest levels of Cairo society, hoping to make a better life, their aspirations to rise on the social scale generally do not mean wanting to emulate the professional aspirations of women of the upper classes. Envy of upper-class women's lives has limits. Most of these women are proud of being Egyptian, proud of their long tradition, attached to their customs, and particularly tied to their strong family life and its place for women. They want the economic well-being of the upper classes, but this does not mean a wholesale desire to adopt all upper-class patterns. While some women are pleased with their new opportunities and proud of their working status and income, many others hope to quit their jobs rather than rise to new responsibilities; they look to the home rather than the workplace for their future. In fact, about two-thirds of these women claim they would quit their jobs if they could. A final third support their new status as paid employees and often extol the benefits of their new situation; but even these women admit that together with the advantages come many heavy costs.

We can turn now to discussing the details of women's account of the benefits and costs of paid employment, to understand their perspective on the work experience. The discussion can be conducted under two broad and overlapping categories: economics and everyday routine. The former concerns matters of income, the way this income is gained, and the way it is used within the family. Under the category of everyday routine, equally crucial questions of everyday experience and problems of role and identity can be pursued.

ECONOMICS

Why are Cairo's lower-middle-class women working in such increasing numbers? The need for income was the nearly unanimous reason given by these working women regardless of their age, educational attainment, or marital status.[27]

Why do I work! To make some money of course!

I work because life is very expensive today, and everyone needs a little more to be able to cover the costs.

I work to have the salary, so that we can buy some things for our home, some extra things we could not afford with only my husband's income.

Women also mentioned a variety of other reasons for working in these jobs, including keeping themselves occupied, meeting friends, meeting future husbands, the fact of being single, the idea that everyone works today and the wish to better themselves.

Well, working keeps me busy, you see, I would be so bored sitting in the house all day. Here I am occupied with this and that, and I have the chance to talk with my friends and see people. I have the chance to see the world!"

I like working in this job, and the reason I keep working is to be able to see my friends and chat with them. I met my husband here too, and we are very happy together. If I stayed in the home I would be bored and lazy all day. Here something is always happening; we can talk among ourselves; we can look out the window at what is passing by; it's entertaining!

Of course I am working because I am not married yet. All girls work these days. After one gets married, then it becomes different. There are so many responsibilities then, for the house and the children. Some women work after they marry and some do not. But until I marry, I will certainly work.

I work because everyone works today. This is modern life, this is the modern way things are in Egypt. All the women work and this is a good thing. It gives women some things to do and someplace to go outside the home; it offers a challenge. I can make myself stronger this way, and offer more things to my children.

Even with these other reasons, nearly everyone stated the need for income first as the obvious and most important reason for working. Indeed, it is hardly surprising that women of this economic level labor primarily for the income they gain. Holding a job for its intrinsic interest is, in all countries, mainly an upper-class prerogative and Egypt is no exception to this rule. As lower-level clerks and secretaries, women generally earned around £E 45 a month in 1984, with wages rising to about £E 60 monthly by 1988.[28] The few who have acquired better jobs, such as departmental supervisor, whether through length of service or exceptional initiative, earned more, perhaps an additional £E 25. However, the newer recruits earned substantially less, with salaries about £E 10 a month less than these averages.

For these salaries women work the typical six-day week with Friday, the Muslim holy day, off. Usually they are expected in the office between eight and nine and they leave around two; this adds up to a work week of approximately thirty hours. Most work in the government bureaucracy where they benefit from protective labor laws barring discrimination on the basis of sex for hiring, benefits, and salary. Unfortunately, as in the United States, men tend to fill the upper echelons of the bureaucracy while women cluster in lower-ranking clerical positions. Nevertheless, women's complaints center not on the difficulty of obtaining higher-ranking positions, but on the size of their salary, which they consider far too small both for the hours they must labor and the necessities they must purchase with these funds.

> My salary is a help to my family, because there are many younger children and this way I can support myself and save money for things for my home when I marry. I plan, God willing, to buy a gas stove this winter and I have also bought two pictures for the wall recently. But before I marry we need many things; there must be a refrigerator and it is very difficult to save any money on this salary; there is the cost of clothes and transportation to consider.

Families of the lower middle class are striving for more than subsistence; they have a clear idea of the type of life they want to lead and have hopes of achieving these goals through sacrifice and hard work. Women measure their definitions of economic need in relation to the immediate social differentials they clearly experience and observe. They are ambitious, believing government promises that they can rise in Cairo's social and economic ladder. They are willing to commit family resources toward this goal and work hard to help attain desired ends. They cite the need to pay expensive rents, to save for key money for a flat, and to buy good food for the children as reasons for working. They have more than subsistence in mind and these levels of expectation are politically and personally important as motivation.

The earnings these women make generally go to fund family needs;[29] typically women make a budget for the month. A normal budget for a young couple of about £E 100–150 monthly (perhaps £E 1400–2000 annually including bonuses and extra informal income earning) is generally expended on rent, food, commuting, clothes, medicine, and education for the children.

A typical lower-middle-class monthly budget (1984):[30]

Rent	£E	45
Gama'iyya payments		20
Food		35
Utilities		3
Commuting		5
Clothing		8
Education		8
Medicine, health care		5
Pocket money, emergencies, contributions to extended family		16
		150
Total income		
Husband's wages		60
Wife's wages		45
Informal sources, or second job		45
		150

Rents require a disproportionate amount of a family's income as the housing shortage in Cairo continues and intensifies; given the lower-middle-class concern with finding a suitable flat which will convey and reinforce family status, this problem assumes even greater importance. Typically, a young couple finds a place to rent after the formal engagement party and before the final marriage celebration, a period of perhaps two or three years. They plan to stay in this flat for their foreseeable future, barring drastic swings in the family fortune. Apartments of the sort that cost their parents about £E 3–7 monthly (because of rent control) will cost these young couples between £E 40–60. In addition, key money, or advance rent payments, which they must give to acquire a home, often amount to some £E 3000–6000, clearly a crippling expenditure on families with only £E 1200–2000 in expected annual income. Utilities—electricity, water, butogaz—add a further £E 3 per month.

Food costs vary with family size of course; a typical expenditure for a young couple with two small children might be £E 30–40 per month. This amount pays for a diet heavy on starches, principally rice, macaroni, and breads. Chicken or fish is eaten about once a week, often on Friday or when visitors are expected. Meat is consumed much less frequently because of its high cost.[31] Fava beans, goat cheese, eggs, vegetables, fruits, and sweets round out the diet.

Commuting also adds to the regular expenses; most people commute by bus or tram to their jobs and if both husband and wife must pay for this trip, then another £E 4–5 must be counted in each month. Remaining funds are used for clothing, holiday expenditures, medical emergencies and savings.

Typically, money is saved through use of *gama'iyya*, traditional informal saving cooperatives, for paying off key money or purchasing expensive items such as electric fans, televisions, refrigerators, radio-tape decks or conversion to more modern plumbing. At one time, the husband's earnings were sufficient to cover the necessities of housing and food, while the wife's earnings could be used to supplement that income, purchasing those appliances which made life easier and more entertaining. Increasingly, as prices climb, the wife's money is also required to cover basic needs.

This typical family budget for a young couple varies somewhat in form from traditional patterns. The traditional approach, according to these women, generally involved the man working for wages or salary; he brought home to the wife enough money to provide for the household.[32] According to Islamic belief, this task is the husband's responsibility, whether his wife has her own money or not. A good husband, by women's standards, turned over his whole salary and the woman in turn made a budget of family assets and expenses and purchased the daily needs for the household; her duty as a good wife was to make the money stretch sufficiently to cover family needs. Many husbands were not quite so good however; they gave money to their wives but women never knew whether it was truly all or only part of the salary. The rest men kept for their own use, buying cigarettes, paying for coffees, eating at food stands with other men away from the house. Often, women complained, men frittered away on cigarettes and coffee money that was needed in the home for necessities. Some men gave their wives money weekly, others daily, others whenever they felt like it.

The typical contemporary pattern for families with both partners working involves the husband and wife pooling their earnings. The wife makes out a budget and the family follows these guidelines in their expenditures. Prices for rent and other necessities are fairly set; larger purchases are debated and discussed at length. Usually the final decision belongs to the husband and he commonly makes the actual purchase. As one young woman described the process,

> First, we spent many months talking about what we need. I wanted a refrigerator. Mohammed wanted me to have a refrigerator too, he is a good husband. But, he also wanted a tape player. Men are like that! They always think about having a good time and sitting with friends talking over tea! They don't think about women like us who have to do the work! How will I store the food? I asked him. I could save so much time shopping and cooking if we had a refrigerator. I could get the fruit and vegetables only twice a week, not everyday. And I could cook one day and put the food in the refrigerator and it would be easy to heat it up the next day when we come home from work. He finally agreed because his friend at work, Mahmoud, bought a refrigerator and he was embarrassed. But now we have saved and we have the tape player too.

When a man has a second job, which is common, he sometimes puts the income from the first into the family pool while keeping income from the second for his own pocket expenses. Unfortunately, a woman's second job, caring for the house and family, does not provide her with extra cash to make personal purchases. These must come out of the family budget and although women manage the budget, they feel that this money should be expended on the family, not on their own personal needs or wishes; as a result women may have far less discretionary income than their husbands in an economy dominated by cash exchanges.

Obviously, a key change for women is the switch to earning cash themselves rather than relying completely on their husbands for funds. "I enjoy working because of the salary I can earn, it is more than I could make from raising chickens or ducks in my home as my mother does. With this money I can buy things as I like! I don't have to ask my husband for this or for that, always relying on him. If I decide we need something, I can just take the money and go and buy." Women know their own earning power, and they are often proud of their ability to contribute cash to the family's income. Further, earning their own salary gives women and their children greater security as they can now purchase food and basic necessities from their own funds rather than relying solely on a husband who might prove unreliable. These capabilities are crucial in an urban environment of cash exchanges, where women are able to rely on social networks and in kind exchanges far less frequently than in the past.

However, there are costs that diminish the value of this new earning power. First, women's salaries are low to start with, making their efforts to fund family needs extremely difficult. Women compare their salaries with those of women working at similar jobs in the private sector and complain that government salaries are unfair. "I work to earn some money, but today the salary I make does not go very far. Look at the cost of meat for instance! Everything is very expensive and my salary is good, but not enough to buy the things we would like to have." Most women focused on what they saw as an unwillingness of the government to provide higher salaries, emphasizing their perceptions of these jobs as a form of social welfare to which they and their families are entitled.[33] Secondly, these small wages can no longer go to fund the extras women initially expected to be able to attain; increasingly, they now must go to fund the family's basic needs. Fewer tapedecks and electric fans can be purchased as families spend more and more of their income just to pay rent or buy food. And finally, women lose the traditional economic resources which their mothers had time to cultivate — both informal earnings and the support of social networks. These costs to the family and the individual woman are hard to quantify, but they certainly cut into family resources, again diminishing women's gains from their new form of earning.

Since women and their families tend to think of these jobs as a stop-gap measure designed to aid family finances, not as a form of personal advancement for women, these encroachments on women's income are very hard to take. Disappointed with the incursions on their earning power, most women, from time to time, question whether these jobs are worth their efforts at all. "Sometimes I think that I should quit my job and just stay home with my son. I could do some sewing too and earn a little. But I'm not sure, this job gives me some security, and pays for some extra things like this barrette, or that picture." Women recognize that other changes beyond the increase in income occur in their everyday life from the challenge of the work experience, and these changes contribute to their overall accounting of costs and benefits. We can consider these alterations in everyday patterns and routines in the next section.

EVERYDAY ROUTINE

In matters of everyday activity, one of the greatest changes was mentioned by Nadiya at the beginning of this chapter. "Now women go outside the home. . . . " This change in women's mobility is expressed as an important reason for working in many ways; women claim that work is interesting, that one can meet new and different people, that one can get out of the home, that one can be busy and not bored, or even challenged. Traditionally, both men's and women's lives centered on the home and the neighborhood. In recent years it has become increasingly common for men to go out of the *hara* to work while women remain inside. Older women, such as Nadiya's mother, are limited to shopping at nearby markets accompanied by their children or occasionally to venturing out to visit relatives in other areas of the city.

One day, for instance, Mervet convinced her cousin that we should all go to the afternoon show at a movie theatre in the center of Cairo. Using me as an excuse, she was able to persuade her mother to accompany us on this special occasion designed to show me a real Cairo theatre. Lunches were packed, clothes carefully selected, and we set out on the bus for Tahrir Square. Mervet's mother, who had always appeared very competent and self-possessed, became increasingly nervous; it was very clear that she was not used to such outings. At the theatre, we ran into a snag with the lunches, filled with aromatic ground meat, which the theatre attendants were determined should not enter the door. After quite a round of arguments, we successfully entered with lunches in hand and made our way to our balcony seats where soda, candy, and popcorn were being sold at loud volume. The film, an action-packed American import, seemed to leave Mervet's mother completely confused, but the younger women were very enthusiastic, enjoying the social occasion. After we returned, Mervet's mother commented with relief, "Well, I am glad to be back on our street!"

Yet her working daughters' lives involve such excursions about the city as a matter of course. Each day they must commute, often long distances, to the office. Women prefer to meet with friends and make the trip together, but often they are alone for at least part of the time. This commuting to and from work gives women a knowledge of the city they never had before. They gain the ability to move around on their own, mastering the bus and tram systems, memorizing the winding streets.

They are also exposed, whether out on the streets alone or in the company of female fellow workers, as they are away from the protection of male members of their family. Men walking down the streets or sitting in the sidewalk coffee shops can compliment and comment. They attempt "accidental" encounters; they touch and pinch. Women are consistently harassed in this manner as they walk the crowded sidewalks and squeezed overenthusiastically on the overloaded trams or buses. Learning to deal appropriately and effectively with these situations without the help of family members is crucial for maintaining one's reputation and avoiding annoying situations. Typically, women cluster in groups on the buses and stroll arm in arm on the streets, signaling that they have no wish for other company. They will walk far out into the street to avoid passing right in front of a sidewalk cafe and to show that they are not loose, but moral women.

Traveling about the city in this manner and in the workplace itself, women are exposed to a variety of customs, dress, attitudes, and behavior. The neighborhood can be a reasonably homogenous place; people vary somewhat in income or morals or family life, but there is consensus on appropriate behavior and reasonable goals. Out in the city women see people from all over the world— villagers from the Sudan, rich sheikhs from Saudi Arabia, mini-skirted tourists from Europe and America. They notice other nationalities and classes; they observe different lifestyles. Women acquire an awareness of the particular nature of their own customs and the knowledge that in other areas of the city, or of the world, people often live quite differently. For instance, one woman's mother asked in the midst of a discussion of religion: "Where do American people go when they go on the *hagg* (pilgrimage)?" Her daughter quickly answered her, explaining that Americans do not go on religious pilgrimages; she was aware that Christians in America differed from Muslims or even the Copts of Egypt and took no special religious trip either to Mecca or Jerusalem. This widened awareness of potential differences allows women to have pride in the uniqueness of their own customs and perhaps provides some tolerance for the customs of others. For instance, an unmarried woman named Fawzayya cited the example of couples who stroll along the Corniche by the Nile hand in hand or sit closely together on benches by the river. "That is all right for women in places like Zamalek, but not for women here!"[34]

At the workplace, women meet new people every day. They spend hours chatting over steaming cups of sweet tea with fellow workers, male and female, from other sections of the city. They make friends outside the *hara* and the family; they sometimes go to visit these friends in their homes just as they would visit relatives. They argue over questions of marriage, childcare, proper dress, engagements and weddings, husband's behavior. They also compare the prices of various commodities and learn that different areas of the city charge different prices for similar goods. They encounter new opinions and multiple points of view, rather than being restricted to the sentiments and behavior available in their home, the homes of relatives or in their own neighborhood.

For instance, one woman had a sick baby and she was doctoring him, according to the advice of her aunt and mother, with some pills from the local pharmacy. These included an assortment of antibiotics, decongestants, aspirins and cough suppressants as well as an unidentified drug to make him sleep. The child had gone into convulsions in the night, but appeared better in the morning and was with the woman's mother for the day. Fellow workers offered various remedies, suggestions, and stories of their own experiences. One woman, who had a sister who studied medicine, counseled the mother to stop the medicines and take the child to the doctor, explaining that they were intended for adults and could harm the child. The mother agreed to try it and took the baby to a private doctor, who prescribed medicine which helped the child recover. Now this woman is much more careful with medicines and passes on this advice to others with children. Helpful information can be passed in this way to women who would have lacked such exposure in the past.[35]

Another advantage, or widened opportunity, is that women may meet men, future husbands, in the workplace. Traditionally, young women married cousins, more distant relatives, or neighbors known to the family. These marriages were arranged by parents and relatives, and the couple might or might not know each other before the marriage. Now, women have added the workplace to the list of possible sources for future partners. Men and women at work sit and talk, joke, and flirt mildly with each other. Through mutual friends they learn about the other's family and consider the potential for becoming partners. The man might then call on the woman's family and be considered for marriage. Usually, women will meet their future husbands only once or twice to discuss their wishes for the future before the formal engagement party and lengthy engagement period. Meeting a husband at the workplace widens a woman's opportunity to know her husband better before committing herself to marriage. Often, husband and wife will continue to work in the same office or building after marriage, allowing them to "keep an eye on each other."

Azza and her husband Magdi, for instance, met for the first time when she was called to a government office to begin work. She went to the supervisor's office and while filling out some required forms, she talked to the other workers in the office, one of whom was Magdi. The next day he came by her newly assigned office to say hello and they talked for a few minutes. On the third day, he followed Azza as she left the office at the close of working hours and walked to the bus stop. He asked if he might visit her family and she said yes. Later that week he paid the visit and satisfied her family as to his suitability as a marriage partner, and they were engaged soon after. In time they were married and now they both continue to work in the same government office building.

This pattern is common for young women workers today and differs substantially from traditional, totally arranged marriages. While men and women of this social stratum do not date before the formal engagement, they do meet each other often in the home during the two- to three-year engagement period and talk over their thoughts and hopes for the future. Women have the right to reject a suitor the family proposes and this right is given practical power by the ability to meet and attract alternative partners at the office. Afaf, for instance, after breaking her engagement to a distant relative, considered several men from her office as possible partners before settling on a friend of her brother. The family was deeply involved in the whole process, but final say rested in her hands.

Another change in women's everyday routine involves moving from the household into the workplace, altering the environment of women's daily activities. In the home, women, including the mothers of the women in this sample, do virtually all housework and childcare. In Cairo, where automated appliances and convenience stores are nonexistent or extremely expensive, women must do most work by hand. Typically, shopping for food is done daily. Women or children go out to nearby vegetable stands and select the best produce for the money. Meals, generally stewed vegetables and macaroni or rice, are cooked every other day on butogaz stoves or small bunsen burner-like gas canisters, and leftovers from the first meal are saved to be served again the next day to save time and fuel. One day a week is set aside for washing, which involves scrubbing clothes in a plastic tub of cold water and hanging them out to dry on clotheslines suspended outside the windows of the house. Another day is for general cleaning; floors are swept and furniture is wiped to clear off the dust which settles on everything in a matter of hours. Children are often the focus of the home; they must be entertained, fed, dressed, and watched. The men of the household, including male children, very seldom help out in any substantial way. They may help when a woman feels sick, or is especially busy for some reason. They may stop for bread on their way home, or get up to make their own tea once in a while, but these duties are all considered women's responsibility.

In families where both husband and wife work this pattern is beginning to change, but not dramatically or uniformly. Husbands are usually not pleased that it is necessary for their wives to "help out" with the earning of income, because they then spend less time on tasks in the home. "In the old days, when I was living at home with my mother I would go out to work and come home tired at the end of the day. My mother would have a beautiful dinner waiting for me as soon as I walked in the door. Now, times are hard and everything has changed. You see me now, I am tired and I sit here and must wait for dinner," complained an irate and discouraged husband. He and his wife had both just returned home from full days at the office and she was busy in the kitchen preparing a hot meal as he rested in the living room.

Even men who recognize the extra burdens on their wives feel there is really little they can do to remedy the situation; men simply cannot do such tasks very well, if at all. Yet, perhaps half of the men admit, with some embarrassment, that they do in fact sometimes help their wives with the housework. Usually they help with the food shopping or light cleaning and straightening up in the apartment. Very seldom will a husband perform such tasks in front of guests, nor will his wife encourage him to do so. Yet, one husband, newly married, actually helps cook and serve dinner in front of friends; he explains that since his wife helps him provide for the home, he must in turn help her with her tasks in the house. However, such an understanding is still unique and most women complain: "I don't know why he doesn't help me at home. I am very tired when I come home in the afternoon and still I must cook the meal and have everything in place or he will be upset with me." Women cope as best they can. They often send one person from the office out to do shopping for all. They sort eggs or pick over rice at their office desks as the hours wind by. They buy fruit and bread on the way to and from work, choosing the more expensive shops by the bus stops rather than shopping for better quality produce further away. They leave their children at childcare centers or with relatives and neighbors while they work.[36]

The problems at the intersection of household and workplace are severe for lower-middle-class women, causing them to reopen the question of the value of working at all. In addition, there are further problems of gender as expressed in the workplace itself, which contribute to women's disillusionment. To get these jobs, most women have at least completed secondary school and have often attended a higher institute or college. In fact, in 1976 over three-quarters of Cairo's female clerical workers had finished secondary school and a further 7.7 percent had finished university.[37] In 1984, among the women in this study, 20 percent had attended or completed university, usually specializing in social work or liberal arts; 32 percent had acquired the *diplome tigara*, a degree from a business institute; 16 percent had acquired teaching certificates; and 24 percent had finished high school. Yet, very few of the skills women have mastered are utilized in their offices. These women hold lower-level clerical positions; one is responsible for running a copy machine, another records appointments for a department manager, another takes money in a cafeteria, another types and files. They are seriously underemployed.

Further, they seldom learn new skills at the office. Generally the work is simple, repetitive, and fairly boring. Women complain of the tedious hours and they spend the time chatting since the work itself requires so little attention. Often, four or five women may hold a similar position and can easily cover for one another while one slips out to shop, pray, run an errand, or go home to visit a sick relative.

The few women who explain that they like their work are usually in more responsible positions. Two women, for instance, supervise their departments; both have worked for about twenty years and regard working as important for women. They are capable and willing to put in extra effort. Like many women of their cohort, women who began working in the 1960s, they are pioneers in the expansion of opportunity for women, and consequently they are very concerned with maintaining their position. Younger women have a different experience, and only a few of them display this extra initiative which would give them the opportunity to rise into jobs that could hold their interest and even satisfy their desire to be "kept busy."

Some opportunities do exist for women who have the time and drive to put the extra efforts into their jobs, but these women are exceptions. For example, one woman working in the government bureaucracy was originally assigned the typical secretarial job; now she does accounting for the department. Another originally had a job in a government office doing typing but was able to mobilize family connections and find a job in a bank. These women, however, see themselves as unusual rather than typical; further, the government could not absorb a significant number of such women since the interesting jobs are few and generally occupied by men or higher class women in a system that works on seniority and favors male applicants.

These jobs present little in the way of career opportunity; the severely overstaffed bureaucracy has little to offer in terms of advancement potential for the majority. And the majority of women do not think of work in these terms; it is simply a way to earn some small income to help out in the home. Thoughts of careers are rare. Most women view work as something people simply have to do; moving ahead and meeting challenges are regarded as useless efforts in a world which sees the workplace as unimportant compared to the home.[38] While nearly all the women claim that they have the same rights and opportunities at work as the men in their departments, a quick glance is enough to ascertain that women hold the clerical jobs and men the managerial and administrative positions. When asked why men fill the upper layers and women the lower, a common response (of both men and women) is "Women have other duties and only put half their time into the office." Men, with little else to occupy their time, are able to advance while women are too occupied with other responsibilities. Women see this as a natural division and not as a social or political problem. In fact, they appreciate being able to hoard their energy for the strenuous commuting and their work at home.

A final aspect of the change in women's everyday routine created by the move from household to workplace is the change in the nature of the environment they inhabit. Women move from home life in which they are very much in charge and involved, to the legalistic and bureaucratic atmosphere of the office. This move is probably not correctly characterized simply as a switch from the private to the public sphere.[39] Home life in the Middle East has many public aspects; the *sitt al-bayt* is involved in organizing the economic and social life of a large family. Housewives prepare budgets, purchase goods, grow chickens for sale, participate in *gama'iyya* arrangements, organize engagements and weddings, and help with the children's education. Life in Cairo still centers firmly on the family and family life is not relegated to a narrow, private corner, but indeed has tremendous political significance.

More to the point, women lose control over their own time which they used to have within the household, and the structure and relations of the workplace now control them and monitor their behavior. They must punch in a timeclock, ask permission to go on errands or take time off, and appear at work most days. The routine of the office is regulated by the clock rather than personal desires and women resent this loss of control. To regain control, women collude to evade their supervisors whenever possible, covering for a friend who has slipped out on an errand or not appeared at work for the day. (In fact, the atmosphere of most offices appears more like a household than a workplace to Western eyes, as women chat, drink tea, and prepare food.) Many women simply do not accept the authority of the workplace or their superiors and evade orders whenever possible or argue vehemently for the right to go on an errand or leave work early. The shift in identity from wife to worker is incomplete at best and resisted strongly, especially when coupled with women's perception of work as something owed to them by the government as a form of security.

EVALUATING THE WORK EXPERIENCE

Women tolerate diminished authority in part because this loss is counterbalanced by an increased ability to earn and to provide. As mentioned earlier, women generally work to give advantages not otherwise possible to their families; they seldom cite personal goals or gains as their primary reason. In fact, it could be argued that personal goals would place women in the home, for in fact women rarely, once married, spend money on themselves and their workload is virtually doubled. Still, they now have the chance to give advantages to their children, particularly better food, clothes, and education, which the husband cannot provide alone. They take great pride in this capability. This new status as breadwinner is double-edged, however. Men, according to Islamic doctrine, are the designated breadwinners and women may resent having to help out once children appear and the work becomes much heavier. Several women explained that although they worked to provide extras for the home, their husbands had no right to expect them to work and that they had the right to control and save their own money. A few, mostly younger married women without children, said they followed the more traditional pattern of keeping their earnings apart and not contributing to the household budget. Once children enter the scene, however, this financial situation is increasingly difficult to maintain. Men are unhappy that their wives must work and women are not necessarily pleased at the opportunity. To be a breadwinner is not an approved or awarded social achievement for women. A woman enters a new relation with her spouse. Typically, the relation of complementarity has been the Muslim goal; now women are entering men's realm and men who cannot provide fully for their families feel diminished. The woman's status in the household becomes uncertain and unsettled.

Woman have gained in independence and self-determination as a result of working and appreciate these gains, but certain traditional rules continue to hold fast. For instance, although women leave the house each morning, traverse the whole city and return from work each afternoon, they still generally ask for permission to leave the house for any reason, such as for shopping or for visiting. And men, according to virtually all of the women, have the right (*haqq*) to say no. A good husband seldom will, women claim, for he assumes his wife is involved in proper activities and gives his permission for whatever she wishes, but he has the right and occasionally or often, in some cases, imposes it. Particularly in the first few years of marriage, this right is often imposed, according to women, causing marital disagreements and occasional divorce. "Today Mohammed and I get along very well. But in the first days of our marriage he was very strict. If I wanted to go to the store, or to see my mother down the street, or even to visit his sister, I had to ask and he often said no just to show me that he could. I had to pretend I did not care. Many couples have problems for this reason in the first few years of their marriage. But usually, men get less worried later on. Today I can come and go as I please, I ask Mohammed but he almost always says of course I can go." Men also continue, again according to the great majority of the women, to hold the right to allow family women to work at all.

To be a worker rather than a housewife offers women certain compensations: some income, increased security, self-determination, pride, prestige. Especially significant for women is the freedom of movement. Every woman, whether she wishes to work or not, endorses the change in women's mobility, the chance to leave the household and venture freely into the outside world. This is a change women have no desire to lose or abandon; they claim that women should be able to go out of the home for education, for friendships, or for entertainment, not only for work, and not only at the whims of their husbands. Most admit that this change occurred because they are working yet insist that they could hold onto this gain even if they were to quit their jobs.

Therefore, although women do not in general articulate as reasons for working the right to equality or personal freedom, nonetheless, in a concrete way, they seek to expand their opportunities. Overall, women view the experience of working as an ambiguous gain at best and hope to surpass the need for such labor, while retaining the benefits they have won through this change, especially the benefit of mobility.

WORKING OUTSIDE THE HOME AND POLITICAL CHANGE

Admission of women into the work force has been promoted as the most effective route for change in women's position in both the industrialized nations and the developing world. Liberal theorists have assumed that allowing women entry into the realms of paid labor will initiate a process of gradual emancipation in all areas of women's lives, finally creating equality of opportunity. Marxist and socialist feminists, from a different perspective, have pursued the same goal, thinking that granting women entry into productive work will help end the stifling round of unproductive housework and childcare women now enact, and initiate women's participation in the wider class struggles which would encourage liberation for all.

Notes of caution have certainly sounded to question this enthusiasm over employment's benefits. Critics of the liberal position have charged that simply allowing women the option of entry into what is essentially the male world of the workplace does not suffice as women are often prevented from full participation by a variety of ideological and economic pressures which are ignored in the liberal lexicon of equality of opportunity and freedom of choice.[40] Also frequently ignored is the fact that most women work because of necessity, to feed not only themselves but their families. Entry to paid labor for most women is not a choice made for reasons of self-development and happiness, but a hard fact of life. Charges against the socialist feminist position have been equally damaging; to simply assume that changes in the economic realm will produce alterations in other areas of women's lives involves a misunderstanding of the unique nature of women's inequality, with its complex interactions of class disparities with forms of patriarchal domination.[41] Emphasis on the mode of production, whether inside the household in domestic labor or outside in paid employment, often leads to attributing too much importance to economics alone, or to relying on an uncertain deterministic framework.[42]

Yet, the most important critique of women's entry into paid employment comes from women workers themselves. Many women question the value placed on paid labor. In both industrialized societies and in the developing world, women often assert that they would rather remain in the household and do not wish to enter the work force. And many working women claim they would like to quit their jobs and remain in the home.[43] Their discontent and their questioning form perhaps the most serious challenge to the attempt to push women into the workplace, highlighting the issue of the imperfect translation of increased economic access into increased self-determination.

Women's questioning of the value of working outside the home raises, in other words, the difficult challenge of understanding the nature of women's special inequality, with its complex interactions of global, class, and gender relations. How, exactly, do economic changes impinge on and perhaps alter women's inequality, and how do women assess their changing situation? Answering such a question requires understanding the interrelated negotiations of the various dimensions of women's inequality from women's perspective. This is a question of consciousness, and we should turn now to a discussion of the interacting ideologies of the lower-middle-class subculture to discover the political implications of the experience of working.

FOUR

Women's Dilemma:
The Ideologies of Gender and Economics

A certain ambivalence about women working, even among working women themselves, arises in nearly all cultural contexts. Complaints of lack of time, too much work, insufficient care for children, and the double load of housework and outside work are common. Despite the benefits of income and security gained through jobs in the government bureaucracy, Cairo's clerical workers certainly experience this ambivalence and question whether it is all worthwhile. Yet, the ambiguity these women feel takes definite shape as a particularly intense dilemma in this subcultural context. By examining the ideological parameters framing women's experience with working, the depth and dimensions of this dilemma can be described.

IDEOLOGICAL INTERACTIONS WITHIN THE SUBCULTURE

Competing ideologies within the subculture of lower-middle-class Cairo interact to create a powerful and confusing dilemma for women, a true double bind. Women's ambivalent evaluation of the work experience arises from and is deepened by these tense cross-

74

cutting pressures and competing discourses. But before exploring the details of this ideological interaction, the term *ideology*, notorious for its nearly infinite variety of meanings, must be briefly defined as it will be used here.[1] Generally, the concept of ideology focuses on the way ideas serve to structure relations of power and inequality. While ideology is sometimes defined, following the Marxist notion of false consciousness, as a distorted view of social relations which can be counterposed to an undistorted, objective, or true view of reality, the term is also commonly defined in a more encompassing sense as the world view or the commonsense set of assumptions that people employ to think about their lives. It is the framework or paradigm within which attitudes and actions are shaped, decisions made, and questions raised. Drawing on Gramsci's reframing of the notion of ideology, I intend an expansion of this latter use of the term, viewing ideology as an overarching arena for both thought and behavior, a discourse that shapes the way people tend to think about and act on opportunities for change.[2] As such, ideologies in fact transcend the old dualities of the world of ideas versus the world of objective institutions, or superstructure versus base; according to Gramsci, ideologies serve to integrate these disparate elements into a "relational whole" or "historical bloc" of both ideas and institutions.[3] Ideologies are "articulating principles" that organize beliefs, behavior, social structures, and social relations within a certain perspective of the world, into a "hegemonic formation." [4]

In lower-middle-class Cairo, the ideologies of gender and economics emerge as most important, shaping women's (and men's) perceptions and consequent actions around the experience of women working outside the home. Within the subcultural context, these two world views combine and compete, interacting to create contradiction rather than unity, and shaping a very difficult dilemma for women. Women are, in a sense, the locus of contradictory ideological currents and despite the political space created by working outside the household, their experience is troubled by this ideological clash.

GENDER IN LOWER-MIDDLE-CLASS CAIRO

Images of the Middle East in Western minds seem to inevitably include secluded and veiled women subject to male whim and to

75

the ideological bonds of Islamic beliefs, including the stress on women's troublesome nature and deserved subjugation. Yet, the reality of women's lives is, of course, far more intricate and complex, with subtle shadings the prejudiced eye may miss.[5] Islamic doctrines are subject themselves to considerable variation and interpretation. Further, Islamic beliefs are only part of the many ideological influences that color the subcultural construction of gender. The "great tradition" of Islam, localized religion, the new Islamist views on women, Western images, indigenous feminism, the requirements of the institutions of family and state, for instance, all contribute to the creation of the ever evolving image of the proper woman in this subcultural context.

In lower-middle-class Cairo, debates over women's proper role and identity in the modern world tend to take place within the framework of Islamic views, which lend legitimacy, security and cultural authenticity to arguments for all positions.[6] The lines drawn by Islamic belief form, therefore, an outline essential to understanding the interpretations, indeed the variations and departures, created by lower-middle-class Cairenes, male and female, on the subject of gender. To begin the discussion of gender ideology, a brief look at classical Islamic doctrine is in order, not because these doctrines describe women's lives, but because they structure the environment for the ongoing negotiation of gender roles and identities.

The *Qur'an* considers the role of women in a number of passages, some specifically concerned with women's place in society, some dealing with women's unique nature, and some including women within the general congregation of believers. Yet even here, in the central source of Islamic belief, there is considerable controversy over the question of women's status. Some claim that women are considered equal and equivalent as believers within Islamic doctrine. "O mankind! Be careful of your duty to your Lord Who created you from a single soul and from it created its mate and from them twain hath spread abroad a multitude of men and women. Be careful of your duty toward Allah in Whom ye claim (your rights) of one another."[7] Others argue that women cannot achieve any clear emancipation within Islam because of the distinct denigration of women as second-class citizens and believers. "Men are in charge of women, because Allah hath made the one of them to excel the other, and because they spend of their property (to support women). So good women are the obedient."[8] Most would agree that women's status was improved with the introduction of Qur'anic injunctions, especially regarding the treatment of widows and orphans of war, problems of multiple marriage, and details of inheritance procedures.[9] Women gained some clear rights with the advent of Islam which they did not possess in pre-Islamic times under the Arab tribes. However, while Islamic doctrine may have liberated women in distant history, the more salient problem centers on interpretations put forth today. What was progressive then may not be progressive now; around this point considerable debate revolves. How will the religious tradition, including not only the Qur'anic injunctions, but also the *hadith* and centuries of interpretation by religious elites, be reinterpreted today?[10]

This controversy over orthodoxy involves far more concrete consequences than mere theological dispute, for Islamic law and tradition form the foundation for legal rights and procedures in the Arab states. In Egypt, the *shari'a* is constantly reinterpreted by religious and legal authorities and then implemented through the courts. This debate and implementation does not, of course, occur in a void and contemporary theological disputes are permeated with state politics. The state relies on the religious hierarchy to lend legitimacy to its policies and religious debates often arise because of political imperatives.

An important example of the theological controversy experienced throughout the Arab world today, with its complex interactions of state, religion, and popular beliefs, can be seen by tracing the history of the Personal Status Laws in Egypt. The 1979 code was advocated and opposed for years before finally being enacted into law by presidential decree during a Parliamentary recess. "Jihan's law," so called by its detractors, after Sadat's unpopular wife, was denigrated by the fundamentalists and by many who simply opposed Sadat's political initiatives in other realms. Considerable debate ensued in the newspapers and among secular and religious elites regarding the status of these laws and their relationship to the *shari'a*. The Personal Status Laws, promulgating reforms primarily of women's rights during divorce cases and in situations of polygamy were, in 1985, repealed. Later in the same year, due in good part to the pressures of elite women's organizations, the laws—with some revision—were passed once again.[11] Controversy of this sort, though not always of this intensity, is common with relation to issues of women's status.

Another example can be found in the debates over women's

status that took place in Iran around the time of revolution in 1979. As different versions of the future Islamic state were being articulated, different versions of women's place and role in this society were expressed as well.[12] Participants in this debate all rejected the secularized image of the Western woman as a proper role for women in Iran, yet they did not concur on the nature or place for women in an Islamic society. Ali Shariati, the main ideological opponent to Khomeini, articulated a vision of women that focused on a reinterpreted image of Fatima, the daughter of Mohammad and the wife of Imam Ali.[13] He argued that Fatima was the model of "freedom, equality and integrity most compatible with Islam"[14] and emphasized her intertwining roles as "devoted, self-sacrificing wife and mother" and as "courageous untiring fighter for social justice,"[15] roles she united as mother of Hasan and Hussein.[16] Khomeini and his followers, on the other hand, argued for a more traditional view of women's role, emphasizing women's seclusion, use of the *hijab*, and a more circumscribed role with regard to public activities. Other voices joined the debate as well, adding to the ferment and contributing to the point that no one Islamic vision of women's role can be identified.[17] The tradition is broad and flexible enough to encompass a wide variety of political positions and considerable political argument.

Such elite discussions, however complicated in themselves, are only part of the picture. How are these controversies and disputes of various elite groups within the "great tradition" perceived by the people of the lower middle class?[18] And what other factors influence how lower-middle-class people consider alterations in gender roles?

First, it must be remembered that the people of this social level are rarely direct parties to such legal disputes and theological debates. Some may read the newspaper to discover what religious leaders have decided is the correct meaning of Islamic doctrine and the proper path for appropriate behavior. For instance, one woman, in a discussion about whether one could be religious and still work, said, "In the past, we (Muslim women) were not allowed to work outside the home, but today things have changed and the demands of modern life are new and different. Now, al-Azhar has said it is all right for women to work." People recognize that tradition, and even religious rules, are subject to reinterpretation and alteration with changing times. But they feel such changes are up to the religious authorities and leave the final judgments to them. When asked about the Personal Status dispute, one man commented, "I read this matter of debate with great concern, and I think that they will discover that the law (of 1979) was not in accordance with Islam. I have read that this is what the religious leaders know. So they must repeal the law because we must go with the way of Allah in all these matters." This reply is common to the attitude of the more thoughtful, but many simply feel that such disputes are all distant debates which have relatively little direct impact on their lives. Others simply find the endless debates both confusing and boring. One young woman commented:

> In my family we have a terrible problem. The husband of my aunt has two wives; this is a great problem because there is much bad feeling, many fights between the two families. For the children it is very bad; children who grow up in such families often become thieves, and we are very worried.

While most people concur that divorce and polygamy are deeply unfortunate events, to be avoided at all costs, the question of women's rights once such events have happened is a thorny problem most would simply prefer to ignore. Further, while this young woman knew about the 1979 laws, because of the immediate problem in her own family, her knowledge was still quite vague and inaccurate. Her aunt was pursuing her "rights" through garnering the support of family members and mobilizing her social networks, not through recourse to the courts. This kind of social knowledge was much more crucial for both the aunt and the niece, than detailed knowledge of the laws and the changing legal status of women.

Women in particular tend to leave the reading of newspapers and the thinking about such elite debates to their husbands. The debate over the 1979 laws filled newspapers and magazines almost daily, and almost all of the women knew that some law had been passed. However, only 20 percent of the women in this study knew the substance of the changes in women's legal status well enough to attempt a statement of their content. Even these women could only express relatively vague ideas about the content: "The law is about women and marriage," or "It is about divorces." Only a very few could articulate more precisely the substance of the new law, such as, "This new law helps a woman if her husband wishes to take another wife," or "The law is about a woman keeping the apartment if her husband divorces her." This lack of precise knowledge is not simply a matter of little interest in current events on women's part, or identification with the private over the public. The avenues of recourse if such events do befall lower-middle-class women will be quite different, after all, based on personal links to more powerful family members rather than direct recourse to a distant and intimidating legal process which they assume will not take their side fully into account.

Whatever they know about such debates, elite decisions regarding women's rights do influence the position of lower-middle-class women. The recognized religious authorities have considerable power through their monopoly on perceptions of legitimacy; people rely on the religious elites to provide the proper path for well-meaning people to tread through the maze of modern life. But these elite interpretations also respond to the realities of power, class position, and expediency, and increasingly lower-middle-class people are beginning to question the legitimacy of their pronouncements. Changing one's religious justifications too often, or too clearly at the behest of political needs, leads to disbelief and cynicism about the religious hierarchy as well as about political leaders. Such cynicism, linking politics and religion, is not uncommon; women, for instance, are quite aware that the dictates of religious leaders are the opinions of men and therefore not necessarily completely in accord with women's best interests. This awareness is most commonly restated in the form of comments questioning whether the religious hierarchy really knows women's exact situation and problems. Women complain that men do not understand the amount of work involved in double labor in the home and at work, or do not comprehend the problem of buying food on very limited wages, or do not realize that women are torn between caring for their children and providing for their families. The right of Al-Azhar or local religious leaders to set the terms of women's status is not explicitly denied, in other words, but women do question specific pronouncements and even disagree on the basis of their own, more immediate, knowledge of their predicament.

But more commonly than questioning Al-Azhar, lower-middle-class people tend to utilize the religious pronouncements to their own advantage and in accordance with their own subcultural beliefs. For instance, it is interesting that questions such as women's right to work outside the home or men's right to have four wives can be argued and debated within the lower-middle-class context, using the pronouncements of religious elites to support positions on either side of the controversy. In the process of subcultural and local reinterpretation, the immediate attitudes and actions of class peers and close class reference groups have great impact on ideas and behavior. The elite world is brought in when convenient, but the real pressures are more immediate.

A story can illustrate this process. Mona grew up in the center of Cairo but now lives with her new husband in a new area on the outskirts of the city. She has a college degree and works as a typist in a government office. Her new neighbors are mostly migrants from rural villages, and since these women rarely have the requisite education, they are generally housewives. Mona believes that women should be able to work and that men should not have the right to stop female family members from working if they want to do so. Before marrying, she made certain that her husband agreed with this philosophy. Now, however, she finds herself in disagreement with him over this very question; she would like to keep working, yet he wants her to quit and stay at home. Normally, in such an argument, she would turn to female family members and neighbors to support her position and strengthen her arguments against her husband, but now she is in the difficult position of being at odds with those she would have relied on in the past. Although her coworkers support her, and although religious leaders proclaim that working is legitimate for women, Mona has been forced to submit her resignation and will soon be staying in the home.

Beliefs and actions are a product of complex negotiations between the discussions and decisions of elite groups and the realities of such subcultural struggles. Women like Mona tend to pick and choose among these religious arguments and select the ideas they find convenient for their own situation; thus, the fact that these matters are subjects of debate and possible reinterpretation opens the way for women to construct their own version of religious justification to some extent but does not ensure them success in setting the future direction of people's interpretations.

The new directions women's exploration is taking will be discussed later in this chapter, but first we must consider the foundation on which such explorations and subsequent struggles are based, the strong consensus about natural roles for men and women that permeates the discussion of gender of both men and women in lower-middle-class Cairo.[19]

Women and men have quite different natures. This simple cultural perception is held most strongly by both men and women and leads to the corollary that they have quite different parts to play in life.

> Men and women are completely different! Men are always going off out of the house, they want to work, they want to talk with friends in the coffeehouses. Even if a child is sick, this does not stop them. Women are different. They could not leave a sick child. It is part of their nature to stay home, to make things in the house comfortable, to care for the family. Women are like this.

Innate differences between the sexes are not perceived as a dichotomy of superior and inferior; on the contrary, men and women both emphasize the complementarity of the sexes.

> Men are strong and hard, so they go out to deal with making money and having a job. Women have strong feelings, so they hold the home together. This does not mean man is better than woman, or woman is over the man. Is the workplace better than the home? No! It is different, that is all. Both are necessary and important.

Men and women are seen as biologically different, having therefore different strengths and weaknesses, and different paths to follow in life. The difference is viewed as a natural, not a socially constructed, dichotomy.

Within this overarching gender construct, women are cast in two main roles, inside and outside the family.[20] First, women are portrayed as wife and mother. The importance of family in Egyptian and Arab culture elevates this role; women as mothers are respected and even idolized. Typically, mothers are portrayed as "self-sacrificing," "caring," "nurturing," "loving" and "indulgent to their children." They are pictured as centering their lives on rearing their children, deriving their pleasures, structuring their routines, and gaining their most important identity from this role. These duties within the home, caring for and educating their children, are not only women's most important responsibility, they are also highly appreciated tasks in the societal context. Women portray themselves as competent managers, capable shoppers, and financial organizers for the household. They emphasize that their position as mother entails great responsibility and is vital for husband, for family, and for society. "Women are the ones who cook the food and care for the children. How could people live even one day without women. We do all this work!" Indeed, women are perhaps especially conscious of their important role in this particular class context as they stretch quite limited resources to gain the style of life that might be called middle class and that is so important to their husbands, and to their children's future.

Further, women are portrayed as having a legitimate sexual nature as well, which gives them sexual rights and creates the foundation for a powerful and legitimate sexuality as long as it is exercised within the institution of marriage and the boundaries of family life. Through the emphasis on family bonds, women's sexuality contributes to the maintenance of society through the strong emotional ties of family affection and through actual reproduction. For example, women have the right to sexual satisfaction; this includes both the right to sexual relations and the right to fulfillment within those relations. Sexual relations, in other words, are not purely for the purpose of reproduction but also for the satisfaction of both partners.[21] The trading of sexual stories and information among women is open and unabashed. Women joke with each other, offer personal stories for entertainment and informational purposes, and discuss how to attract male interest. Handbooks about sexual activity are popular, and women spend considerable time and wit initiating newly engaged young women into this field of knowledge at female gatherings.

At the same time, beyond this role of wife and mother and center of the family, women are also seen as a potential danger outside the boundaries of family life, as the "temptress" and "seductress."[22] In general, women are perceived as having a very strong sexual nature, which must be controlled if society is to maintain order. To curb this overpowering appetite, society has developed various rituals, customs, and traditions to insure that women's sexual urges—and women's power to disrupt society—will be constrained. Veiling and seclusion are examples of society's check on women's unruly nature. The generalized image centers on the notion that women cannot be trusted, so they must be controlled by outside forces, for they can be tricky, petty, and malicious, although they can also be kind, generous, and strong. The corollary of this image of women's sexual nature is a view of man who also cannot control himself; if he sees a woman, by his very nature he desires her. "Men see women who have a nice body and they want her. This is how it is. So, if I want to go to work I have to expect this." Inevitably men will be tempted and inevitably women will be unable or unwilling to control their actions. "Whenever a man and a woman are together in a room, the devil is the third."[23] The prevailing view, held by both men and women, is that sexuality is such a strong force that individuals are relatively powerless to resist its impulses. Therefore both men and women must be kept from temptation. Women admit their own "immoral" urges and agree that social sanctions and family constraints should remain strong. Yet they also wonder aloud why men have more freedom to give way to sexual misdemeanors than women and ask why men seem to be unable to control their sexual nature to the degree that women can.

Thus the image of women in lower-middle-class Cairo is divided between the woman as family member and the woman outside the bounds of family, and therefore of respectable behavior. Essentially, lower-middle-class society deals with the question of women's nature by making a division between women who "belong" to a certain man and those who do not. Women in one's family are due respect, appreciation, and a measure of dignity; women outside the family are fair game. This dichotomy emerges in the comments men make about women they see on the streets or in their workplaces. "That woman is alone; she must be looking for someone to walk with her!" commented one young man; when I mentioned that his sisters often walked alone on their way to work, he countered, "That is completely different!" The contests of honor between men, with women's reputation at the center, can range from simple challenges and teasing on the streets to serious feuds involving entire extended families. In Cairo, despite changes in women's mobility, women are still honored and protected within the family, but vulnerable, in reputation and reality, once outside its confines.

The family structure emerges in this account as all-important for maintaining a reasonably well ordered society and practical morality. Women's role at the family center therefore acquires a social importance and political relevance far greater or at least more obvious than their role in family in the West. The lower-middle-class family remains organized on this principle that men and women simply have different natures, talents, and inherent tendencies and therefore different parts to play within family arrangements. The natural divisions suit both sexes to the roles they will perform. Men are suited to going out in the world, thus they are responsible for providing financially for the family. Women are suited to remaining within family boundaries, creating and caring for the home, the children, the husband. The family roles of both men and women are fundamental in maintaining societal structure; gender constructions therefore support keeping women in the home, and oppose women working and abandoning their key role.

ECONOMICS IN LOWER-MIDDLE-CLASS CAIRO

Clearly, this perception of male and female roles as naturally derived from innate tendencies and character dispositions is not one that would promote change in women's family responsibilities. That women would venture out of the home to work, except under conditions of absolute necessity, would seem unlikely.

Yet, necessity is a relative term. In Cairo, the interesting situation exists that women of the "poor," the lower classes, often do not labor outside the home despite the extra income this would bring to their families. The jobs they could gain, without education, as domestics or street peddlers would be too degrading in status for even these very poor people to contemplate; instead, they adjust their economic desires to suit their situation. Women participate in informal labor avenues, they sew for neighbors, they cook for other families in their *hara*, they help sell goods with their husbands, they raise poultry. Many of the lower-class women who do work are in fact widows or divorcees who have no family to fall back on and who must work to cover the most basic needs. Once any discretionary income comes into the picture, even the smallest amounts, the cultural prohibitions on women working come into focus. Indeed, lower-class women will mock lower-middle-class clerical workers, saying that they abandon their families for a very small wage and questioning their femininity and morality.[24]

Yet, women of the lower-middle-class almost universally go out of the home to work. How can this be explained? This difference between lower-class families and the women of this study involves a specific economic ideology of this transitional group, trying to edge their way up from lower to middle-class status. This ideology emphasizes gaining a higher status and a level of household goods commensurate with middle-class standing. Especially crucial is the type and size of apartment a family should inhabit. As mentioned earlier, the families of this study totter on the edge of the divide between the "poor" and the "middle" classes; they are families who are strongly committed to attaining a firm situation of middle-class status and living standards. Therefore the economic ambitions of this lower middle class become particularly compelling as the standard for beliefs and behavior. The lure of the working woman becomes strong in this sector of Cairo society because of this economic ideology.

The main component of this ideology is an ambitious orientation toward the end of gaining secure middle-class status and the proliferation of consumer goods such status entails. These goals, realizable by the professional upper-middle-classes, may be very difficult for these families to even begin to attain, never mind consolidate— especially given the worsening economic situation in Cairo for this group.[25] Yet, since they exist on the very margins of the middle class, their entire class identity rests on their ability to realize at least some of these hopes.

These desires have been fueled by government policies dating from the Nasser and Sadat regimes. The Nasser era reforms in education made it possible for women to leave the home to work in respectable jobs. To send one's daughter or wife out to work peddling on the streets or as a domestic in someone else's home is regarded as a last resort, reflecting very badly on the men in the household, but sending them into the government bureaucracy advertises their educational achievements and earning power, lending some prestige and economic power. Families who hope to leave the lower class behind are inclined to seize the option of utilizing women's earning power, and so powerful is the lure of respectable jobs that many lower-class women strive to educate their daughters to give them this chance that they themselves did not have.[26] And many men now claim they want to marry a woman who will work after their marriage, at least for a few years until the children arrive; such a partner is an economic advantage, enabling the household to acquire appliances, pay rent, and buy extras that would be otherwise impossible.

However, the enormous swelling of the government bureaucracy over the last twenty years has produced a most inefficient system which gives jobs to many but satisfying and well-paying jobs only to the highest ranking officials—who tend for the most part to be men. Most who work in the government ranks serve in extremely low paying positions where salaries have risen only slightly in recent years, not nearly enough to compete with inflationary prices.[27]

Furthermore, the jobs themselves are most unsatisfying and do not provide productive work or a sense of accomplishment. Both men and women complain that anyone could do their job, that their educational skills are wasted, that their days are boring and un-challenging.[28] Finally, these problems have been compounded in recent years by the government's inability to absorb all of the graduates; long waits of four to five years have become the rule as jobs become more scarce. Young women sometimes sit at home or they try to find alternative employment for the short term, but such work is considered degrading and women complain bitterly about losing the jobs they feel have been promised to them. For all these reasons, the status of government employment has fallen dramatically in recent years.

This marginalization of women's labor is the consequence in part of government economic policies interacting with class pressures. During the Sadat era, the *infitah* or open door policy, was designed to promote foreign investment and economic development. Its unintended consequences include an inflationary spiral of rising prices not matched by rising wages, an influx of foreign luxury goods accompanied by aggressive advertising to promote conspicuous consumption, and an increasing disparity between social classes due to the growth of a relatively wealthy upper middle class working in the private sector. It can be argued that the lower middle class has been especially hard hit by these unintended consequences of state policies and the global economy. Low government salaries cannot cover the drastically rising prices in basic goods. Over and over, women cited the fact of rising prices as the heart of their families' struggle to survive and rise in the class ranks. The most serious problem for these families has been the increase in housing costs, which, because of rent control, affects families at different stages of the life cycle quite differently. Young families seeking an apartment must pay these much higher rents as well as considerable sums in key money. Wages have not risen sufficiently to make this kind of increase palatable, or even, it would seem, possible. Costs of food and clothes have also increased, though not so drastically.[29] This increase has been partially offset by an extensive food subsidy program, which keeps the prices for such goods as bread, oil, sugar, rice, tea, and clarified butter relatively low.

At the same time, advertising and the lifestyle of the upper middle class promote the attainment of luxury goods—cars, jewelry, perfumes, clothes, expensive appliances. Women are encouraged by the media, and by their class goals, to spend their earnings on cheap imitations of these expensive luxuries—matching handbags and shoes for each outfit, plastic jewelry, children's toys which break overnight. They watch these television ads for perfumes, evening gowns, and fast automobiles with avid interest, or they stroll along the luxury streets in downtown Cairo with the nervous feeling that they do not belong; purchasing the goods in these store windows is far beyond their economic capacity.[30] Instead, these women go to their local shoe store in Helwan or Sayyida Zeinab and pay for their shoes on credit over a period of several months, one or two pounds at a time.

Thus, lower-middle-class men and women are affected by the "open door" but in a negative way, for they generally do not have access to the private sector jobs it has created. As a result, their expectations are raised but their means are severely curtailed, and indeed the goals they wish to attain are always advancing in front of them. This lower-middle-class group now finds its position most precarious.

Further, they are losing ground relative to their immediate reference groups in the society. The upper middle class is becoming wealthier, benefiting from access to the private sector.[31] The luxuries they can purchase have pushed the standards of an upper-middle-class lifestyle ever higher, further and further away from lower-middle-class realities. The lower class, ironically, is also often better off; men who migrate to the wealthier Arab nations can send home large sums of remittance money which are used to buy appliances and furnishings, making lower-class flats better equipped than many lower-middle-class homes.[32] Lower-middle-class families continue to strive, but their efforts to seek upper-middle-class goals are becoming increasingly unrealizable. The reference groups these women use to measure their gains and losses demonstrate to them that they are increasingly squeezed; they need the income of two earners simply to support a household and the hope of upward mobility is becoming more and more dim.

In short, the economic ideology of the lower-middle-class encouraged the entrance of women into the government offices, spurred by hopes of increased purchasing power and the chance to secure middle-class position. In the last few years, however, this encouragement has developed more urgency and necessity as prices have continue to rise ever higher. Now women are pushed into the workplace for they must work simply to be able to maintain their current standard of living. As one woman commented:

> When I married, we agreed that I would work until we had our first child, and then I would stay in the home and care for our children and do the household work. We were able to buy a refrigerator with my earnings and we planned to also buy an electric fan since our apartment is very hot in the summer. But prices for food are very high, and for clothes, and transportation—for everything! My son is two years old now, and I am pregnant again, but still I am working. My mother cares for the children because we need the money from my work for their clothes, and medicine, and education. I want to quit my job and stay home, but I cannot and I am always so tired.

Virtually all the women cited this "need," which they defined as the acquisition of a larger flat and some household appliances and furnishings, and the education of their children as the justification for working outside the home. This class defined need shapes women's participation in the workforce and is regarded as a sufficient and acceptable reason. "Everyone works today," explained one young woman, "prices today are very high and we must work to help out our husbands and to give opportunities to our children." They see this need for women's added income in the home as universal in their class level and could hardly think of any women they knew who were not working, except for those waiting for government jobs or on leave with small children for a temporary period.

Women accept the lower-middle-class economic orientation, even though some question the possibility of achieving their goals for their families. Many women expressed dismay over the inability to realize their hopes, despite their exhausting efforts.

> I work everyday here in the office, and then I must pick up the children from my sister and do the shopping. Then I go home and start my housework, which is never finished before my husband arrives, making him upset with me. I am saving to buy a washing machine, but my husband would like a tape deck with cassettes to play with his friends. My son was sick this winter, and we had to buy very expensive medicine for him, so I have not been able to save very much anyway.

89

Despite their anger and increasing cynicism, these women accept the idea of ever expanding need and the goal of getting ahead—of consumerism and mobility. Dealing with the burden of working full time, and for the foreseeable future, is the confusing problem the women, and men, of lower-middle-class Cairo face.

THE WORKER—WIFE/MOTHER DILEMMA

By definition in this subcultural context, working out of the home and being a good wife and mother are simply at odds. Married women universally raise the problem of performing their role as a good wife; they cite the inability to cook intricate meals, the necessity of leaving the house dusty, the difficulty of dressing up and being sexually attractive to their husbands at the end of a long work day. For women with children, these difficulties intensify, compounded by their desire to be home caring for the children, rather than leaving them in daycare centers or with relatives. Because of the push and pull of cross-cutting ideological pressures, women of lower-middle-class Cairo face a difficult dilemma. An economic ideology linked to their class position strongly supports women going outside the home to work by focusing on women's responsibility to help the family in its ambitious push toward firm middle-class status. Yet, this new role of working woman is not supported, and indeed strongly opposed, by the subcultural images and ideas about women's nature which locate women's place as within the home. Women are caught in a classic double bind. As the necessity for women's economic input into the cash resources of the household becomes increasingly crucial, the question of whether women should be working at all has assumed even greater salience, becoming the focus of considerable controversy.[33]

While the economic problems of their class status affect both lower-middle-class men and women, it is women who face the double difficulty of trying to reconcile economic problems with gender role. Placed in a compromising situation in which they can no longer perform their key role as mother and wife correctly, women feel that their position is especially troubled. Some feel considerable empathy for their husbands' need to work very hard to bring home the income to support a family, but they protest at the same time that they help with this burden and then come home to care for the family as well. The double load of work is common to many cultures and many class situations, of course, but the double bind that women in this subcultural setting face is especially acute. Not only do women face a double load of work, but they also receive virtually no support for their role as working woman.[34]

It is a double bind that raises some problematic questions. Why does the economic need for women to work outside the home overcome the gender-dictated need for women to stay in the home?[35] Will gender roles, after some undefined period of cultural lag, follow economic imperatives and alter to accommodate a new identity for women?[36] The interactions of gender with other relations of inequality are always complex, and in this case it does appear that economics triumphs over gender in an uneasy victory. On the one hand, women have been propelled into a new identity and role, a situation of widened opportunity which has some clear benefits, such as increased exposure and mobility, that all agree have bettered women's situation. Yet, on the other hand, lower-middle-class women find themselves with an exhausting workload, with little support from society. This may be merely a transitional period, but it is also clear that this transition creates real strain for the women who must live through these times.

Further, the signs do not seem to point toward a situation of widened opportunity for women. Gender roles are being reinforced, rather than redefined. Islamist visions of women's role, government actions on women's legal and political status, and cultural assertions against the West reinforcing traditional identity all contribute to a reaffirmation of women's role within the home.[37] For women who have to work, and for those whose class ideology effectually forces a decision to work, the reinforcement of traditional gender ideology creates a terrific burden.

CONFUSION AND CONSCIOUSNESS

The conflict between gender and economic ideologies in this class subculture creates a dilemma for women, and it is unclear how serious this situation may be for their future opportunities. To understand the struggle that is taking place, we can turn now to women's interpretations of their position. Women's consciousness demonstrates a great deal of confusion and questioning regarding women's proper role and place in a changing Cairo.

Around the question of the proper identity for women, as worker or as housewife, for instance, considerable controversy arises. Is it permissible for women to work? Nearly all of the answers given relate women's working status to the effect on family life. The great majority of women feel that women work for the economic needs of the household, and that if these reasons were to magically disappear, all women would return voluntarily to the home.

Yet a few other justifications for women's work do appear. Some women, especially older women, or women with divorces or absent men in the family, cite the necessity for women to gain marketable skills which will insure economic security.

> Girls have to go to school and be educated today. This is the modern world. Women can't stay in the house anymore. Their husband needs them to help earn and pay the rent! And many husbands disappear—my cousin's neighbor's husband just left last week. Her brother is trying to get him back, but what can she do. She has two small children and no education. It is not possible!

Several women claimed that women should work because it entitles them to stand up to men when both bring home a salary. "If I want to buy a new dress, then he cannot say to me, no, you cannot have this dress; I can simply do it." This ability to gain bargaining power for decision making is seen as important, again primarily by older women. Younger, single women tend to romanticize the marital relationship and assert that love will dissolve all such decision-making conflicts. "My husband and I will not have such problems. I mean, I will not marry someone who would be like that. We will love each other and if I stay home, or I go out to work, what does it matter!" Only one woman cited the need for women to be fully self-sufficient and approach men on an equal economic and social footing. "I need to work outside the home, so I am looking for a husband who will allow this. It is important for women to be equal to men and to stand together side by side." Yet, she too emphasized the effect this would have on the family, rather than her personal position, in that an equal relationship is a more lasting relationship. "All women are afraid of divorce, or even of a husband who goes off to work in other places, like my father, so it is necessary to stand together on the same level, not one over the other, to keep a family together."

On the other hand, certain kinds of jobs are seen inappropriate justifications for leaving the home by almost all lower-middle-class women. Waitresses, hotel chambermaids, and airline stewardesses are singled out as women involved in especially suspect forms of labor—although many women also joked they would like to get such jobs and live such lives! These jobs are seen as potential bases for illicit romantic liaisons. Clearly, such liaisons would threaten rather than strengthen the family. Wanting to be out of the home and thereby neglecting one's children, would be another suspect reason for working—but in general women could not perceive this as a reality for anyone they knew. For these women, the reality is the reverse; they want to be home caring for their children. For the most part, they are sure that women work to provide income for their families, and that therefore their working is justifiable, perhaps even noble, and certainly worth more respect than it is receiving at present. Most are quite sure that their sacrifices and difficulties are unappreciated and even unnoticed.

Women's feelings about their upper-class counterparts reflect the importance of this feeling of sacrifice. Women who work when extra income is clearly unnecessary are portrayed in an unflattering light. If wealthy women are able to avoid neglecting their housework by hiring maids, this is seen as partially acceptable. But leaving small children for work, when not necessary economically, and whatever the childcare arrangement, they found problematic. "Children need to have their mother with them; maybe a sister or grandmother can replace her for a few hours, but the mother should be teaching the children, not strangers."

Answers to the more focused question of whether women are allowed or permitted to work according to the *Qur'an* and Islamic beliefs vary considerably. All women state the belief that women's major and proper role is in the home acting as wife and mother. "A woman is meant to be a mother, all her feelings are toward this tie." "Women know how to turn little odds and ends into a comfortable home, it is their nature." However, some claim that when it may be necessary for a woman to work outside the home for the sake of her family, Islam countenances this arrangement. One woman cited the example of the prophet's wife Aisha who worked as a nurse caring for the wounded after war. This public working role, she said, provides a model for women, justifying their work when it is really necessary for their families or for their society. Others claim, however, that working is forbidden absolutely by their religion and that they were violating its tenants by having jobs. "I think it is wrong, *haram*, for women to work," said one typist, "but my father says I am finished with school and must go out to work. I will find a husband who is more religious, and follows our beliefs, and then I will stay in the home. Oh, I will go out to visit people and everything, but not to work."

Generally, women feel that it is possible for women to work under economic duress but not ideal and that in any case, women should work only temporarily. Overall, the majority of 72 percent said it is possible under certain circumstances, although never ideal, for women to work, reflecting the class-based ideological conflict of economics and gender. Only 8 percent asserted that working is acceptable, or even a good thing according to Islamic beliefs, marshalling arguments about women in history, or citing nationalistic exigencies. However, fully 20 percent of these working women actually felt that it was *haram*, forbidden by their religion, for women to work outside the home. Most of these women claim they want to quit their jobs but economic conditions will not allow them to do this, and argue that they are being forced into the position of doing something wrong, whether by general economic circumstances or by men in their families. Some are less disturbed and say simply that although it is wrong for women to work, they have decided to work anyway and go against their religion. Their reasons include security, spending power, keeping busy, and sociability; in short, for personal reasons, they like their jobs and want to continue working. They were hardpressed to justify their action given the ideological context in which they must search for legitimation. "Well, I know it is wrong to work, but I like it here; it is too boring at home and so I work. I have time to be religious later!" said one young woman, blushing slightly.

A few women changed the focus of the question, however, by emphasizing that working had been forbidden in the past but had become permissible today, making the question of women and work a historical and therefore alterable situation. They cite the authority of al-Azhar's dictate that working is now possible under certain conditions. "This is the modern age and everyone works now; in the past it was forbidden, but today we all work. This is life and civilization; things change. It is not forbidden, it is not even shameful (*ayb*)." These women, though few in number, show an evolving notion of women's place, and make society, rather than themselves, responsible for the dilemma in which they are enmeshed. However, most women remain uncertain and confused about the question of women's appropriate activities.

Questioning of identity and role is widespread among women, demonstrating turmoil and some bewilderment about appropriate gender roles, and contradictory beliefs which create some political space and perhaps some potential for real change. Vehement conversations about proper behavior and beliefs are frequent, as women seek to define their proper role in the context of uncertainty and competing demands. The focus on household and family needs by nearly all the women raises the important point that the kind of liberation they may be looking for is perhaps quite different from the autonomy and individual self-sufficiency that Western women often seek. Women's attempts to define a new identity and female nature in Cairo will probably focus on family needs, rather than individualistic emancipation.

Women's questioning is part of a much larger search for a settled identity which can reconcile traditional values with the demands of modern life. The problem of unsettled identity is a major political issue throughout the Arab world today. Since the end of the Western colonial era, much energy has gone into the formation of national and pan-Arab identities to fill the ideological void. Nasser's pan-Arabism and Islamicism are two examples of efforts to end this turmoil and confusion of identity. This effort has assumed even greater intensity in Egypt since the defeat in the 1967 war with Israel and the ideological questioning of the late 1970s. Because of the political salience of the household in the Middle East, women's role will remain at the center of these debates. Yet, while part of this larger movement, women's questioning in lower-middle-class Cairo is also unique and particular. Their problems and their efforts cannot be reduced to generalizations about the difficulties of creating nationalism or the problems of Islamic fundamentalism. Their questioning responds to the specific demands of their situation and they use the larger cultural symbols to confront their particular dilemma.

There has been some change in women's commonsense, some disruption of their everyday ideas and images of what it means to be a woman. But the ideological pressures are strong and the power of tradition is still considerable. They are caught between the drive toward ambitious economic goals and traditional female identity, between the roles of worker and wife-mother. Yet, the

95

women of Cairo, contrary to the Western stereotype of the power-less Middle Eastern female, are in fact extremely resourceful in manipulating their situation. It is time now to examine what women do to remedy their problem. Women do take action against their difficult situation; one example of their struggle can be found in a symbolic form of behavior—the new veiling.

FIVE

Women's Symbolic Action: The New Veiling in Lower-Middle-Class Cairo

For women in Cairo the new veiling offers a compelling and pow-erful form of symbolic action. The *higab* expresses women's feelings of confusion and conflict over the dilemma they encounter with the new experience of working, the loss of identity they face with the competing pressures of the lower-middle-class subculture. In ef-fect, the veil serves the need women feel to bridge the gap between traditional and modern values and behavior. Yet, the *higab* does not symbolically revive the traditional covered dress of Cairo, but rather creates a new, revised form of traditional dress; it creates in symbolic fashion a new way to be a woman in a changing Cairo.

WOMEN'S DRESS AS SYMBOL IN THE MIDDLE EAST

Veiling symbolizes the mystery of the East to many Westerners, the hidden and unknowable, the elusive ambiguity of women's world and the coercive manipulation of female conduct. But the reality of Middle Eastern dress reaches beyond this "orientalist" conception to encompass much more complex and subtle relations.[1] What does veiling symbolize to those who do it? and to those who, as members of the culture, observe it?

Veiling has, of course, a long and varied history as a cultural gesture, and it has been and continues to be employed in a wide variety of contexts, many falling outside the realm of simple or stereotypical gender relations. The range of economic and cultural situations in which the veil has symbolic importance or impact is wide; the veil is even used by men in one culture of the Sahara.[2] The historical and anthropological evidence of incredible variety in forms, degree and function of the veiling motif points to its position as a central symbol in the Middle Eastern cultural tradition.[3]

Veiling involves the use of dress to convey a public message— both about the wearer and about the relationship between the wearer and potential viewers. The dress itself may involve many degrees of actual coverage, from a simple scarf over the hair to an enveloping black drape of heavy cloth covering the entire body and hiding the face and eyes.[4] It may, or may not, be accompanied by various degrees of seclusion. Yet, all these variations carry the central notion of hiding certain parts of the body, which to some degree must be hidden and unrevealed to certain culturally designated viewers.

Contrary to Western stereotypes, veiling is not a specifically Islamic custom, and certainly not an unequivocal religious dictate. Indeed, veiling and the linked practice of seclusion are found in many cultures and supported by religions other than Islam.[5] The *Qur'an* itself advocates only limited covering of the body and limited seclusion from inappropriate viewers.

> O Prophet! Tell thy wives and thy daughters and the women of the believers to draw their cloaks close around them (when they go abroad.) That will be better, that so they may be recognized and not annoyed.[6] . . . Tell the believing women to lower their gaze and be modest, and to display of their adornment only that which is apparent, and to draw their veils over their bosoms, and not to reveal their adornment save to their husbands or fathers or husbands' fathers, or their sons or their husbands' sons, or their brothers or their brothers' sons or sisters' sons, or their women, or their slaves, or male attendants who lack vigour, or children who know naught of women's nakedness.[7]

However, the *Qur'an* admonishes not only women to practice modest behavior, but also men: "Tell the believing men to lower their gaze and be modest. That is purer for them."[8] More restrictive advice was given only to the wives of the Prophet, who had both the religious and social status of the elite and the special problem of being permanently in the public eye.[9] The *hadith* add to this distinction between the wives of the Prophet and ordinary women by emphasizing the prerogative of seclusion and veiling of the Prophet's wives, emphasizing the links between veiling and raised status, while the advice provided for ordinary female believers is very contradictory.[10] In practice, these multiple contradictions in the religious texts have resulted in a great deal of controversy over proper translations, and therefore over the exact requirements for women's behavior and dress.

Further, veiling was evidently a relatively common practice in the Middle East before the advent of Islam.[11] As it was gradually incorporated into Islam, past meanings linked to politics, economic status, and religious prestige, as well as gender beliefs, shaped the local variations of women's dress and the rules for its use. From the time of its adoption into Islamic culture, veiling has been strongly associated with sexual beliefs and with standards of appropriate behavior, yet also with evaluations of social status and with political concerns, making women's dress a much more complex matter than simple religious dogma, or mere fashion, or a straightforward attempt by males to disable women from full participation in public life.

In the family-centered world of the Middle East, veiling often functions within the circle of kin relations to define and delineate in a public way appropriate relations of familiarity and distance. It represents the dialectic of separation and association; women raise and lower veils depending on their particular social relationship with a specific viewer. In this way, the veil designates who is family, who is more distantly related and who is complete outsider. It symbolizes, therefore, who is stranger and not to be relied on, and who is kin and able to be called upon for certain kinds of aid. Women's dress serves as a form of public recognition of kinship networks and social distance. As a result the social rules for appropriate wearing of these clothes may, and do, vary considerably depending on the particular and local patterns of kinship relations.[12]

Veiling also, by virtue of its public nature as a type of perfor-

mance, is linked to the concept of honor which frames moral relations in many areas of the Middle East.[13] The public orientation of
this morality system means, for one thing, that morality is in large
part recognized by social behavior rather than individual, internalized beliefs, a point that leads to the corollary that public manifestations of ideals often do not coincide with actual behavior in
Middle Eastern culture.[14] For instance, veiling may or may not be
linked with more private, less ascertainable manifestations of reli-
giousness or morality. Further, the focus on the woman's body as
the locus of morality for the entire family highlights the importance of the dress symbol in maintaining the structure of familial
institutions and the morality that supports it.[15]

The public and social orientation of veiling in Middle Eastern
society is further reinforced by reading the signs linking women's
dress to connotations of status. It is most common for veiling and
seclusion to be carefully observed when it is economically feasible.
Upper-class women, particularly urban women, have been more
likely to be veiled and secluded than lower class women, who
generally must venture into the public realm to labor, in the fields
or as petty merchants or domestics, or who are more exposed
simply because of the lack of affordable private housing. Thus
historically, more seclusion and more extensive veiling have been
associated with upper-class position. In the past, as well as today,
rising in class status often involves the veiling and perhaps partial
seclusion of previously unveiled women in the family.[16] In more
recent years, it has been common for urban upper-class women to
dress in Western clothes, a move which has in turn been emulated
by the lower-middle-class in their attempt to gain firm middle-
class status. Women's dress, like all clothing, is accorded importance as a key designator of class status, economic prestige, and
social place in many Middle Eastern contexts.

Of course, veiling also emphasizes gender boundaries. It clearly
organizes male and female appearance and, by implication, orders
appropriate behavior and encourages appropriate beliefs. As an
expressive measure, veiling sets women off as a unique group,
creating a strong feeling of gender identity for both sexes, which
even overrides to some extent the very strong class boundaries.
This powerful gender identification works two ways, both locking
women out from certain opportunities and binding women together to create strong female ties and a women's community built
on important social, economic, and emotional networks. Therefore,

while it is true that women are often secluded and excluded from certain, particularly public, forms of social, economic, or political activity, it is also very clear that men are restricted to their realm as well. In the Middle East, with its very important household and family context, men are in effect excluded from this quite central world, with its maneuvering for influence, gossip over family and neighborhood business, and strategies for economic or social gain.[17]

Finally, veiling functions as a form of communication between wearer and viewer; subtle alterations in the dress can send distinct messages which reveal much about the wearer and also about the relationship between wearer and viewer. This communication can operate on several different levels, ranging from the interpersonal to quite public and political statements. The Iranian revolution is probably the most familiar example in recent years of the use of women's dress as an overt political signal; the *chador* became a symbol in a complex political battle in which the future direction of the Iranian state as well as the direction of women's situation were being debated.[18]

Yet, veils may serve to communicate on a more immediate and personal level as well. How the clothes are worn by an individual woman can be as important as whether covering garments are adopted at all. Over this aspect of their dress women have direct control and they do, in fact, employ their clothes to send social messages; for instance, women may vary the heaviness of the cloth, drape their scarves in certain ways, or pin their head covering in a unique or socially acknowledged fashion. These subtle signals send multiple social messages, including clues to the personality and intentions of the individual woman manipulating this dress.[19] This ability highlights the important point that veiling is a two-way mode of communication, not merely a form of dress imposed on women against their will and depriving them of control. Women have always used veiling, to some extent, for their own purposes, as a signal of status, as form of shelter, as "mobile curtains,"[20] as attractions to some men, as reminders of kin relations to others.

Therefore, veiling is used by women, and confines them; it carries many cultural messages, messages which move in both directions, from women to men as well as from men to women. These clothes are both subject to women's control and symbolic of women's constraints, and this fundamental ambiguity is crucial to understanding the privileged nature of the veil as symbol in Middle Eastern culture. On close inspection, veiling emerges as much more than a symbol of women's constraint; instead, it must be read as a subtle and evocative sign of the negotiation of power, of the intersection of domination and resistance, highlighting the interpretive struggle to define women's place within the family and the larger society.

WOMEN'S DRESS IN CAIRO

In 1923, Huda Shaarawi and Saiza Nabarawi, returning from a trip to Rome for an international feminist meeting, removed their face veils in a symbolic action that launched a movement among upper-class women to abandon the face veil and move about the city without its protective cover.[21] And until recently upper and middle-class women in Cairo wore reasonably modest versions of Western dress both on the streets and at home. However, the last ten to fifteen years present a startling picture. Many women now appear on Cairo streets wearing different varieties of "Islamic dress," ranging from fashionable turbans over the hair, to gauzy headscarves wrapped about head and neck, to top-to-toe dark and heavy coverings.[22] Why are women reverting to veiling in Cairo today? And especially, why are working women, supposedly modernizing in outlook, putting on these coverings? Their action startles and puzzles because it runs against both intuitive and theoretical expectations. Why would working women who are part of the modern sector of the city return to traditional behavior, particularly behavior that was rejected by women only a generation ago? Why would women reduplicate conditions which seem to represent or contribute to their own subordination?

Answering these questions requires a look at the specific history of veiling in Egypt and especially in the urban context of Cairo.[23] The 1920s movement to discard the veil, while symbolically important, remained primarily an upper-class phenomenon. It was linked with upper-class women's entrance into political life through participation in the struggles of Egyptian nationalist groups and political efforts to rid the country of the foreign presence. Predictably perhaps, women's special needs were often subordinated to the larger struggle; still, this participation offered women a route to gain status and skills previously outside their realm of everyday routine. For instance, many women became active in the volunteer organizations which sought to alleviate the poverty, health problems, and educational needs of the poor. Management skills previously utilized only in the household now were exercised on a larger scale and many upper-class women benefited from this training which opened the way for their later entrance into public service.[24] Thus, discarding the veil was linked with politics from the beginning, and with the entrance of women into a wider realm than that of the household.

For Cairo's lower-class women this movement was essentially foreign. They never contemplated altering their dress, and in fact, these women continue to wear some version of their traditional outfits to this day. These clothes, while they cover a woman, generally do not hide her face. Lower-class women in the villages and the city must attend to their work, which often involves physical labor, making it impossible to inhibit their movements to the degree required by face veils, and certainly, seclusion. Lower-class urban women wear a wide variety of styles, depending on which part of the country they came from, their family position, their marital status, and the type of work they must do.[25] Very generally, this outfit consists of a colorful dress, smocked at the top and falling to mid-calf. An equally colorful kerchief is tied tightly around the head covering the hair. Then a black overdress is put on when a woman goes out of the home or neighborhood, and a black scarf is draped over the head. Variations on these clothes are still the usual garb for the lower-class women in Cairo's traditional quarters. However, middle-class women, including the vast ranks of female employees in Cairo's bureaucracy, have generally worn Western clothes which, until the last few years, even included pants, short dresses, bathing suits and sleeveless blouses.[26] These clothes were homemade or tailor-made copies of the latest Paris and Milan fashions which upper-class women wore in public. Western dress showed, in fact, middle-class status and was one of the signs of entering the world of middle-class prestige and prerogatives.

This dress situation existed until the mid-1970s. Then, however, in the aftermath of another period of Egyptian nationalism and soul seeking, the years following the 1967 and 1973 wars with Israel, a new movement commenced, again voluntary and initiated in good part by women. Once more, the change in women's dress began primarily with the comparatively well-to-do; this time its center was in the universities. Egyptian women began to participate in a new veiling movement, putting on covering dress rather than removing layers of clothes. This movement was associated with the widespread resurgence of allegiance to Islamic values and behavior then popular in the universities.[27] Soon women wearing floor-length gowns with wide sleeves and skirts and covering their head with long, nun-like coifs appeared in the Cairo streets. Many of these women were connected with Muslim groups which advocated a return to the traditional ideals of Islam in the context of modern life, or which expressed an "alternative," "oppositional Islam" against both the state and the religious establishment.[28] Despite this veiling, most, although not all, of these women continued to participate in normal life; they went to classes at the university, practiced medicine or law or whatever profession they had studied for, taught school children, attended social affairs, and generally continued to enjoy the freedom of mobility and expansion of opportunities in the workplace and in public life which Egyptian women had encouraged since the turn of the last century.

This movement to wear Islamic dress has not, of course, been limited exclusively to Egypt. In Iran, for example, the *chador* has become a central symbol in the battle over the nature of an Islamic state;[29] in Turkey some women are using the headscarf and covered dress to express opposition to the modernizing direction of the government; in parts of North Africa, including Tunisia and Algeria, women use Islamic dress to signal nationalistic opposition to the colonial experience and continuing cultural and economic dependency;[30] in Pakistan, Afghani women in refugee camps are donning traditional dress for the first time to uphold traditional values in a new environment where more people are strangers.[31] This widespread symbolic gesture has spread throughout the Muslim world, expanding in a variety of different cultural contexts.

The *higab*, or headscarf and covering clothes, is clearly an important symbol for many Middle Eastern and Muslim women— but what does it mean? Western assumptions that the veil automatically means subjection and limitation, or a return to a restrictive or medieval version of the Islamic religion must be questioned in the face of these large numbers of intelligent, often educated and modernized women who choose voluntarily to put on this dress. Becoming *muhaggaba* speaks, in a symbolic way, to some feeling that many women hold in common; but this should not lead us to ignore the fact that the *higab* clearly means different things to women in different cultural, national, and class contexts. Veiling, in the past or the present, has local meaning, which is most crucial in trying to understand the nature of the power struggles which it carries on and illuminates.

In Egypt, as elsewhere, this local meaning of the new veiling movement may not be agreed upon, much less supported, by all; in fact, this movement provokes much controversy, between the classes, between men and women, between political factions. Some Egyptians support the idea, while others vehemently oppose it, and the newspapers often carry comments and debates over the propriety of veiling or not veiling in the modernized world. For example, in a typical article in *al-Ahram*, the author argued that women wearing this dress are in effect going back to the harim. The veil over the face leads, he maintained, to one over the mind as well. While women and men do have different natures, he argued, they are like two branches of a tree—in other words, their parts in life are complementary, not those of superior and subordinate. Women are forgetting this and forgetting all the gains they have made in the last fifty years; and some men, unfortunately, are rejoicing in this mistake.[32] This negative portrayal of the new veiling provoked considerable contention; two refutations in *al-Akhbar* illustrate the arguments for the opposite position. The first states that the *Qur'an* supports the covering of women and therefore women are recognizing their religious responsibilities by returning to the *higab*; the second argues that the West puts women in an inferior position and sees them in a most derogatory light and that therefore Western customs should be no model for Egypt or for Egyptian women.[33]

Despite the controversy, by the early 1980s it became apparent that many women were switching over to this "Islamic dress." Indeed, a significant and highly visible number of women now wear some version of the new outfits, and the decision to wear the *higab* seems to be consistently growing, particularly among women of the lower middle class.[34] In 1983, at the beginning of this study, about one-third of the lower middle class working women wore covered dress, while many others, at least another third, seriously discussed their plans to become *muhaggaba* in the near future. The remainder of the women generally claimed indifference toward the issue and only a tiny minority declared that veiling was unnecessary for women or was reactionary.[35] By 1988 the picture had altered even more dramatically and about three-quarters of the female workers of this study had adopted some version of Islamic dress.[36] The *higab* in some form seems to be approaching the norm for these women.

While the new veiling in Cairo originated with a small and vocal minority in the universities and in association with Islamic groups professing an alternative form of religion and politics, it has developed over the last decade as a movement with considerably wider appeal. The current mass nature of this movement, its great popularity among lower-middle-class women, and the changed social, economic, and political context signal that to assume the same goals motivate women to wear the *higab* in the late 1980s as motivated women in the late 1970s may be problematic. Indeed, as the *higab* has been adopted by this particular social group in increasing numbers, changes in motivation and meaning are most likely.

One clue to such change is that the outfits women wear when they become *muhaggaba* have altered. Early versions of this dress, and those of the very religious today, tend to be loose fitting, with a head-cover somewhat like a nun's coif which hides all the hair, the neck and the shoulders. The colors are dark or drab, beiges, browns, greens, or navy. Dressmakers have been busy, however, making new and much more fashionable *muhaggaba*wear; there are even fancy ready-to-wear shops specializing in these clothes in the wealthy quarters of the city. Often, these more fashionable dresses, while long, are narrow in line and follow the body more closely; they are made of silky and gauzy materials in colorful shades and prints. Heads are covered with a gauzy scarf which wraps over the hair and around the face but leaves the shoulders free; alternatively, a turban is placed over the hair. Matching bags and shoes and elaborate jewelry complete the outfit which conforms with the custom of covering the hair and body but is clearly focused on being fashionable and alluring as well. Many women also continue to wear some cosmetics with these outfits, especially kohl on the eyes and bright shades of lipstick to match one's dress.

Although women debate the fine points of proper apparel, such as the question of whether earrings should peek out from one's headscarf, or be covered over completely, clearly the message signaled by these new forms of covered dress varies from that of its more somber predecessor. The early extremism of the new veiling movement persists in a peripheral way, women wearing very heavy, long gowns and complete face veils (and perhaps gloves and sunglasses) can be seen occasionally on the streets.[37] But by and large, as this dress has been adopted by the mainstream middle class, including the women government employees of this study, the dictates of fashion have modified the symbol; the *higab* of these women depicts a modified message.

How, then, can the compelling character of covered dress for this particular group of women be explained? We must look to the subcultural context to really comprehend what these women intend to say through their choice of apparel and why they are attracted to the adoption of this symbolic motif in such numbers. The message of this dress involves more than mere fashion and cannot be explained by simple reference to a generalized reactivation of tradition, or an Islamic resurgence. Instead, it must be firmly situated in the context of global, class, and gender relations as they operate in Cairo's lower middle class.

THE NEW VEILING AND LOWER-MIDDLE-CLASS WORKING WOMEN

The differences in clothes worn by younger women and those worn by their mothers are a good place to begin the discussion of veiling among lower-middle-class women. The mothers of all these women wear cotton dresses which were once quite colorful but are now faded to tones of grey and beige. These dresses are long, reaching to the ankles and covering arms at least to the elbow. They are generally quite plain. In the home, they wear a kerchief which partially covers their hair, and when they go out they carefully adjust the headcovering to cover all the hair and usually change their dress to a newer version of their stay-at-home dresses, perhaps in a shade of green or blue. At special celebrations, such as weddings, they often wear colorful dresses and fancier headscarves which more closely resemble their daughters' everyday dress.

The daughters, unlike the girls of lower-class families who continue to wear these traditional clothes, generally (at least until recently) wear Western dress. Usually, they prefer skirts and blouses in brilliant shades. Skirts tend to fall to midcalf and sleeves reach to the elbow. Hair is often carefully set and curled, and women like to wear dramatic makeup. They carry handbags to match their shoes, and plentiful jewelry, including gold or plastic earrings, bracelets, necklaces, and watches, completes the outfits.

Becoming *muhaggaba*, for these women, means abandoning these Western clothes for more modest dress of various degrees and

107

styles. Some women cover their hair with silky turbans or cro-cheted wool caps. Others wear Western-style skirts and blouses lengthened to cover their legs and arms, accompanied by head-scarves wrapped to cover their hair and neck. Still others adopt stricter guidelines for dress, wearing long, wide gowns and an enveloping headscarf which wraps around the face and falls to fingertip length. All these clothes meet the basic covering require-ments but obviously convey different messages about the wearer.

This new veiling is not a peripheral phenomenon among lower-middle-class women, something unusual or odd, but something commonly discussed, considered, and adopted. An argument in Karima's home among a gathering of the family women over whether veiling is necessary or right can illustrate some of the different positions women take, and the general aura of controversy surrounding this issue. The conversation began with a query from one of the unveiled women, addressed to the group at large, asking: "Which do you think looks better, Karima in this photograph (taken before she veiled—wearing a blue dress of a satin material, low cut and dramatic) or in this other one? (wearing a long covering gown of wine-colored polyester with a matching soft scarf wrapped around her head to cover hair, neck and shoulders)?" Both photos were passed around and commented upon amid much laughter, spirited argument, and general discussion, which included occasional com-ments from the men sitting around the table in an adjacent room. The general agreement among the women was that, of course, Karima looked better before but that her current dress was much more appropriate. "Look at how beautiful she is here, you see her hair is very smooth and nice. And she has a good figure, you can really see that!" "She is very pretty in this picture, but this is for a husband only! not for everyone!" One younger sister strongly pro-tested, however, claiming that she would never wear such covering clothes and that it was not necessary. "Why should she hide herself now? She still looks very good even if she does have children! I will not wear these clothes, a woman should be free to wear modern dress and look nice. I am very pretty; why should I make myself look like that!"

Another discussion took place in the office among a group of workers, all but one of whom were already wearing the *higab*. They teased a young woman, Mervet, asking her, "What are you waiting for?" She laughed them off but eventually said, with some embar-rassment and discomfort: "I'm not ready to take this step. It's very serious you know to put on the *higab*; you can't just put it on one day and take it off the next. I don't feel this need in my heart yet, so the time is not right. God willing, I will feel it someday, and then of course I will put on the *higab*." She voices the prevailing idea that putting on this dress is an important personal decision, and that it is wrong to take such a move lightly; without the proper feelings inside, it would be wrong to veil.

Although in private conversations Mervet admitted that she had no intention of putting on this dress and was very comfortable with her current skirts and blouses, she still avoided making these comments to her colleagues. Instead, she confronted them within the prevailing ethos of appropriate behavior, indicating that it is necessary for a woman to put on these clothes willingly, after feeling in her heart a personal desire to dress in this way. Force, or mere custom, is regarded as insufficient; this new veiling is a decision based on personal reflection. Clearly, however, it is also subject to the pressures of peer interaction as well and Mervet was uncomfortable enough that she could not confront her friends and colleagues with an argument that women do not have to veil at all.

These stories illustrate some of the controversy and confusion displayed by women in their conversations about why women would become veiled. Of course, the variety of personal reasons that might motivate any individual woman is wide. However, most women, about 80 percent in fact, initially and immediately cited the fact of being a Muslim woman as the main reason why a woman might choose this dress. "We are Muslim women, and so we dress this way, with long sleeves and not showing hair, or neck or shoulders." Being a Muslim women is generally defined with a sense of cultural belonging, which may or may not be accompanied by personal religious feeling. These women see themselves as part of a larger community which holds certain beliefs and follows certain patterns of behavior. "Muslim women hold their families as very important. They work hard to get the things the children need." "We Muslim women dress in a modest way, not like Western women who wear anything! We cover our arms like so, and also our hair with a scarf, like this. That is the way we do it." "Muslim women are careful about their reputation. Egypt is not like America! In America women are too free in their behavior. Americans walk up to anyone and kiss them on the street! Even strangers! I have seen it on the television. That is not our way."

Women realize that there are other ways to believe and to act, and they define their own behavior as distinct from that of other groups, such as Western women.[38] They are, after all, part of an urban culture, with access to media images of women of other classes and countries. They realize that dress has become a matter of decision, not simply the customary clothing which everyone has always worn. Emphasizing being Muslim provides a sense of belonging to a specific group and also a sense of continuity and security in what have become controversial cultural decisions. These cultural and social connotations seem more important than purely religious feelings.

In fact, only a very small percentage of these veiling women seem to be actually turning to religion in a genuine way; women who read the *Qur'an* on their own, attend meetings for women at their local mosques, pray daily the prescribed five times, or concern themselves with fulfilling their other religious duties remain a tiny minority.[39] Only one woman I encountered could truly be called very religious and she did pray daily, she sometimes read the *Qur'an* on her own, and she attended neighborhood mosque meetings specifically for women on occasion. While a few other women could be called moderately religious, fulfilling daily duties such as prayer at least a third of the time and being generally more serious and thoughtful than most, the remainder—veiled or unveiled—seldom performed any religious actions or indicated personal religious emotions, with the exception of fasting during Ramadan or celebrating various holidays, such as the birthday of the Prophet.

Non-veiling women sometimes commented that women wearing the *higab* were especially religious, but they just as often claimed that the *muhaggaba* just wanted to be considered religious, although she was really no different from everyone else. Although it is true that one important gain for women from the current "return to Islam" in Egypt is access to the classic sources of the religion and the ability to shape their religious heritage in a public way, few women of this social group seem very interested in pursuing this new opportunity. When questioned, they reply that they are too busy, too involved with their duties at home and at work, or even that they are just not interested.

Therefore, although the new veils are often taken as a sign of support for the Islamic resurgence, it would seem that for this subgroup of women in Cairo this interpretation is misguided. It seems, just in terms of sheer numbers, that the reasons motivating them could not all be traced to membership in Islamic organizations. In fact, women were quite negative about the beliefs or actions of Islamic groups and called the followers "bad Muslims" or even "criminals." They saw such groups as political, not religious, organizations and as inappropriate areas or activities for women in general. Regarding one woman who did pursue neighborhood mosque reading group meetings and who wore a severe form of the covered dress, for instance, the other women in her office building were succinctly derisive. When she was not around, several women commented that it was misguided and inappropriate for women to take such an aggressive political and religious stance. "She goes too far! It is because her family comes from the village. They are not used to life in the city and so she wears this dress. She wants to show that she is more religious than us and always tells us how she went to read the *Qur'an*. That is all right, but wait until she is married; she won't have time for reading and meetings and talking all day anymore." Her officemates saw this woman as unusual and suggested that her more recent village background (her parents came from the Delta region) was responsible for what they considered rather odd beliefs and behavior, and her overenthusiastic conversion to an extreme version of covering dress. One of the more cynical of her deskmates, also dressed in the *higab* in the form of a gauzy scarf over her hair and a long colorful gown, suggested: "Tuha wears that dress because she is not pretty. And being religious, that is all a show! She just wants to get married; do you know that she is 32! She thinks she can find some one religious to marry her, and she has a good excuse for not being married and having children by now—no one anyone suggests is religious enough!"[40]

Rather than participating in an overtly religious revivalism, these women express a general sense that people in their culture are turning back to a more authentic and culturally true way of life, and they perceive the veil as part of this cultural reformation. This much more typical and widespread cultural attitude, rather than religious or political Islamic feeling, is very strong; the movement seems to have more to do with returning to roots, to a set of values important in the past which women feel need re- emphasizing. This need for cultural tradition and authenticity is a feeling perceived by the women as widespread: "Everyone is more religious now." "Everyone is realizing that life is difficult now, and that we must return to the true values of our religion and way of life."

These comments begin to shed some light on the puzzle of why women who previously wore Western dress would now be advocating the *higab*. For when they are asked about the cause of this widespread feeling and the resulting changes in behavior, the idea emerges from their accounts that a major social transformation is occurring in Cairo society and in their own lives as daughters, mothers and wives trying to cope with a challenging situation. Accounts of the exact nature of this challenge within their society and their own lives emerge when women are pressed to explain why, at this time and after wearing Western dress for their whole lives, women would suddenly decide to alter their dress so radically. As mentioned earlier, although veiling is generally interpreted as an Islamic custom, the actual evidence for mandatory covered dress is contradictory within the sources of Muslim doctrine and tradition. Custom advocates veiling, and people tend to coalesce custom and religious imperatives. But for all these women putting on the *higab* is a relatively recent decision. Very few have worn this dress for more than a few years, and most started to veil after they left the university and entered the workplace. Veiling, in other words, is a dramatic change for them, and a very recent change, hardly the maintenance of a Muslim custom they routinely cite at first.

To account for this change, about half of the women say that people were thoughtless and misled in the past, but that now they see the light and realize their previous behavior was wrong. "Before I did not know that what I was wearing was wrong, but now I realize and I know, thanks be to God." "In the past, people didn't understand that these values are so important, but now everyone has come to see that they are good and strong. So we know now that we have to act like Muslim women, that it is important."

Even stronger for many is the claim of beauty and fashion; 56 percent of the women associated the *higab* with the dictates of fashion. Some argued that before it was stylish to wear Western clothes and now it has become fashionable to wear more traditionally styled dress. Since everyone is becoming *muhaggaba*, it has become the thing to do. "I don't know why fashions change in this way, no one knows why; one day everyone wears dresses and even pants. I even wore a bathing suit when I went to the beach at

Alexandria one time. Then, suddenly we are all wearing this on our hair!" Some women claim that women who wear the *higab* look very beautiful and they wish to look that way as well. Saniyya, for example, complained, "I want to wear the *higab*, even though my husband does not like it, I think it looks very beautiful. But my face is too long and thin and it does not look beautiful on me. This is why I do not wear it." Others assert, as in the story of the family controversy presented earlier, that Western dress is more "beautiful," but that looking too attractive may not be socially acceptable outside of one's household.

A large proportion of the women queried, about 60 percent, answered that they simply did not know why things had changed; but that they were participating in the movement, whatever its fundamental causes. "I don't know why everyone wore modern dress before and now we do not, but this is the situation." Such women simply accept the new styles and go along with the general trend. The sense that there is a trend and that veiled dress is becoming less one option among many and more the correct thing to do is strong. Whether women actually wear this dress or not, they comment that the pressure to put on the *higab* is a compelling trend.

A few women, however, particularly somewhat older working women, associate this trend or movement with general hard times, with a sense of crisis in both political and economic realms. They claim, "Life is hard now, much harder than before, and maybe because of this many people are thinking about God and their lives and this becoming covered is part of this thinking." Having perhaps more historical perspective, these women are able to articulate the sense of crisis many women seemed to feel in more generalized political terms. It is interesting to note that these older women were also the most opposed to the movement. "Well, these girls can wear the *higab* if they want, but I will never wear it. I worked very hard to be in my position today (supervisor) and these girls do not know how hard it was in the past for women. Really it does not matter what people wear, but I will not wear it."[41]

Many women, about 40 percent, maintained that the *higab* functions as a form of protection for women, warning men and strangers that the wearer is a good and virtuous woman. "When I wear this kind of dress, you see, all the people on the street realize that I am a Muslim woman, a good woman. They leave me alone and respect me." Or, "Men do not bother a woman who wears the *higab*, be-

113

cause she makes it very clear that she does not wish to be talked to, or flirted with. This makes the bus ride, or shopping, or even working in my office much more simple. You see, in my office, the men will just walk in and start chatting away, and this is a problem for my reputation." Married women, in particular, find such attentions troublesome, for husbands generally come to hear of their wife's popularity, or witness their wife talking to other men. Jealously is viewed as a natural reaction and the *higab* as a natural way to calm men's disturbed feelings. "My husband did not like the way the men at the bus stop would talk to me as I left for work. You know, they would ask me the time, or how are you, or whatever. It is very innocent, but my husband is a jealous man. Well, I guess he loves me and that is all that is important, and so I decided to put on the *higab* to prevent him from these strong feelings. Why should they come between us?"

Finally, a small number of women did discuss the *higab* as a religious form of dress. "She is very religious, she is always praying, you know. For instance, right now she is out of the office so she can go to pray. That is why she wears the *higab*, to show she is a religious woman." "Women who wear this dress are very religious, they want to be very good Muslim women. It is so important to them, they decide to wear the *higab* as a demonstration of their feelings. People respect them for this."

The variety of answers given to the question of why women would decide to start wearing the *higab* at this particular time, or what the change is in people's lives that would provoke this symbolism, demonstrates that there are no set or pat answers to these questions. These women do not all agree on the reasons why a woman would decide to wear the *higab*, nor on the proper timing for such a decision, nor on the necessity for such dress at all. The question of why these women veil, therefore, has no one simple answer.

Even among this one social group, the variety of reasons expressed suggests extreme caution in making generalizations about the nature of the new veiling movement in Middle Eastern society. Most discussion of the new veiling centers on its political import, as a movement directed either against the West or against the State. Links to state-level politics and especially to Islamic groups and their oppositional politics are often suggested.[42] The information gathered here, however, suggests that we should be most cautious about assuming such oppositional politics or religious militancy among the majority of veiling women. That there is no consensus most likely argues for the view that these women are not part of some militant or political movement which has a settled program of behavior and interpretations, such as fundamentalist groups or political organizations. As this veiling movement has made a transition from a powerful, but limited, university phenomenon to a mass movement, the symbolic politics have apparently altered as well. Clearly the reasons offered here are focused more on the immediate relationships in which these women are immersed rather than on larger questions of politics or international relations. For these women the idea of being Muslim has more to do with their role as wife and mother in the family, than with expressions of nationalism or anti-Western feeling. Their answers point to localized power relations as the essence of the meaning of their veiling.

VEILING AS A SYMBOLIC EXPRESSION OF WOMEN'S DILEMMA

Lower-middle-class working woman see the issue of veiling as an option, and they interpret this option within a wide range of frameworks including cultural authenticity, fashion, feminism or reactionary behavior, socio-economic crisis, and, finally, religion. They see veiling, most importantly, as a personal decision they must consider, forced by various social pressures. In fact, it has become nearly impossible for them to ignore the question. Every woman must take some sort of stand. She may decide to become *muhaggaba*, or assert it is not necessary, or claim that she intends to veil, whether at a specific time, such as after marriage, or less specifically, after feeling strikes in her heart. There seems to be no general consensus on when or why a specific woman should alter her dress from Western clothing to the *higab*. Yet, very few of the younger women at this point are willing to say they do not intend to veil at all. Few are willing to oppose the idea of veiling, even if they have no specific intention of becoming veiled themselves in the foreseeable future. Overt opposition to the *higab* seems to be very difficult for women, since few are willing to argue that their religion or cultural traditions are in some way wrong. Instead, women tend to avoid the issue by saying that the feeling has not happened to come

115

upon them yet, and others are expected to respect this personal decision.

Just as the traditional veiling served as a symbol carrying multiple overlapping and even contradictory meanings, the new veiling, likewise, evidently serves multiple purposes. Women's answers reflect their personality, their family position and background, their neighborhoods and their politics; therefore the query why do these women veil? has many answers. These converge, however, on the sense of meeting an individual need or social crisis, of meeting the challenge of change in their culture. Women's conversations about the *higab* center on the need to make a statement of identity in the face of questioning and change. The problem of understanding the new veiling in Cairo can be approached by exploring this sense of meeting a challenge in greater depth.

Working and mothering provide women with two very different roles, which, given the economic and ideological climate in lower-middle-class Cairo, women must try to balance with little hope of success. Clearly women face a crisis of cultural and personal identity, created by the new experience of working outside the home, which erodes women's traditional identity without providing a reasonable alternative. The naturalness of women's role has been disturbed but this, in itself, offers no new answers to women on how to be a modern and yet Muslim woman, on how to be a worker and yet also a wife and mother.

How does veiling fit into this picture? Islamic dress serves as a highly charged symbol in this society, a symbol which women are clearly finding a compelling way to make a statement of some kind. As women's own articulated reasons for veiling show, the *higab* acts as a highly condensed and complex motif, capable of carrying many meanings and embodying many ambiguities. While it carries important messages on gender relations, the new veiling also crosses the boundaries of gender to affect the renegotiation of class and status, and, most distantly for this group of women, the negotiations of national standing and identity. As a symbol, veiling is a public messenger, operating on many levels, sending messages to men, (and to other women), to other classes, and to the world.

Much can be learned about this symbolic response by looking at the distinction between single and married women in the use of the *higab*. Single and married women are affected in different ways by the experience of working, and this has consequences for their sense of identity which they express in their dress. For single women, leaving the household to work does not produce the same degree of ideological conflict that ensues for married women. The economic ideology that pushes women into working and the gender beliefs shaping the understanding of women's proper role, so contradictory in this lower-middle-class subculture, can for single women be at least partially reconciled. This is true because single women, while using some of their earnings to help their families, reserve most of their income to build a trousseau of household goods for future married life. This saves the parents the considerable expense of providing these items themselves, and the young women are working for their future marriage and family life, something they personally look forward to and of which society strongly approves.[43] The economic goals of the family and the gender beliefs of the lower-middle-class subculture are both satisfied. Single women also work to earn a salary they can spend on attractive clothes and jewelry. Again, these are socially approved purchases, for these women are making themselves noticeable and attractive to the men they meet in the offices, who are often considered highly eligible marriage candidates. And at work, in fact, they are able to meet many more men than they could possibly meet if they stayed in the home. As most of these potential marriage partners are very concerned with dress and beauty, women spend quite a bit to create the appropriate image. For single women, therefore, work actually promotes traditional goals of gathering an elaborate trousseau and household goods, dressing attractively, and finding a good husband,[44] enabling women from families of lesser means to pursue these traditional and valued goals in a way they could not before women left the home to work in the government offices.

Yet, for married women the situation is quite different. Rather than funding desirable extras, the earnings of married women often must go to pay the rent and food or clothing costs of the family. This is the first point of tension; the man is traditionally responsible for providing for the family and if the woman works only for extras, such work is considered reasonable. But if she works to provide basic support, the traditional family alignment of responsibilities is altered, fostering resentment on both sides. Further, the attractive clothes that once were a legitimate way to attract men now become a problem. Husbands become jealous when other men look at their wives or pay them compliments at work; and according to subcultural beliefs, a good wife should not display her attractiveness but keep it for her husband alone. Both men and women

117

accept such jealousy as a natural reaction, and, as one woman commented, "I find his jealousy a problem sometimes, because I have to work; our family needs the money that I earn to pay the rent which is very expensive in our new building. But I know it means that he loves me, so I don't really mind."

Beyond these conflicts which arise between husband and wife, married women's load of work increases, first at marriage and then again with the birth of children. Women simply cannot take care of children, cook and clean, and then be able to pamper their husbands when they get home from work if they too have spent a good part of the day in the office. The immediate reality of this double load quickly alerts these women that they cannot fulfill their dream of being a good wife and mother or their feminine social duty of performing these tasks. They are caught in a bind between a social change that sends them out to the workplace and a gender ideology which has not appreciably altered and continues to demand that a woman place the role of mother and wife above all. The economic ethos and gender requirements clash, with married women caught at the center of the conflict.

The clothes of single and married women point to these different experiences with the double bind of economics and gender. The stories of two women, Hoda and Karima, can illustrate this single-married distinction and its symbolic expression through the *higab*. Hoda, who is single, always dresses in very attractive and carefully organized outfits, emphasizing bright shades of red or yellow. Her hair is carefully set and styled, her nails polished to a deep crimson. A considerable portion of her salary goes toward making these clothes; she buys the material and sews every Friday over at her married sister's home. At work, she is always the center of attention, laughing and joking with everyone as the workers drink tea and chat, waiting for two o'clock to arrive and the end of a day's office duties. She likes to talk with the men who work in the next office as well and often stops by the door to chat for a minute on her way to and from an errand. She hopes to find a husband at the office who is educated like herself. Her family assumes that she will, just as her older sisters did, and meanwhile she purchases her outfits and occasional knickknacks for her future home, such as pictures or plastic flowers.

When asked about donning Islamic dress, Hoda laughs and says, "Well, I need to find a husband first!" In a more serious vein, she says that perhaps she will become a *muhaggaba* one day. She admires the women in her office who have decided to dress this way and respects their commitment. But, she continues, "I do not feel the decision in my heart; to put on the *higab* a person must truly feel this matter in themselves and I do not. Maybe I will in the future, only God knows."

Karima, on the other hand, is married and has small children. She decided to become a *muhaggaba* a few months after the birth of her first child. Many factors influenced the decision, including her sense of increased responsibilities, her husband's discomfort with the compliments men paid her at work, and her feeling that her proper place was home with her children. When these factors were coupled with the realization that probably she could not afford to stop working, her sense of a conflict became overwhelming. "I am so busy that I don't know what I am doing, and I am always so tired. Now I am pregnant again, and it's very difficult to take the bus to work and then come home and cook the food. My sister helps me with the cleaning, I couldn't do it all. Still it's impossible! If only I could stop working, but we need my salary for the rent; it's very expensive."

Karima spends her busy days tending to both workplace and household, beginning early in the morning and continuing well into the evening. Her hours at work are actually her time to relax, before the real work at home begins. In the office, she answers the telephone and chats with her friends. At home, she must shop, cook a hot meal in the small and inconvenient kitchen, clean the rooms in preparation for her husband's arrival home, and care for the children as well. At the end of the day, things are never finished to her satisfaction; Karima is proud of her home and wants to have the time to sew some curtains, to help her niece with her homework for school or to fix a special meal for her husband. But she barely has time and energy to complete the absolute basics of housekeeping, despite her efforts. She feels frustrated, and the *higab* is an expression of her realization of the constraints on her life—of the diminishment of her hopes for a better future for her family, and of her inability to fulfill her own notions of what a woman should be able to do in her life. She explains that the *higab* helps her feel at peace. "I know that my husband and my children are the most important thing, and I try to do everything in the proper way for them. But I am always very tired, and sometimes the apartment is not clean, or the dinner is not cooked, or the children stay with my mother and I have no time to visit there. This is not a good thing. I want to quit my job, but we need the money. When I wear this dress, it says to everyone that I am trying to be a good wife and a good mother. The *higab* is the dress of Muslim women, and it shows that I am a Muslim woman."

The stories of Hoda and Karima illustrate the way in which working coincides with women's roles when they are single, but conflicts once they marry and especially once they have children. The pressures of Karima's life differ considerably from those that Hoda experiences, and society offers approval to the single working woman but not to the married worker, despite her greater sacrifices. These pressures cause most single women to say that they do not feel the need to veil, while many married women have a strong personal feeling that there is a central conflict in their lives which they need to express in some fashion. The dress of the *muhaggaba* can serve this purpose. Indeed, among the women of this study, veiling was much more common among married women (and even more prevalent among women with young children) than among single women. Only about ten percent of the wearers of the *higab* were single in 1984.[45]

Yet, the *higab* does not seem to be put on routinely upon the marriage ceremony; many newly married women continue to wear their normal clothing. Women insisted that there was no necessity to wear these clothes simply because someone was or was not married. They argued instead, quite emphatically, that these clothes are an option, not a necessity. "There is no reason to wear the *higab* just because a woman is married! Some married women wear this and some wear that. It is not important. What matters is the feeling in a woman's heart, which tells her to wear this dress." Only after some variable length of time, or especially after the birth of children—and, I would argue, after a woman is struck by a personal sense of conflict—do women decide to put on the *higab*.

VEILING AS A SYMBOLIC RESOLUTION OF WOMEN'S DILEMMA

Veiling, however, does more as a symbol than express women's dilemma; the *higab* also serves to resolve women's conflict. The new veils enable women to regain control and create a new self-image, offering in symbolic fashion a partial resolution of the pressures women experience at the intersection of competing subcultural ideologies.

The act of veiling resolves, symbolically, the tensions between household and workplace which women feel but cannot alter to their satisfaction. "When I wear the *higab* I feel at peace. Before, I was very troubled. I did not know how to act or how to behave. My family sensed this problem in my heart and they were also very upset. Once I made this decision it was completely different. I knew who I was." The veil defuses the conflict working women feel by asserting the primacy of the traditional helping role, the traditional faithful to her family role, which both men and women value. Work can then be viewed as a temporary aberration, taken on for the sake of the family, rather than for any personal or selfish satisfaction. This attitude is clearly portrayed by the veil which says, in effect, I am a traditional woman who holds the traditional values. I am not to be taken lightly while I am here in the workplace and away from my home, because all my thoughts are with my home, as they should be. Further, the *higab* portrays these values in a very public and pronounced fashion, making women's symbolic presentation of the reasons for working outside the home an easy and an unequivocal matter for others to read. To neighbors, strangers on the street, colleagues in the offices or family, the *higab* emphasizes women's role as traditional wife and mother.

Veiling is primarily women's idea and women's decision; the new dress is a voluntary movement initiated and perpetuated by women. Its popularity rests on this ability to resolve the question of whether women can work outside the home, yet resolve it in a way that both satisfies the economic values of lower-middle-class families and pacifies disturbed gender beliefs. Veiling settles the to-work-or-not-to-work question by tabling the religious and ethical problems involved; even if working is actually wrong (*haram*), it is not so wrong for women to work for their families as it would be if they worked purely for themselves, and it is not so wrong if they are demonstrably good Muslim women in all other ways. Thus, women may continue to work outside the home. The *higab* offers a symbolic reconciliation of the competing economic and gender ideologies of the lower middle class.

Veiling helps resolve the identity questions which are raised with working outside the home and trying to raise a family and run a household all at once. Women who veil have selected one identity, the family role, and their work then fits into this context as a supportive and socially approved effort, rather than as a disruptive break from their main duties and values. For instance, veiling helps women with the question of a prolonged period of work. Temporary work for a year or so, or working while one is still single, is considered fine, but when women look ahead to a future of years in the office, they naturally feel they will never be able to take the role and place they have always envisioned. Veiling helps clarify to themselves, to husbands, and to coworkers, that they work in the face of economic uncertainty to aid their family and not because it is their personal desire. Thus husband's fears are calmed and women's own uncertainty laid to rest; a decision has been considered and clearly made.

This sense of making a decision is important; all the women speak of feeling the necessity to make some decisive step. The symbolic action of becoming a *muhaggaba* is a culturally available way to make a statement. And, once such a decision is made, certain questions no longer need to be considered, for they are in a sense already answered. Women feel this relaxation from tension and as a result are less troubled about the work-family dilemma.

This conflict is, after all, a difficult and seemingly insoluble problem. Further, women cannot ask their mothers for advice since their mothers never faced these problems. Involved in a new situation without culturally approved answers, many feel alone and confused; and they turn to debating these matters of proper behavior with their peers. Whether a particular individual should have gone to visit her aunt on the other side of the city, or stayed home to have dinner ready for her husband, is debated at some length and with considerable heat. Such arguments are part of an ongoing reassessment of women's proper behavior, duties, responsibilities, and privileges.

In a changed social context, where it has become difficult to know what is right and what is not, the *higab* can, in part, answer women's questions. It functions as a bridge, an alleviator, a kind of balancer for these women, compensating for their otherwise inappropriate behavior, and putting women's actions in a different, and within this cultural setting, a more flattering, light.

Aida, whose story was told in chapter 1, embodies all these complexities clearly and poignantly. Her story illustrates the difficult decisions women encounter and resolve through adopting the symbolism of veiled dress. As mentioned, Aida loves her work, in fact she had broken off a previous engagement because that man demanded that she quit her job after the wedding. On becoming engaged for a second time, she explained that she intended to marry, set up housekeeping and continue working. She also planned to become a *muhaggaba*. "I was troubled because I like to work, I enjoy being busy and meeting people. You see my office, there is much commotion and coming and going here. And there are all kinds of people; this is very interesting and fun for me." Yet, Aida, like many other women, feels that working is actually wrong for women. "To work, outside the home I mean (of course women always work in the home!), to work outside is forbidden (*haram*). You see, women have other duties; they must take care of their families." Working conflicts with the responsibilities of the home, with being a woman at all, in fact. "When one is still a girl this problem does not make too much difference, but once I get married my first and real responsibility is at home. I have to prepare the food, and clean the rooms, and God willing take care of the children." Neglecting the house by going out to work is never good, and if not absolutely necessary is in fact a religious transgression. "Working," Aida says, "is forbidden to women in the *Qur'an*" and so, after she marries, she will, by continuing her job, be committing a worse infringement than she was when a single working woman. This, she explained, was why she would probably become a *muhaggaba* at some point. Asked to discuss her reasoning, she responded, "Life is like an account book, and one accumulates credits and debits with good deeds and sins. Working falls on the wrong side of the ledger. Veiling, of course, falls on the good side. So this can help balance things out for me in the end." Veiling before she marries is not really necessary because she is not committing too large a violation. But afterward, she continued, "my neglecting my family is a large problem which I need to fix in some way." The symbolic act of veiling can help balance the accounts for the afterlife.

Wearing the *higab* can also compensate in public fashion for the otherwise questionable behavior of leaving home for school and eventually for the office jobs that degrees are meant to ensure. The veil does not completely solve the problem, but it deintensifies the sense of conflict to more manageable levels. Women feel they have made a choice in the face of conflicting claims and are able to carry on with their work and with their ideas on proper womanhood. They have made a statement about their values, about their ability to work and to still be proper Muslim women, and finally, about

123

how men should therefore treat them. Women feel more at peace with society, their reputation becomes more secure, and their freedom of movement remains assured.

Thus, when we view the issue of women's new veils without the usual stereotypes accorded to veils and veilers, the symbolic politics of women's behavior become clear. In traditional society, veiling focused on the female body because of its position as the central link in a familial system of honor, shame, and reputation. Similarly, veiling today recalls these powerful values and expresses a new struggle which again centers on women and the repercussions of their new roles. Since women's traditional identity and role are challenged by their new option of working outside the home, women who work in Cairo's lower-middle-class face the dilemma of opposing forces pushing them into two quite different roles; their traditional identity is being eroded in the process, and they must struggle to define a new identity in the political space which has arisen. Veiling, as a public symbol, expresses the tension women feel and further, serves as a method for resolving their problem by creating a new identity—the covered working woman. The combined ability to both express and resolve explains the compelling power of the movement in this particular subcultural group of Cairo society.

This focus on the female body in a symbolic and political struggle should not surprise us, for, as Foucault reminds us, what often seem to be quite personal struggles over the individual body can be read as political struggles over self-determination, distribution, or opportunities—in short, over power. Indeed, Foucault argues in *The History of Sexuality* that in more modern times, in situations of rapid change and rapid dislocation of traditional patterns of role and identity, overt political battles tend to become submerged into what appear to be personal and individual struggles for control over the body.[46] Perhaps this new veiling, this renewed focus on the question of the covering of the female body in Cairo society, is a key to the reality of relations of power in the process of renegotiation.

SIX

The New Veiling as Accommodating Protest

This study began with the story of Aida, who personifies the modern working woman but who has nevertheless decided to wear veiled dress. Her story, illustrating the paradox of modernizing women who seem to pursue and reenact their own subordination can now be reexamined and reconceived.

One compelling attempt to account for perplexing behavior on the part of subordinates in relations of power, such as this situation of the new veiling in Cairo, can be found in Gramsci's notion of hegemony. Hegemony, he argues, points to the problem of the endurance of power relations which constrain and limit people's lives. It attempts to answer the fundamental puzzle of obedience and acquiescence within relations of inequality; why do people consent, why do they seldom rebel, why do they sometimes actually seem to assist in their own subordination?[1] In one relatively common interpretation of Gramsci's hegemony, such behavior is characterized as the shaping of beliefs and behavior of a subordinate class by a dominant group.[2] Consent is achieved through the molding of the common sense of subordinates, directed toward the interests of the upper class. This interpretation essentially argues that the ideology of the ruling class structures a social situation in

125

which the lower classes are unable to perceive the way they are subordinated. Hegemony is framed as ideological control and manipulation by the dominant group, in the interests of the dominant group, as the creation of a false consciousness.

Aida's case, and that of other women like her, initially appears as the classic example of hegemony so defined, for in deciding to veil, she seems to reproduce her own inequality. After all, why else would women decide to wear the veil again, in a sense to reject opportunity and actively seek to reinstate old patterns of identity and role—patterns that have limited women in the past and would seem to predict and even ensure further constraint in the future? The motivation for this unlikely and baffling behavior must arise from some clouding of her evaluative abilities; she must be somehow duped and deluded into this decision. Hegemonic relations, conceived in this manner, indicate that these working women must be unclear about their true interests and somehow persuaded into supporting a dominant ideology with beliefs that reinforce their own subordinate behavior.

Yet, our examination of women's experience in Cairo argues against this interpretation. Clearly, the new veiling by the working women of lower-middle-class Cairo cannot be seen as a reactionary attempt to revert to tradition, a point that leads us to a more encompassing reading of Gramsci's hegemony and of Aida's action as a form of struggle, rather than as pure domination.[3]

Certainly, other recent studies suggest that the role of subordinate groups is a great deal more ambiguous and more active than the narrowed model of hegemonic relations suggests. For example, Willis, in his book on the perpetuation of class relations in England, argues that working-class boys actually do not believe in the promises of social mobility which the schools and society teach.[4] In fact, it is precisely because they do not believe that they do not strive to better their situation, thus guaranteeing that they will end up in working-class jobs. The existing inequalities therefore endure. Consent of a sort is achieved, furthering upper-class interests, yet this is not a consent deriving from belief in the system, but rather a very different kind of consent emerging from a lack of belief in alternatives. This difference in lower-class perspective, while ending in the same practical result, is crucial for understanding the actual hegemonic interaction which has taken place.

Another example, centered on peasants involved in the "green revolution" in Malaysia, is suggested by Scott; he notes that consent is not present among the lower class in the village to any appreciable degree. [5] In fact, a whole range of resistance can be discovered in which peasants act against the upper class to present their own, alternative view of justice. Their "little tradition" argues against the idea of hegemony as consent and points to the fact that obedience can be achieved despite conflicts in belief. Again, the existence of such everyday and often subtle struggles, conducted by subordinate individuals and groups, must be incorporated into our understanding of hegemonic interactions.

These accounts of the process of hegemonic interactions suggest that we need to look more closely at what appears to be reactionary behavior and beliefs. Our understanding of power relations must be reconceptualized as an ongoing struggle and must encompass the consciousness and conduct of subordinate groups, who function as active players within power relationships. Any narrowed view of political interaction that ignores or downplays the role of subordinates will lead to a distortion of the actual process of power relations, for struggle involves both subordinate and dominant groups in a linked interaction, an often lengthy and prolonged attempt to define and interpret current reality and the options for change.

Aida's story, as she changes from single girl to engaged young woman and then finally to married mother, demonstrates this fact that a much more complex story underlies what first appears as reactionary behavior. It illustrates the development of the tension between work and family, and the power of the symbolic solution many such women are selecting, the *higab*. The symbolism of the new veils in lower-middle-class Cairo thus tells a story of struggle, and in the process it allows us, and indeed forces us, to rethink the question of women's part in the clash of tradition and modernity and the negotiation of power relations which inevitably occurs during such times of transition and transformation.

UNUSUAL FORMS OF STRUGGLE

Not only does the new veiling express a struggle in lower-middle-class Cairo, it also expresses a particular style of struggle, involving an ambivalent mixture of both resistance and acquiescence, protest and accommodation. The powerful symbolism of the veil carries this ambiguous mixture, and indeed perfectly conveys women's contradictory intentions.

127

First, we must consider the idea, perhaps more startling, that veiling serves as a form of political protest. The usual definitions of political protest focus on a different style of behavior—revolutions and rebellions, labor strikes, acts of civil disobedience, attacks on state institutions. These forms of behavior are overtly political and easily recognizable within the framework of common definitions of political behavior. They include strong organization, a focus on established institutions, and a conscious attack on existing structures and relations of political import. But definitions of protest that encompass only these forms of behavior become inadequate when considering the protest of many subordinate groups—particularly those in non-Western societies or women in general. Our ideas of what should be termed political protest must be expanded to include these less obvious and often submerged forms of struggle.

In this case study, as an example, the mode of protest under discussion comes down to a change of clothes. Are choices of dress really political matters? Or is this a question of fashion and fad rather than a political struggle over self-definition and opportunity, over relations of power? The political essence of all such cultural struggles was raised by Marx and stressed by Gramsci, who emphasized the importance and even the autonomy of the cultural realm with respect to the potential renegotiation of power relations.[6] While women's protest is indirect and displaced into the symbolic realm, these statements of dress can be read as signs that significant negotiations of power are taking place.

Clothes, of course, do communicate—defining the image the wearer would like to present, making a statement about mood and personality, and revealing social class, occupation, or family status. This communicative function has long been recognized as part of the symbolic construction of power relations. Purple, for instance, has been the prerogative of royal wearers; silk was reserved for upper-class wearers in France; and in the Middle East, women's clothing has been used to frame in symbolic fashion the hierarchical structures of kinship, class, and gender for many generations. Perhaps this communicative, rather than confrontational, pattern makes changes of clothing a particularly attractive style of symbolic behavior for some subordinate groups. Certainly many dissenting groups do make alterations in apparel part of their endeavor to differentiate themselves, strengthen their identity, and shape their future in opposition to the existing mode.[7] For example,

Puritans in England wore round helmets and cropped hair to signal their religious protest and the creation of a new form of religious and political community. And some militants in the Middle East wear Islamic dress to demonstrate their participation in a movement of religious revival and political protest. To see veiled dress as a component of overt political protest is not unprecedented; women in Iran have, quite clearly, used the veil in their political demonstrations against the Shah and for greater democracy.[8] Similarly, in Egypt, women in the universities in the late 1970s used *al-ziyy al-Islami* to express their discontent with secular government and the domination of local politics by the West.[9]

Although these examples point to groups who also participate in overt protest, making the political message of their dress easier to read, the protest of some subordinate groups may be quite submerged and expressed through kinds of messages that need more subtle deciphering to be accurately read. They may be displaced symbolic expressions rather than head-on articulations of displeasure, and subtle tactics rather than obvious strategies, but their meaning remains linked to negotiations of power. For example, Cloward and Piven argue that deviance from accepted norms ought to be considered as an implicit form of protest, as "hidden protest."[10] They argue that deviant activities such as suicide, prostitution, drug and alcohol addiction, and neurosis, all of which occur frequently in the female population, should be read as a kind of resistance to oppressive social conditions. Deviant activities, especially for women, who generally are taught to be less aggressively confrontational, can express protest of existing standards of acceptable behavior, or the desire to individualize oneself against prevailing conformity.[11]

Similarly, in his book *Ecstatic Religion*, I. M. Lewis argues that women are very likely to participate in religious rituals and ceremonies which stress the possession of their body and soul by various spirits. These times of possession allow the woman to express certain needs and desires which could not otherwise be articulated, without a head-on confrontation with men. Conveniently, the spirits do the asking, and men can grant these wishes without losing the appearance of authority; giving women an ability to obliquely protest their situation and sometimes to gain measured results.[12]

Beyond these examples of social deviance and spirit possession, there are other potential places to search for hidden protest. Small sabotages and obstructions may also signal such implicit protest, as Scott argues in his book *Weapons of the Weak*; peasants, he maintains, may withhold grain from landlords, purposefully damage or not maintain machinery, or attempt to avoid fulfilling rent requirements by hoarding and pilfering grain or other food supplies.[13] Petty vandalism and theft may not initially appear as political protest, but when considered within the context of power relations, Scott argues, their meaning as part of the ongoing struggle to negotiate distribution becomes clear.

These quite different forms of behavior, at first sight unlikely sources of political protest, reveal on closer examination a fundamental unity linking them to highly political struggles over distribution, control, identity, and opportunity. If political protest can be understood as part of the common tendency to try to gain more control over one's situation and ability to shape one's future, then such displacement into symbolic expression is not unique, nor even unusual. In fact, recognizing protest in its multiple forms is possible once the barriers of searching only for Western, male-oriented styles of political activity are surmounted.[14] In Middle Eastern contexts women may use "dozens of less dramatic acts: an unkept house, noise when the husband is entertaining, insufficient food for guests, unruly children, and so forth, all of which cast an uncomplimentary light on the husband and his supposed control over her."[15] It stands to reason, after all, that people will protest against those values, actions, or institutions in which they immediately experience the beliefs and behavior to which they object. In Western cultures, and among men, this protest naturally focuses on the institutions where workers labor, where offenders are tried, or where political participation might lead to increased voice and control. Their protest is aided by the belief, most likely true, that these are the arenas where they, as knowledgeable members, could actually have some impact and effect.[16]

In non-Western societies, and particularly among women, these economic and political institutions are often not the focus of resentment or protest, or even of much interest. In Cairo, for instance, the numbers of women and the role they play in the Parliament is of little interest to many lower-middle-class women; they are concerned with much more immediate problems and protests—protests directed at the problems most affecting them—problems centered on the family. Perhaps predictably, then, the protest of these lower-middle-class women does not take the standardized forms of political participation. Their protest originates within their subcultural setting, not as foreign forms of struggle or strikes, but as the easily accessible, immediate, and even quintessential female communicative medium—clothing. Their complaints and desires are articulated through the symbolic and relatively subtle statements of dress.

While the form or style or site of these unusual struggles may differ from more conventional notions of political opposition, the issues negotiated in these submerged struggles demonstrate absolutely central political content. Michel de Certeau groups these small protests together in his discussion of what he calls the "oppositional practices of everyday life."[17] He argues that the small tactics that individuals employ to bargain over the encroachments of modern forms of power form, in the end, a significant resistance, and perhaps the only viable kind of protest for some subordinate groups, or even for any subordinate groups given the growth of modern, more invidious, forms of power.[18]

THE NEW VEILING AS PROTEST

The case of lower-middle-class women in Cairo is especially interesting for its expression of such localized and immediate struggles against inequality; the lack of an overt ideology of political opposition should not blind us to the fact of its implicit message of protest, but should instead guide us to the question of what, if not state-level politics, these women consider worth protesting against or arguing for. If we grant that lower-middle-class women are upset, as Mona certainly is when she says with some heat, "I don't see why he does not help me in the house, when I go out to work and help him to maintain the house and family," the next question is, what exactly are these women protesting? And how does the veil act as a symbolic expression of their implicit resistance?

While protest can run the range from simple negation and rebellion to a quite organized and coherent articulation of alternatives, for these women formulating exact reform ideas in words seems very difficult. When asked, very few were able to name a specific reform they thought should occur in women's situation, yet their complaints were clearly voiced. As one woman commented, "I don't know why men are so rough and hard. They really have it easy, you know. Women have the hard time, we have to take care of the house and go to work too. I'm tired all the time, and my husband just snaps his fingers like that and wants his dinner. He can't even make his own tea!" When added together, women's objections and complaints over housework arrangements, grumbling and resentful husbands, an overwhelming load of work, the inability to maintain their economic status, and the manner in which they are treated on the streets and in the offices point to the problem of eroding position. Women object to the untenable position they hold in a changed Cairo. No longer the dignified women of the household, they now occupy an uneasy seat somewhere between the home and the workplace. Their complaints center on this dilemma, the inability to be a good wife and mother and still go out to work.

> I was married last year in the winter, and my husband and I live together in our own apartment, which is very nice. I keep it clean and cook very fine meals for him. After all, I learned how to cook as a small girl and often cooked the meals for my family. But it is difficult to get the best vegetables as I must take the bus very early and go to the office, and there is not time to shop on the way to work. On the way home I stop in to buy, and my friend saves me some of the best potatoes, or onions, or tomatoes. Still, they are so expensive! I get so tired, and then my husband does not seem happy; he says his mother and sister are better cooks, and he wants me to stay home. But how can I not go to work? We couldn't pay the rent, and I need to have security and save money. It's not possible for a woman not to work today, but it is always very difficult.

Women object to the loss of their traditional identity, in which they were valued and respected as women in their roles as mother and wife. Particularly upsetting is the problem that this eroded identity has not been replaced with a new, valued—modern—identity.

> I thought that I would be respected for having a job as a *muwazzafa*, but instead, in my neighborhood, all the women tell me I am a fool. They say my husband will divorce me because I am never home to iron his shirts or cook him good hot meals. I think they say this because they are jealous, but all the same they are right. We are always in a conflict, my husband and I, because he is upset with the way I manage the house, or spend the money, or dress the children for school. A

good wife would be at home, but today women like me have to work. It is very hard.

The ideological clash of their particular class context leaves women in the difficult position of needing to leave the home to work but being devalued for this very action. Women expand on this dilemma in concrete examples, focusing on immediate, and seemingly trivial everyday instances of this devaluation of their position. For example, Usrah complained,

At home, my mother was the queen of the house. When I was growing up, what she said, we all did. Even my father, because he liked her cooking, and the neat and beautiful way she kept the house. He treated her very well. But today, my husband treats me badly; he is always grumbling and complaining. His shirt is not clean, his tea is not hot, his dinner is not ready, his relatives cannot come to visit because everything is in a mess. He does not see my position. I work very hard here in the office, and then again in the house, but I never get caught up and never get ahead. He does not help me, just complains, complains, complains.

The *higab* voices the protest that many women dare not voice directly to their husbands, and perhaps that many cannot articulate completely even to themselves. The veil, above all, demands respect for the wearer. "When I put on the *higab*, men must respect me. It says that I am a good woman, and if they are a good man, they will see that it is right that they treat me with dignity."

Further, the new veils can protest, and perhaps ameliorate women's situation in at least three dimensions of inequality—in relations of gender, of class, and of global position. In the realm of gender, for instance, veiling, as adopted and adapted by these women, conveys a certain vision of womanhood, encompassing the traditional values of honor, virtue, dignity, competence in the home and household affairs, and modesty. "This dress says to everybody, 'I am a Muslim woman,' and this means, you know, that I am a good woman, not a loose or immoral woman doing forbidden things." "When I started to wear the *higab*, I felt that everyone looked at me with new eyes. I was not just any woman that they could come up to and bother, but a good wife and a good mother and they could respect me, because they would know who I was."

133

In my neighborhood most women are not educated and they do not go to work, so I am different from them. They talk about me and say that 'her arms are showing,' or 'she has no shame.' This makes me very upset. My husband says I should not care because what does it matter what these women think, they are not of our social level. But I feel so uncomfortable. When I put on the *higab* it shows that I am a good Muslim woman and then I can be at peace with myself.

Veiling also signals in the area of class relations by focusing on the rising status of these women and their families. The new dress, adopted in part in imitation of the clothes of better-off women in the universities, symbolizes women's aggressive adoption of middle-class values. These values include the accumulation of consumer goods for the household and the drive to acquire a better and bigger flat; for these family goals women are willing to enter the workplace and suffer its pressures. The adoption of the *higab* allies these women with their more affluent veiled counterparts who are able to acquire such goods and live such a life. Because this dress does not reduplicate the outfits of traditional urban women, but forms a new style, it allies women with modest middle-class women and further differentiates them from lower-class women. "This dress is not the same as those *baladi* women wear! You see the way the scarf comes over my head, and the pin I use to hold it on. And also the soft colors and material. This *higab* is not the same at all; this is the dress that women of the middle-level, the middle-class, wear." Further, dressing in Islamic clothes tends to dissolve the more obvious differences in dress between upper-middle-class and lower-middle-class women. Upper-middle-class women can afford expensive materials, ready made clothes, and the best tailors to sew their garments. Lower-middle-class women generally make their own clothes or have a friend sew them; the quality of material and the workmanship clearly establish lower economic position. Even the quantity of clothes and of accessories signals class status.

I decided to put on this dress after I left school. You see in school I could wear my uniform everyday and look okay, and I waited for the day when I would have a salary and could buy all the clothes I wanted. But you see the prices! It's not possible! For one pair of shoes I have to pay five pounds! Some women in my office started to wear the *higab* and they

said, 'Why don't you put the *higab* on too?' and I thought
about it. Now with this dress I can look very chic everyday,
even though I have just two outfits. Before I never had the
money to look good every day of the week. Now it is easier.

By adopting covering dress women can demonstrate their middle-
class position and evade the revelations Western dress would inevitably make about their exact position within the middle-class
hierarchy. The new veils can also convey women's somewhat ambiguous feelings about the goals and lifestyle of women higher in
the social hierarchy. While lower-middle-class women seek to emulate upper-middle-class women, they are also often uncomfortable about some of the customs they see or hear about. For instance, Awatif mentioned: "I have a neighbor who does cleaning
for a woman who lives in Zamalek. This woman works in a travel
agency and they give her discounts to buy plane tickets, so she can
travel anywhere for very little money. My friend told me that she
leaves her husband and children at home and goes on these trips
alone!" Another woman commented, "These women who work as
secretaries in the private companies are very snobby, they do not
act as we do in a friendly manner and talk in a neighborly way to
people in their building. They spend their time all alone, talking to
no one, just like the Americans!" Although desperately trying to
identify with more upper-class women, women feel a certain uneas-
iness about too close an identification with upper-middle-class values. Wearing the *higab* allows women to associate themselves with
the economic values of upper-middle-class women while still dis-
sociating themselves from the customs they find problematic. Thus
the *higab* signals women's resistance to the economic pressures of
their class inequality, and expresses their attempt to rise in the
social hierarchy while retaining their subcultural identity.

Lastly, veiling conveys women's strongly felt anger over the loss
of traditional values that has accompanied the overwhelming thrust
of modernization and development. The resulting economic and
political crisis for this class in Cairo of rampant inflation and
inadequate wages which do not rise to compensate, means the
inability to maintain their class position and the threat of further
hardships when they feel they have already been pressed as far as
they can go. Women who once experienced the luxury of deciding
whether to work or not and shared an optimistic outlook, now must
work to help feed their families and furnish their homes in the

most basic way. Their sense of outrage focuses on the loss of their tradition. The general statement, "I am a Muslim woman," clearly signals women's intense identification with a vibrant and powerful culture, one which can reaffirm the values they hold as important and which has the potential to make these values once again a reality. For better-off women this nationalist and anti-Western aspect of the veiling movement has been perhaps the most salient; they are protesting the vision of womanhood presented by the West, the image of the future imposed by modernization, and the inflation caused by economic dependency on other powers. But for their lower-middle-class counterparts, these issues are but less important. The much more immediate reality of their particular struggle includes reaffirming their belonging to the world of Islam but lacks the specific knowledge of or interest in the West which might lead to more militant feelings or action. The family role is much more important to their particular struggle and attempt to negotiate a wider and stronger foundation for their newly acquired role of working wife and mother.

Women's feelings, condensed into the symbolic motif of the veil, center on the belief that women have experienced a loss, and on the intention that women should recoup this dignity of identity and role they have somehow been cornered into abandoning. The veil is a form of symbolic remembering which seeks to recover this lost dignity and place.[19]

A clue to exactly which values women wish to reinstate through this process of cultural memory (and which they do not wish to recover at all), can be discerned in their discussions of what is appropriate behavior for a veiled woman today. Most insist that veiling does not impinge on a woman's right or ability to move about, accompanied or not, in the city, whether to work, to visit, or to shop. Most do not feel that veiling need be accompanied (nor is it) by increased religious activity. Most declare that veiling does not imply that a woman need stop working outside the home. Women, it seems, want to reclaim their position as the valued centers of the family but without losing their newly acquired abilities "to go out of the home and do everything." They want, in other words, to capture the gains of working outside the home, without losing the status and sources of power they once had by staying within the household. Veiling is a protest of an erosion of power women experience at the intersection of household and workplace, and an attempt to maintain the gains women have made with the opened political space of the employment experience.

Thus, the new veiling conveys messages within the interactions, constraints, and struggles of power relations; its signals are related to questions of control, distribution, identity, and opportunity. The *higab* calls on a privileged motif for communication in Middle Eastern societies, and women take advantage of its energy to select the aspects of their eroding tradition that they consider useful and necessary elements for a widened future identity. Therefore, while the veil is often taken as a symbol of the new fundamentalism in the Middle East, it seems clear that this veiling recalls the past, but with a selective vision, recreating certain values, while neglecting to resurrect others. The *muhaggabat* are not blindly returning to old principles; instead, they are advocating a reconsideration of important cultural values which are becoming lost in a changing Cairo, to the detriment of women's status. As a revised form of traditional clothing, the *higab* may seem an unusual vehicle for carrying women's feelings of anger over the loss of traditional values which supported their status, but protest can be discovered in odd places and carried by unlikely symbols. This is probably part of the appeal, in fact, for subordinate groups like women who run considerable risk in protesting at all. The new veils symbolize lower-middle-class women's selective advocacy of certain cultural values and women's protest against their eroding position in a changing city.

THE NEW VEILING AS ACCOMMODATION

Veiling, however, carries a double edged message, conveying protest but also symbolizing women's need to acquiesce and accommodate to the existing structure of power relations. It is to this other side of women's symbolic action that we can now turn.

Just as understanding the veiling movement as a mode of submerged protest requires looking beyond surface stereotypes, to understand veiling as accommodation requires the same effort. Western images of the veil simply assume a reactionary meaning, dwelling on images of the *harim* ladies and the symbolic denigration of all women. Yet, veiling, as stressed here, has a much more varied cultural meaning and symbolic life; any discussion of its drawbacks for women must go beyond prejudice to an evaluation of its symbolic part in women's actual struggles as they occur within particular interactions. There are, as it turns out, more clues than Western indignation that veiling may include a form of acquiescence to existing social and cultural relations of inequality. Many upper-class Egyptians are puzzled and even angered by the movement. And many lower-middle-class women, particularly older women who recall the struggle to gain some of the rights they now hold, also associate veiling with a past they would rather forget. Comments that "these young girls don't really understand what they are doing" are frequent from older working women.

Not only a symbol of women's submerged protest, the new veiling also symbolizes women's acquiescence to the existing power relations which structure their lives. Through accommodations which range from questions of convenience to more significant matters of self-determination, the dress of the *muhaggaba* expresses compliance and the desire to be obliging, accepting, and grateful for concessions granted.

There are many examples. Veiling, for instance, is often impractical. While the clothes can be inexpensive, they are also awkwardly long, heavy, and stifling hot in the summer since they are often made of the polyester fabrics which are so popular with the middle classes. Women often complained and commented that they were too hot in this dress on summer days, especially walking to and from the offices. Arriving home, they would quickly pull off their headcovers and long dresses and put on the cotton gowns they wear in the home, which are much cooler and more comfortable. These clothes can be more than merely uncomfortable; for example, on a hot day in July on a city bus, there was a woman seated beside her husband for the ride. He wore a light sport shirt and Western pants while she was wearing a long sleeve, long dress with a high neck covered by a long scarf wrapped about her head. As the trip progressed the bus became extremely hot and the woman's color became more and more flushed; she finally fainted and had to be carried off the bus. Further, long clothes can be awkward and even dangerous for moving about in a crowded city like Cairo where jumping on and off moving buses, and walking the pot-holed streets amidst the traffic are daily necessities.

Some women insist that the *higab* is convenient, as it is quick and easy to dress in the morning and as headscarfs keep the dust off one's hair. Yet, other women claim that the *higab* is difficult to launder as the long skirts gather dirt. Some women suggest that veiling is cheaper than wearing Western dress, since only one or two outfits are necessary. However, *muhaggaba* dress has now entered the fashion world and women often have just as many outfits as others who wear skirts and blouses, so even this advantage is rapidly disappearing with the multiplication of expensive boutiques and forms of covered dress. Finally, these outfits are restrictive; women who (from the evidence of family photographs) once swam on the beaches in Alexandria now only wade a bit in the water, lifting their heavy skirts as they go.

More significant than these inconveniences are the ways in which veiling conveys women's attempt to accommodate to, adjust to, and accept existing conceptions of appropriate female behavior. One example is women's expectation that veiling will help to lessen the teasing and harassment they receive from men on the street. "I wear this dress so that when I go back and forth from my home to the office, people will not bother me. I have to take a crowded bus and people have more respect for a woman who wears the *higab*." Rather than placing the blame, and the need for change in behavior, onto men, women accommodate by altering their dress to fit the prevailing norm that men should not be tempted by women.

Another example centers on women's desire to alleviate the jealousy of their husbands. Men are uncomfortable hearing other men discuss the physical assets of their wives, so women accommodate by dressing in the *higab* to remove temptation from the eyes of their husband's colleagues and talk from their wagging tongues. "When I first started working in this office, the men used to talk about me. You see I have a very good figure, just the kind of round body Egyptian men like! Of course, that was before I was pregnant as you see me now. Well, the men were always saying to my fiancé how lucky he was, and how beautiful I was and so on. He was very jealous! Finally, I decided to just wear the *higab* and avoid this problem." Again, the necessity to change is placed not on men, but on women, who accommodate to the norm of women's proper behavior by adopting dress which will avoid improper comments.

Another signal of accommodation touches on issues of women's identity and self-determination. Veiling allows women into the workplace by, in essence, removing the reminders of gender; this step can perhaps be helpful to women in accomplishing some acceptance, but it in no way contributes to creating a gender-neutral workplace where women can work equally and comfortably alongside men. Instead, it emphasizes the fact that women are allowed into the offices only by special exception, by altering their dress to accommodate to the men who work there and who, by implication, have priority. The office remains a male preserve, even though most of these offices are filled almost exclusively by women.[20]

Thus, the *higab* demonstrates women's belief that venturing into the male world of the workplace requires special efforts and concessions on their part. "After all, its not so terrible if I wear a scarf on my hair; what does it matter! I still come to work everyday and earn the money that we need. I wish I didn't have to worry about what men say, and the neighbors talking and my husband being upset. But that's how it is here; Egyptian men are this way." It is crucial to note that women are not willing to give up this newly discovered right to walk the streets or "man" the offices, but they are willing to make concessions to make this right a possibility. However, these concessions go beyond mere prudence; they offer more than a strategic calculation or rationalized exchange with men. Not only do women concede that the veil is necessary; many women also actively assert that it is right to wear the *higab* in such contexts, and they voluntarily and often enthusiastically make the decision to wear this dress. "I am happy to dress like this, with a long skirt and cover over my head. This is more proper, and I am more comfortable." Women are not responding primarily to male pressure, but to an internalized feeling that they wish to make this accommodation to the traditional ideals of woman's identity and proper role. "Wearing the *higab* makes a woman secure; no one can say anything about her. But the reason I wear this head-scarf and dress is that it makes me feel right. I know that I am a woman and that my place is with my family and my work can make my home a nicer place. I am proud of this. This dress lets everyone see who I am, a Muslim woman." Their action of veiling symbolizes acquiescence and active acceptance of the primary female role as wife and mother; it signals women's accommodation to the strictures set by tradition and supported by men.

AMBIGUOUS SYMBOLISM AND POLITICAL STRUGGLE

Lower-middle-class working women in Cairo are using a potent and ambiguous symbol to express their conflict over work and family identity. As a symbolic expression, the veil may seem a displaced and indirect statement, yet the new veiling conveys a powerful political message which cannot be disregarded. Indeed, such struggles in the symbolic realm can be as crucially important in the negotiation of power as more concrete or overt battles. Michel Foucault even claims that as history progresses, such struggles become increasingly important; the negotiation of social relations will increasingly take place in the worlds of discourse, art, and symbol, in increasingly muted and indirect modes.[21] Symbolic statements in the power struggle, evoking complex and even contradictory layers of meaning, become the center of the negotiation of identity and role; they become the key to negotiations over the opportunities which arise as traditions alter and change. Women's struggle in lower-middle-class Cairo, waged through the ambiguous symbolism of the new veil, is just such an immediate, personal, and fundamentally equivocal struggle—a form of accommodating protest.

SEVEN

Accommodating Protest and the Reproduction of Inequality

The new veiling has a double face; it both expresses women's protest of a situation in which valued identity and status are being eroded and it signals women's acceptance and acquiescence to a view of women as sexually suspect and naturally suited only to the home, emphasizing the belief that women invade men's world and abandon their own when they leave the home to work. The resonant symbol of veiling condenses and conveys a contradictory message and the negotiation of women's self-determination and future position is colored by this combination. Foucault argues that this kind of ambiguity, this duality of intention, is located in the nature of all resistance to power but emerges as especially apparent and important within the forms of symbolic struggle required to combat the more subtle forms of modern power. He argues that in situations of resistance "one is dealing with mobile and transitory points of resistance, producing cleavages in a society that shift about, fracturing unities and effecting regroupings, furrowing across individuals themselves, cutting them up and remolding them, marking off irreducible regions in them, in their bodies and minds."[1] Resistance to power, in symbolic struggles such as the statement of veiling, cuts across individuals, dividing them into both protesters and accommodators.

WOMEN AND ACCOMMODATING PROTEST

The persistent fact of women's subordinate position throughout history and across many cultures not only presents discouraging evidence against women's ever obtaining equality of opportunity or self-determination; it also presents a confusing picture of women's part in these relationships of inequality. For we also know, from surveying the same cultural diversity, that women appear in many contexts as assertive actors, often using unusual or informal sources of influence to struggle for better conditions for themselves and for their families. Yet, women's endeavors to change the boundaries of their lives seem to produce limited and ephemeral results in many contexts. Inequality persists, despite women's efforts at change. Or rather, inequality is recreated and reproduced continuously, even as political, economic, and social contexts evolve and alter, often opening windows of opportunity, when the relations of power are renegotiated and might be changed. With the idea of accommodating protest this reality of women's persistent inequality can be accounted for, providing an answer to why the old adage "the more things change, the more they remain they same" so often describes the disappointing results of apparent opportunity.

In the endeavor to understand how this persistence is perpetuated it is important to emphasize the point that women do initiate action within the context of power relations and that protest is one dimension of this action. Yet, the fact that struggle occurs, in whatever form, is not in itself sufficient reason for optimism. Drawing on the evidence of history and the results of this study, the uncomfortable reality emerges that women's resistance to control and constraint is neither direct nor unequivocal. It is instead inextricably coupled with elements of acquiescence and accommodation.

Consequently, we need to examine carefully the exact part that women play as subordinates in the interactions of power. The unsettling linkage of acquiescence and resistance leaves us with the puzzling problem of trying to understand why women would choose such an equivocal and ambiguous manner to ameliorate their situation and what effect this style of struggle has on the results of their efforts. These problems return us to the questions raised in the first pages of this study, questions of the potential for either the reproduction of inequalities or for real change which accompany alterations in power relations, and the part subordinates play in such decisions.

Why not manipulate events and outcomes more directly and perhaps more effectively? One answer to the underlying question of why many subordinate groups seem unable to formulate unequivocal forms of protest focuses on the inability of subordinate subjects, who are not capable of formulating a clear idea of the values they seek, of realizing their own true interests, or envisioning any coherent plan for reform of power relations. Exposed constantly to the values of the dominant group, subordinates have no ideological space, in a sense, to think in a coherent way about alternatives.[2] Gramsci, for instance, portrayed the lower class as an incoherent and unorganized mass, characterized by fragmented, often inconsistent, and even contradictory views; the dominant class, on the other hand, he characterized as purposeful and organized, capable of coherency in belief and behavior. He emphasized this distinction through his discussions of the differences between the world view of the lower class and that of elites; the inconsistencies of common sense are opposed to the coherence of philosophy.[3] The mixed message, the accommodating protest, then, which women in this study portray, would be regarded as inevitable because of the structural position these women inhabit within the larger society, a position effectively precluding the ability to think progressively on their own about their situation and to act in accordance with their ideas.

However, this account ignores the reality that subordinate actors, like these women in Cairo, actually exhibit a great deal of ability to appraise consciously their situation and devise a plan of appropriate action.[4] Their awareness of the dimensions of power constraining their lives argues that their accommodating protest is not a matter of incoherence of thought or inability of action.[5] Instead, we must wonder whether it reflects and responds to the reality of the social relations in which these women are enmeshed.

What are these realities, these social relations that impel women to adopt these accommodating tactics of ambiguous symbolism? First is the unique situation that women occupy with respect to the relations of power which constrain their lives. Specifically, for women there is no clear-cut enemy or other to confront directly. The implications of this fact lead to the corollary that women face a web of crosscutting power relations; they participate in numerous overlapping dominant—subordinate interactions. Their relations of inequality are consequently different from those of other subordinate groups.

Women do not have the luxury of knowing their enemy. Facing a layered and overlapping bastion of oppressors, women are at a loss to know which dominant group or relation of inequality is the source of their problems. Relations with men, class relations, even the distant world of global inequalities all affect women in lower-middle-class Cairo. Yet none of these is exclusively responsible for their subordination, although each contributes to constraints which restrict women's opportunities in different ways.

Locating the exact source of women's oppression has been the focus of considerable debate. Marxist feminists have tended to emphasize the importance of class relations over gender, while radical feminists have centered on the sex/gender system as the fundamental source of inequality. The flaws of both approaches lie in their exclusive focus on one source of women's inequity, rather than viewing the interactions between the multiple sources of women's subordination—an argument made by socialist feminists, who sought through discussions of "the unhappy marriage of Marxism and feminism," to use Hartman's phrase,[6] an understanding of the combined effect of class and gender on women's experience.[7] Yet, the attempt to envision the interactions of class and gender have been troubled by a lack of understanding of what this interaction might mean in practice.[8] One way to solve this dilemma is to focus on concrete cases and note the ways in which class and gender intersect, as in this case study, where class inequities push women in one direction and gender inequities force them in another, creating a tense situation of inequality through their crosscutting interaction. In effect, for these women in Cairo, there is no one oppressor, no one to single out or work against, no one to define as the source of the problems women perceive. Therefore, although the reality of coercion and constraint may be entirely clear to women, as their comments and complaints demonstrate, the origin of this force remains elusive. Women recognize this problem of multiple sources of oppression quite acutely:

My husband works very hard at his job as a car mechanic, and then he works sometimes at a small shop in our neighborhood in the evening; I know he is very tired and wants his dinner and some special care when he comes home. Rich men and women have it easy, but we are always working and always tired. Sometimes he is rough and shouts at me, for no reason at all. But what else could I expect? He is too tired.

Of course, women realize that the abuse they receive is unfair, but they also perceive that they are enmeshed in a web of power which constrains their husbands as well as themselves; the men cannot be held to blame for all problems, even though they are generally the most direct source of constraints on women's routine activities. In fact, it is the combined effect of different sources of inequality, as they intertwine and crosscut within the subcultural context that shapes women's opportunities.

In this way, women's accommodating protest becomes far easier to understand. The nature and root of the inequality that women face remain undefined and nebulous; women can neither comprehend nor certainly confront it. They are reduced to complaining that life seems to be worsening, that despite some gains their lot seems to be harder than that of their mothers. Specific complaints are easily perceived, but the source of these problems, much less a solution, remains hidden from their view. An ambiguous symbolic resolution like the veil suits the special nature of women's power constraints.

Another factor influences women's style of power negotiations; women's goals differ from those of other subordinate groups. Women's power relations are often entwined with other ties—love and family bonds, an intertwining that produces different intentions in the context of power negotiations. For instance, a peasant might wish that he or she were a landlord or a worker might wish to be a capitalist owner, but women, on the whole, do not wish to become men, nor to rid the world of men. Simple reversals and overturnings of the power tables cannot be women's end. In Cairo, husbands and wives are key partners in the family structure, with clearly delineated roles and responsibilities. Each believes that what the other does is important and valuable for the good of the family. Neither wishes to switch roles nor to dissolve the difference between male and female character. Inevitably, even the purpose of women's power struggles becomes more complex and confused by

146

these uncertainties. Power relations, in other words, do not exist and reproduce entirely against women's will; women accommodate as well as resist, in part because they perceive the value of many aspects of current social relations.[9]

Further, women, again unlike peasants or workers, daily inhabit the world of their "oppressors" rather than only occasionally and impersonally intersecting the lives of the dominant group. Women live with, among, and in some ways, as part of the dominant group. This complicated and even contradictory position as part of both the dominant and subordinate groups means that the character of women's power relations evolves and alters depending on the particular context, participants, and event.[10] The everyday interaction of husbands and wives insures that women will often identify with and unite with their husbands against outsiders despite the occasions when these husbands might or do act as oppressors. Husbands are friends and lovers as well as a source of restrictions and constraints. Indeed, in the lower middle class, where the ideas of romantic love and the importance of the couple are becoming significant as indicators of a more upper-middle-class status, this tendency to support the husband may in fact be increasing. Lower-class women, whose husbands are less often in the home, who live more fully in a women's community, and who may have had little part in selecting a marriage partner, need not feel this identification so strongly. The freedom to select a marriage partner oneself means for middle-class women the social need to appear to have selected wisely.

Yet, this identification should not be confused with ideological domination, with the ability of the dominant group to dupe the subordinate into believing their interests are the same. In this interplay of strong emotions of deference and mutual dependence, oppression and mutual affection, women truly do inhabit a unique position; they are full members of the larger society as well as part of a subordinated group.

Because the nature of women's power relations is quite different from that of other subordinate groups, the existence of different styles of struggle makes sense as well. Women employ different methods when they wish to make a social statement, and accommodation is involved because women are part of the dominant culture as well as the subordinate subculture. Therefore, women tend to avoid overt confrontation, a method which only makes sense when the enemy is clearly separate and identifiable.

147

In fact, when women do unite in an overt political confrontation, it is often to combat problems that emerge from other forms of oppression, rather than gender inequities, such as political repression. The protest mounted by Las Madres de Plaza de Mayo in Argentina offers a good example. There, women were able to call on their role as mothers and wives as a way to unite against the injustice of the disappearance of their children, emphasizing their gender role and place within the family even as they mounted a public protest.[11]

Women's position as subordinates in society is unique in the way women are intricately involved and tied to dominant groups. As a result, women's power negotiations are often pursued in a manner consistent with the nature of their inequality, within a framework of linked accommodation and resistance. Of course, all subordinate groups find it necessary to accommodate to some extent. But the accommodation of women differs, extending beyond mere strategy to an expression of intentions and purposes. Women accommodate, in other words, not only to evade the heavy hand of power, but also as part of their ultimate goals, given the involving ties of love and family which cut across the restrictions of gender relations. At times, women may also accommodate in the strategic ways of other groups, but women's accommodation goes beyond such strategies—beyond evasions, calculated prudence and lip service to an active acquiescence to the existing society, including at times its power relations.

A third important reason for the form of women's power struggles centers on the ideological problem of a gender discourse of inequality. In fact, the working women of lower-middle-class Cairo have few viable ideological alternatives to the gender constructions of their immediate social context; they are bound within their cultural and social tradition and all beliefs and behavior are shaped within these walls. A kind of limited vision, in other words, forms their actions within their cultural tradition. These women are not duped into an ideological misreading of their subordination, nor is there an actual lack of all alternative visions, yet their actions are limited by the constraints of the existing social discourse.

There is a kind of limiting of vision that differs from the narrowed interpretation of hegemonic politics as the obscuring of reality from subordinate participants. Gramsci also describes a more encompassing notion of hegemony as a limiting of available discourse.[12] Hegemony in this case is defined as a process of creating constraints on imagination, thought, and discussion, rather than as a matter of buried interests or a veiled reality, withheld from the subordinate subjects conscious perception. Within this widened view of hegemonic politics, the struggle of dominants and subordinates is reconceptualized as a constant negotiation of identity and proper roles.[13] Women's struggle over the linked questions Who am I? and Who might I be? naturally centers on the symbols and signs of gender identity, and the veil is the most obvious symbol for women in Middle Eastern culture.

This struggle, however, not only binds the minds and imagination of the subordinates; it also limits the dominant subjects. The hold of the natural structures and constrains both masters and subordinates. Ideology, therefore, is not so much a tool in the hands of a dominant class, as an enveloping version of reality in which all social encounters are interpreted and conducted. Bourdieu calls this enveloping atmosphere of rituals, routines, beliefs, and images the "habitus," a term which he says signifies the habitual nature of the choices we all make on an everyday basis, a habitual structuring of our opportunities which leads to the selection, over and over, of the existing social structure and its accompanying relations of power.[14] The all-encompassing version of reality defines the parameters of available argument and prejudices the choices the participants will make in their various social encounters. It is not impossible to select an alternative outside of the habitus, but all forces cohere to make this unlikely and unusual. The enveloping discourse of gender inequality continues to shape power negotiations and prevent potential changes in the notion of male and female identity and role.

This view of the struggle of dominants and subordinates as a struggle over meaning which takes place within the limiting boundaries of available beliefs helps in the attempt to understand women's ambiguous actions and the potential for new gender relations in a changing Cairo. It helps, first, by explaining why women's fund of alternative ideas lacks scope and clarity. For instance, women's descriptions of male character, which include the rather unflattering adjectives "hard," "rough," "stubborn," and "stupid," are interesting for the underlying assumption that male character is set by nature and therefore unalterable. Individual men may more or less fit this natural mold (and a lucky woman finds a "good" man for a husband) but in general men act in certain set ways which women can never hope to change. Their characters are perceived as biologically set. "Yes, yes I would like my husband to wash the dishes, but what does this matter! After all, everyone knows that men do not want to wash dishes and how will they become different? They will not change! Women are the ones who deal with things and are flexible; men are hard and rigid. They will never change." Thus, while women may utilize social networks for their own purposes, manipulating men toward their own goals, they nonetheless are ultimately stymied by the natural "fact" that men cannot be expected to change.

This lack of compelling alternatives to the perceived natural roles of men and women leads to a feeling of some powerlessness on women's part. Women consistently insist that one can manipulate within the barriers of natural facts but altering nature itself falls outside human capacity. Veiling occurs in a context of social relations which women perceive as essentially immutable rather than subject to possible change. Manipulating within the boundaries of this social structure and using social networks to the fullest advantage is women's area of expertise. But the leap to considering a change in the overall structure of male—female relations is rarely made. For example, many women complain about the problems that arise because they must ask their husbands' permission before leaving the house. They grumble over specific times when their requests were denied; they argue over whether their husbands were right in not allowing them a particular visit or shopping excursion; they spend hours working to convince their husbands that they should be granted the favor of going on a specific visit to mother, sister, or other female friend. But they all accord men the right (*haqq*) to deny such requests. Although they continuously chafe against this restriction, and although they spend considerable time and effort seeking ways to evade or alter their husband's dictates, they are not prepared to argue that women should have this right as a matter of course. They struggle within the discourse that makes men the arbiters of women's actions, rather than attacking this fundamental barrier.

Of course, there must be other images, other realities, available and possible within the larger cultural context. In fact, there are options supportive of other images and practices, but the key and most widespread image available to the women of this study is that of the Muslim mother and wife. Other images appear but never attain the compelling state of the feasible, the natural, the normal—they are alternatives, but in the sense of oddities and not real options. For instance, while the image of the Muslim woman embodies the virtues of family orientation, modesty, cleverness, and hard work, the Western woman is imagined according to the pictures available on television. These include the women portrayed in imported serials, such as "Dallas" and "Flamingo Road"; the glamorous women in the commercials advertising cars, perfumes, and cosmetics; and the scantily clad singers featured in the European nightclub shows.[15] None of these images, focused as they are on women as sexual object and glamorous consumer, fit the lives of these women or offer a viable or even attractive alternative image. This factor may be intensified by women's position in a Middle Eastern culture trying to protect itself against the incursions of the West; the traditional culture is defended, whatever its problems, in a form of "cultural loyalty."[16]

The accommodating aspect of veiling as a symbol of women's struggle derives from the fact that women see no possibility of men altering, and therefore, they feel that they must adapt and accommodate. The symbolic area of dress is perhaps the least costly realm in which to acquiesce, given the constraints of their current situation; women can then retain their mobility in the city and the right to leave the home and go to work, if they offer this compensation. So women alter their looks to conform to the prevailing norms and expectations, leaving themselves covered, literally, and not vulnerable. Unfortunately, they also leave the prevailing discourse of gender inequality intact.

Thus, for these women in Cairo negotiation is possible and submerged struggles frequent, but a true ideological alternative does not emerge to engage their beliefs, an important distinction. Women are free and make frequent use of their ability to negotiate within the boundaries of the existing gender discourse, but within this discourse their efforts are those of the subordinate—manipulations, negotiations, evasions—but not confrontations or the creation of coherent alternatives.[17] Their actions seek to influence but not to confront or change the existing discourse. All these factors shape the style of struggle women employ into accommodating protest, making the use of an ambiguous symbol such as the new veil a most appropriate mode of political action.

ACCOMMODATING PROTEST AND THE REPRODUCTION OF INEQUALITY

However appropriate to women's situation, the accommodating elements of their use of the veil and their style of political struggle against the inequities of power are not without cost. Indeed, the realization that women's power relations take the form of accommodating protest requires us to rethink the problem of the reproduction of inequality to accord with this understanding of how women actually pursue their struggles for wider opportunity.

Veiling is linked in people's minds with the past, with traditional ways, with a cultural authenticity, but it also expresses limits which served to constrain women in the past and are partially resurrected whenever the dress is worn. De Certeau, writing about popular uses of received social forms, notes, "A way of speaking this received language transforms it into a song of resistance."[18] However, while women's way of speaking with the veil may, in part, intend protest, nonetheless the fact of adopting a received language means that connotations and implications accompany the intended idea. Inevitably, suggestions of seclusion, limitation to the household and family, and constraints on educational opportunity and professional options are raised whenever this dress is worn.

Gender constructions in all cultures are certainly some of the most strongly held and persistently believed components of common sense reality. In Cairo, despite the opportunity presented by economic changes in everyday routines and habits, women and men remain enveloped in traditional ideas of male and female character, roles, rights, and responsibilities. Veiling calls on the Muslim tradition, not in an indiscriminate recollection of all traditional values, but as a highly selective attempt by women to revitalize some of the old values.

Veiling, as an attempt to manipulate the past, is dangerous and double-edged, for there is always the danger of recalling not only the desired and valued beliefs of dignity, settled identity, and respect but the accompanying emphasis on seclusion, constraint, and lack of opportunity. The uses of tradition in the struggle to define the future are well known by all holders of power.[19] But particularly for those who seek to recall the past not as holders of power, but as those constrained by power, the dangers must be considered as well.

Because veiling involves both accommodation and protest, women's protest is not only limited but often lost. The acquiescing and accommodating aspects of this mode of hegemonic negotiation are relatively easily coopted. Thus women's relations of inequality are reproduced, not behind their backs, but through, in part, the way their efforts are structured. Because these women in Cairo struggle against aspects of their tradition, but using it symbols and signs, they remain enmeshed in its reality, including its power relations.

Women's accommodation is used and co-opted in the continuing interactions of power relations. Men, for instance, reject or reformulate many of the ideas that veiling is intended to promote and tend to denigrate the statement the veil is intended to make. "These women who wear the veil, they are no better than any other woman. They put on this dress, but under it they could be any kind of women. It does not mean they are more religious, or more Muslim. They are not better. They are probably worse!" Men repeatedly claim that women who wear these clothes are no better, no more virtuous, no more family-oriented than those who do not. Thus the veiled women do not deserve any special privilege or any special respect. "I respect all women when I walk on the streets. Why should I think this one woman is better than the rest because she wears these long clothes? No, this is ridiculous. Clothes can cover any kind of woman."

Further, there has been a troublesome increase in men's attempts to influence women's decision to veil. Veiling is understood by women as a personal decision requiring serious and sincere reflection. While a husband may tell his wife she cannot leave the home to work, for example, or that she must ask his permission to visit her relatives, he cannot insist that she wear the veil. This right *(haqq)* belongs to her alone, a social fact that all women mentioned, and that men also agreed to. However, the stories of two sisters, Iqbal and Sanayya, show the pressure women are increasingly subject to from family men. Iqbal relates that she decided to put on the *muhaggaba* clothing after a request from her husband. They work in the same office building and he was tired of hearing other men complimenting and conversing on the charms of his wife. For her part, Iqbal was relatively indifferent; she had just had her first son, she was happy in her marriage, and as long as she continued to work, she was acquiescent to the idea of veiling and to the underlying idea that her beauty belonged to her husband alone. She even stopped wearing makeup to the office and applied red lipstick and kohl only at home in the evening, for her husband.

Her younger sister, Sanayya, on the other hand, was not indifferent. She vowed she would never wear those clothes even though nearly all the women in her extended family were veiled. Some time after her engagement, however, she acknowledged that she had decided to put on the dress after her marriage to please her fiancé who had requested it. "But at least I have two more years of freedom!" she laughed, referring to the time until her wedding ceremony.

In 1983 and 1984, such successful attempts by men to influence women's decision were quite rare. All women asserted that this movement was under their control and at their initiative, and their behavior demonstrated this truth. By the summer of 1988, many more women were wearing some version of covered dress, for most the change in dress continued to involve a personal resolution. Yet unfortunately, several women admitted that they had put on this dress recently to avoid men's constant harangues. For example, two women working in the same office who had said, several years before, that they would never veil now wore loose scarves over their hair. They were annoyed to be asked about the change and admitted that it was not their choice but that it seemed expedient. Both had succumbed to the insistence of male family members and growing conformity in the office.

When I asked about such stories, women remarked that concessions are often necessary. If women must make some concessions to their husbands for the chance to do other more important things, such as going to school or working, perhaps what they wear should not be seen as so very important. And it is certainly true, and should be emphasized, that through such symbolic moves as the new veiling women in Cairo have been able to keep their jobs and the right to venture outside the home on a regular basis. But these successes now appear more fragile. Sannaya, for instance, who had put on the *higab* to please her fiancé, now finds herself involved in a struggle to be able to continue working at all. Her sister was very worried about her and said, "She is so unhappy, and sits at home all day. And it won't be any better if she has a child because how will they pay for everything! Her husband is a good man, but he is too rigid on this matter. Women have to work today, that is the reality of the economic situation." Further, stories blaming women's position in the workforce for the ills of overcrowded buses, overstaffed offices, and increasing crime in family life have become common. Concessions in one realm apparently are leading to insistence on further retreat.

Another disturbing sign is the increasing involvement of conservative religious leaders.[20] Some women, for instance, decide to veil because of the pronouncements of their local religious leader; several mentioned the existence of such pressure in their neighborhoods, although only one claimed this influence as the origin of her decision to change her dress. More common than this direct influence, and more problematic for the majority of women, men often cite the authority of religious figures in their attempts to persuade fiancés, wives, or sisters to veil. The symbolism of the *higab* is manipulated by these religious leaders to create a certain idea of Islam and women's place, and although this idea varies, it nearly always involves an emphasis on women's family role combined with a belief in the dangers of women's sexuality for society and a defense of Islam and Islamic practices against the cultural imperialism of the West.[21] While women who don the *higab* may or may not believe the rest of the arguments about women's proper position in the larger society, still the character of the movement as women's struggle is being affected and perhaps fundamentally challenged.

Beyond these examples of the turning of women's accommodation to men's advantage, response to the status implications of veiling within the class structure in Cairo can also be discerned. Veiling, for lower-middle-class women, had helped to cut across class lines by dissolving the dress distinctions that had previously differentiated upper and lower-middle-class status. Lately, however, the dress of the *muhaggabat* has become increasingly diverse and there are even fancy boutiques catering to those with modest but expensive taste. The former advantage of the new veiling is being lost as class differences are once again reinforced.

Women's message of protest, clearly, is being countered. Whether women will ultimately succeed in promoting the protest they have to make against existing relations of inequality or even maintain the gains they have already achieved is not clear. The odds are not with them, of course. The possession of power implies weighted results; the potential for promoting the acquiescent angles of women's symbolic gesture of the new veiling, rather than the aspects of protest, appears much the stronger.

ACCOMMODATING PROTEST AND ALTERNATIVES

The women I came to know in Cairo are involved in important choices in the symbolic struggle to define both their own identity and women's place in a changing city. Their struggle resonates with the larger struggle of the Arab world to discover an appropriate modern identity which fits their tradition as it redefines their future. Negotiating the future is the task these women confront with their move into the working world, and the veil is one symbolic statement they make to express and resolve their dilemma of identity and role. Because they are women, both accommodation and protest are intertwined in their style of struggle, a fact that helps explain why reproduction so often occurs.

But it need not be that way. Accommodating protest is not only an explanation for women's part in the reproduction of inequalities; it could also offer a foundation for encouraging real change. Just as the acquiescent aspects of women's behavior can be singled out for cooptation, so could the protesting elements be encouraged and developed. The logic of reproduction and real change are the same, and each time there is a political opening, either result is a political possibility.

Michel de Certeau writes: "Memory comes from another place, it is 'beside itself', it can dis-place. The tactics of its art depend on these properties, and on its disquieting familiarity."[22] The use of the veil is a use of memory in middle-class Cairo to dredge up a forgotten dignity for women by reawakening a potent symbol. De Certeau calls such an action a political "tactic" in the ongoing warfare of negotiation and struggle which forms the web of power relations.[23] In his discussion of "the ingenious ways in which the weak make use of the strong, (lending) a political dimension to everyday practices,"[24] de Certeau tries to articulate the multiple forms of resistance which the weak use on an everyday basis against the strong. Memory, he argues, is one of the strongest of these tactics, for it allows "exits, ways of going out and coming back in, and thus habitable spaces."[25] The calling on memories, for example by wearing the veil, creates a political space, in other words, a space where power relations might be reconsidered and redefined. Thus, women's use of memory, of the veil, constitutes a most astute political tactic, embodying the potential for protest to turn into altered power relations.

However, tactics are the art of the weak, as de Certeau also notes, and he counterposes them to the use of "strategies," which are the privilege of the strong.[26] Strategies are firmly distinguished from tactics by the terrain on which they operate. "The space of a tactic is the space of the other. Thus it must play on and with a terrain imposed on it and organized by the law of a foreign power."[27] de Certeau celebrates the use of tactics, for they are often the only weapon of the weak and quite capable of wearing down or immobilizing the dictates of the strong.

Indeed, there are a number of studies in recent years which celebrate the informal powers of subordinate groups. Janeway, for example, discusses the "powers of the weak," including mistrust and disbelief;[28] Havel argues for the "powers of the powerless," focusing on the political potency of "living truly" as a form of dissent;[29] Scott celebrates the "weapons of the weak," maintaining that the everyday sabotages of peasant-landlord relations signal political resistance.[30] Each argues that small, everyday actions have a potential to turn into larger, fully political, modes of protest.

Similarly, in his study of Petersburg, Russia's most modernized and most troubled city, Berman argues that confrontations initiated by lower-class individuals, which begin on a personal and even quite trivial, level may still grow to have significant political implications and impact.[31] Berman relates Dostoyevsky's story of a petty bureaucrat, an insignificant clerk who develops an obsession from the contradictions which shape Petersburg life, the "politics of enforced backwardness in the midst of forms and symbols of enforced modernization."[32] The clerk's overwhelming obsession is to "think the unthinkable,"[33] to create a small confrontation with the object of his obsession, an aristocratic officer, by bumping into him on the street. "And lo and behold, the most astounding idea dawned upon me! 'What,' I thought, 'if I meet him and—don't move aside? What if I don't move aside on purpose, even if I were to bump into him? How would that be?"[34] The agonies of indecision that the clerk undergoes to reach this idea, and eventually to put it into action highlight the way resistance to traditional relations of power begins with the most mundane and seemingly inconsequential of actions. Yet, even such a small, individual, and ultimately unnoticed symbolic confrontation builds the foundation for the eventual mass public demonstrations of protest that will rock Russia and alter the relations of power. Berman's account, centered on the tensions and turmoil which color the experience of change in Petersburg, and by implication in other developing areas of the world, highlights the confrontations and contradictions, the uncertain struggles and difficult individual moments which are the pathway for more overt, confident, and conscious attempts at reforming the inequities of a class-structured society. De Certeau also concentrates on these unremarked moments, petty difficulties, and discouraging failures which characterize the confrontation of the weak with the strong in any political encounter; tactics, he argues, while perhaps the most effective or the only possible form of struggle for some subordinate groups, have great limitations.[35] They cannot confront directly the discourse and structures which organize the inequality of the weak. "The place of a tactic belongs to the other."[36] Tactics remain a limited and defensive kind of power and therefore inherently fragile, liable to cooptation from the start. Turning these forms of struggle into overt and successful protest is an arduous and uncertain process.

While most of the women quoted in this study firmly maintained that veiling was an individual decision, the fact remains that the action of veiling is distinguished from the modes of behavior discussed by Janeway, Havel, and Scott, by its quite public nature. Disbelief, living truly, and sabotage are all partially masked and hidden forms of protest. The interest of the participants is to keep their actions to some extent under wraps, unacknowledged and thereby relatively safe. Berman's account of a planned bump on a crowded boulevard begins to enter the public realm and seek some acknowledgment of its audacity. Veiling, however, goes even further and demonstrates a public and obvious flaunting of women's point of view. Its drama draws attention, and points to the fact that women are attempting to make some form of public statement. The clever ambiguity of the gesture, which allows women to express protest and acquiescence in one symbolic message, safeguards their resistance and avoids direct confrontation, yet makes nonetheless, a public point. Veiling has already moved, in other words, from hidden resistance to a form of open and overt protest. It carries a symbolic message coalescing women into a potentially unified group. The transition from this implicit unity to a real collective resistance which could be called a fully developed movement of protest is a political potential. This move into the public realm, however symbolic, is a very difficult and important step toward full political protest. Women, in fact, seldom mount such public demonstrations, preferring individualized manipulation and even self-destructive forms of behavior to alleviate the stresses of subjugation to collective, and potentially confrontational behavior.[37]

Yet ultimately the new veiling is limited by its own ambivalence and by its nature as a received symbol from the cultural tradition. Encouragement of the resisting elements of the new veiling relies on the accompanying creation of an alternative discourse of gender (and class), that could reinforce resistance rather than undermine it. Gramsci uses the ideas of counter-hegemony and the war of position to discuss the attempt to create true alternatives in the patterns of social discourse, alternatives which might provide a base for the future growth of more powerful forms of protest.[38] His concept centers on the belief that concrete change in class relations can never occur and be maintained without an alternative vision of human nature and social role to support its structure. Hegemony and counter-hegemony are linked parts of a chain of historical understanding which concentrates on the human role of interpreting and thereby defining the reality in which they live. In times of political space, questions of definitions and interpretations—symbolic struggles—become crucial to the outcome.

Thus a key task for those interested in promoting emancipatory change is to create this alternative culture, an alternative commonsense and worldview which will then be in place when economic changes occur and create openings for possible political reorganization. The crucial question, however, is exactly how such alternative visions can emerge, engage belief, and finally, successfully confront the old discourse of inequality. Gramsci comes to the conclusion that such a countervision can come only from the outside, from thinkers within a political party committed to the role of leader in encouraging social transformation.[39] A vanguard political party is necessary, he argues, to develop an ideological, cultural, and political alternative strong enough to oppose the consistent and powerful upper-class ideological coherency.

In other passages, however, Gramsci suggests the idea that the very contradiction and confusion characterizing the lower class worldview may provide a fertile ground for the growth of alternatives. He was, for instance, especially interested in situations of "contradictory consciousness" where beliefs articulated by the subordinate group support the dominant ideology, yet their behavior expresses an alternative.[40] Women who express the belief that working is wrong, yet continue to hold their jobs present an example of this "contradictory consciousness" and such confusions and conflict in ideological relations could offer a foothold for the creation of more conscious and more complete political struggle.

Indeed, women's confusion about issues of roles and beliefs, while not systematic, clearly does raise questions about the linked power relations through which women are subordinated to men, to the upper classes, and to people and nations outside the developing world. Beliefs about gender roles, although centered on the notion of naturally defined places for men and women in the family and the larger society, also include some suggestion of alternatives, including the humor over certain aspects of male identity alluded to earlier; "backstage" behavior such as poking fun at men who are allegedly stupid and stubborn;[41] and manipulative attempts to control and influence the household, even while granting men the "myth" of their dominance.[42] These forms of behavior offer women some informal forms of influence and perhaps have the potential to confront the existing gender discourse; however they do not yet challenge the overarching belief, or the behavior which supports it, that women belong in the home and men in the workplace, that women's lives should be more constrained than those of men. Therefore the discourse of gender inequality remains unchallenged.

Women in Cairo are aware of and do resist the manifestations of inequality. They are certainly seeking to promote change toward the eradication of some of the inequalities and injustices which bind them. But, as has been demonstrated, their resistance, for several reasons, is fundamentally ambiguous and ultimately carries messages of accommodation along with those of protest. And unfortunately, the potential of the new veiling to create an alternative image for women, combining the strengths of women's working and family identities, seems to be wavering. There are signs that the potential for reproduced inequality is becoming stronger.

The veil evokes a calling up of memories which create an alternative idea of women's identity, yet it also operates on the terrain of the powerful. A symbol of traditional society, it carries a load of significations which women hope to forget but others choose to resurrect and remember. The accommodating aspects of women's mode of protest perhaps safeguard their resistance, yet they also allow, and even encourage the loss of protest's potential. Working has opened a political space for women in which major renegotiations of routine, habits, role, and images are regularly occurring. Women, through veiling, are participating in this reconstruction of identity. But their efforts are not fully successful. True, veiling provides women a cover under which they can keep their jobs even as they emphasize their identity as wife and mother. This is a major gain for women, who clearly argue that being able to leave the home freely and move about the city is the most important new freedom in their lives.

But work is not merely an option for most of these women; they must labor to provide for their families. They need more from a symbol, from their protest, than merely to be allowed grudging entry into the workforce. They need to be able to believe in the value of their work, or at least in the dignity of their double identity as both worker and mother. The economic change of going to work opens up new options for women, but if women (and men) continue to see women only in old pictures, women cannot seize and mold the new opportunities which are coming their way.[43] Women are able to continue their work but at a high personal and social cost. The discourse of gender inequality, if not confronted, counters and absorbs women's efforts to alter their situation and create an alternative. As accommodating protesters, working women who wear the new veils face a difficult and uncertain struggle for new opportunities.

WOMEN'S STYLE OF POLITICAL STRUGGLE

The paradox of the new veiling among working and modernizing women is not only confusing to outsiders of the upper classes or to Western readers, it also points to a dilemma these women are currently experiencing. They live in the midst of dramatic change, in a web of conflicting tendencies, opportunities and constraints created through the vagaries of the modernization process. State policies and economic conditions have pushed these women into the labor force, an important change fostering opportunity for change. Openings in the matrix of social relations appear, as established roles and images become temporarily unsettled. This new political space has exciting potential for women in the search for greater self-determination. Women meet this challenge with a unique form of struggle, accommodating protest. Active and aware, women's style of protest still incorporates acquiescence along with resistance, a suggestive notion for women not only of lower-middle-class Cairo, but for women involved in other struggles elsewhere. This ambivalent style of struggle leaves us with two linked and difficult questions. The first centers on how the shared reality which shapes women's actions and beliefs could be altered and the continual reproducing of an ideology confronted. How can alternatives not only emerge, but gain the power to engage belief and encourage action? The results of this study argue against the perspective that simply lifting the restraints of power will lead to the accomplishment of these goals. The alleviation of power constraints, the creation of political space—which occurs in this case with the economic opening of a new working status—is not in itself sufficient. Such openings create opportunity, but turning opportunity into successful protest is another matter. Modernization, the code word for the massive social changes taking place in cities like Cairo today, is not a process that will sweep human subjects into its grasp and mold them into "modern" beings, complete with all the prescribed attributes of the modern personality and attitude. It is instead a movement that creates pressures, tendencies, fissures, and ambiguous political spaces which require interpretation and action, and elicit both consciousness and choice on the part of human actors. Recognizing the patterns of women's struggle, the challenges of intersecting gender, class, and global inequalities which women must negotiate, is a first and necessary step toward a better understanding of women's prospects in the development process.

The second question, how can we deal with the somewhat disturbing realization that women are active, yet ambivalent, actors who wish to accommodate as well as resist? raises some uncomfortable issues. Women have exchanged the everyday reality of life in the home for a double life in the home and the office. This widened space, both physical in the sense of a new territory, and political in the sense of the potential to alter relations of power, faces women with new chances for change. The hold of the everyday, the habitus, the world of commonsense, has been driven apart and women now inhabit, in a sense, two worlds. But women are prevented from reaping the full advantages of their often courageous struggle by the tension in the very foundations of their resistance to inequality. The resistance is accompanied by acquiescence, and thus their own actions inadvertently strengthen the inequalities they would like to escape—despite their awareness and despite their active resistance. Recognizing such accommodation as women's very reasonable attempt to retain the aspects of traditional social relations they value, rather than assuming that all accommodation is some version of false consciousness or subordinate incapability, is a positive step in the direction of building some movement for change which incorporates women's intentions.

Interrupting and ultimately altering the subordination of women must begin with an understanding of their struggle as a combination of double intentions—as accommodating protest—an understanding which deals with the uncomfortable problems such ambiguous struggle inevitably raises. Only with this recognition might the attempt to encourage the resisting dimensions of women's struggle begin to lead to changed patterns in the interactions of power.

NOTES

PREFACE

1. The classic studies are Lerner, *The Passing of Traditional Society*, and Halpern, *The Politics of Social Change in the Middle East and North Africa*. Also see Perlmutter, "Egypt and the Myth of the New Middle Class." Two excellent recent articles which explore the middle classes with reference to women in Egypt are Hatem, "Egypt's Middle Class in Crisis," and Mohsen, "New Images, Old Reflections."

2. Percentages of responses given throughout the text refer to the sample of 58 working women, unless otherwise identified.

3. The ongoing debate over appropriate methodologies is discussed by Mernissi, in *Le Maroc raconte par ses femmes*, pp. 13–32.

4. This is a result of the fact that women have moved to outlying areas of the city because of the housing crunch, rather than living in traditional areas, where they would have known or even been related to most of their neighbors. This loss of a neighborhood-located frame of reference is one of the major distinctions between the lower and the lower-middle-class.

5. Indeed, when he went back to America to continue his graduate studies, this resulted in some confusion and I was questioned all over again as to what I was about.

6. In this process, I have gained insight from the work of Clifford

Geertz, Paul Rabinow, Kevin Dwyer, Paul Ricoeur, Stanley Fish, and Jim Scott; the volume by Rabinow and Sullivan, *Interpretive Social Science*, gathers together many interesting articles supporting this methodological perspective.

1. WOMEN, POWER RELATIONS, AND CHANGE IN CAIRO

1. In 1984, an Egyptian pound (£E) equaled about U.S. $1; by 1988, it took £E 2.3 to equal $1.

2. In a recent study of the Egyptian bureaucracy, the main advantages of a bureaucratic career were listed as steady income and permanent position. See Palmer, Leila, and Yassin, *The Egyptian Bureaucracy*, p. 39.

3. The word *veil* has no exact equivalent in Arabic; many words are used to convey the many different styles of covered dress. See Rugh, *Reveal and Conceal*, for a full discussion of the great variety of women's dress in Egypt. Most women of the lower-middle-class use the term *higab* to discuss the new forms of covered dress they might wear, which means curtain, cover, or screen.

4. It is important to remember in this context that not all Middle Eastern women are Muslims. In Egypt, for example, there is a sizable Coptic minority. For these women the dictates or language of Islam are not binding, yet many of these women have also worn covering forms of dress and stayed within the household, and today they also face the conflicts of tradition and change that Muslim women encounter. Islamic doctrine alone simply cannot provide a complete explanation of women's status, much less of women's options for the future.

5. For general background on modern Egypt, see Ansari, *Egypt*; Waterbury, *Egypt*, or *The Egypt of Nasser and Sadat*; Marsot, *A Short History of Modern Egypt*; and Hopwood, *Egypt*.

6. On the Islamic revival in Egypt, see Ayubi, "The Political Revival of Islam"; el Guindi, "Is there an Islamic Alternative?"; Ibrahim, "Anatomy of Egypt's Militant Islamic Groups"; or Marsot, "Religion or Opposition?"

7. On the Egyptian political economy, see Abd al-Fadil, *The Political Economy of Nasserism*; Abd al-Khalek and Tignor, *The Political Economy of Income Distribution in Egypt*; Mabro and Radwan, *The Industrialization of Egypt*; and Waterbury, *The Egypt of Nasser and Sadat*.

8. See Tucker, *Women in Nineteenth Century Egypt*; Cole, "Feminism, Class and Islam in Turn of the Century Egypt"; Marsot, "The Revolutionary Gentlewomen in Egypt"; Badran, "Dual Liberation"; Phillipp, "Feminism and National Politics in Egypt"; and Shaarawi, *Harem Years*.

9. For a comparative discussion of labor legislation for women in the Middle East, see Hijab, *Womanpower*, pp. 83–92.

10. On the Personal Status Law debates, see Hijab, *Womanpower*, pp. 29–35.

11. See the discussions in Zurayk, "Dawr al-Mar'a fi al-tanmiya al-igtima'iyya al-iqtisadiyya fi al-buldan al-'arabiyya," and Hijab, *Womanpower*, pp.18–19, for a comparative table on Personal Status Laws in various Middle Eastern countries. Also, see Elizabeth White, "Legal Reform as an Indicator of Women's Status in Muslim Nations," in Beck and Keddie, *Women in the Muslim World*, pp. 52–68.

12. See Toubia, *Women of the Arab World*, esp. pp. 1–26, for an explanation of the organization's goals by Nawal el Saadawi.

13. The discussion of Algiers and Istanbul rests in part on the literature on women in these cities and in part on my personal observations on visiting Algiers in 1989 and Istanbul in 1984 and 1989.

14. See Fanon, *The Wretched of the Earth*; Minces, "Women in Algeria," in Beck and Keddie, *Women in the Muslim World*, pp. 159–171; Gordon, *Women of Algeria*; Tillion, *Le harem et les cousins*; Inger Rezig, "Women's Roles in Contemporary Algeria," in Utas, *Women in Islamic Societies*; and Knauss, *The Persistence of Patriarchy*.

15. See Ahmed, "Early Feminist Movements in Turkey and Egypt"; Cosar, "Women in Turkish Society," in Beck and Keddie, *Women in the Muslim World*, pp. 124–140; Deniz Kandiyoti, "Urban Change and Women's Roles in Turkey," Nilufer Kuyas, "Female Labor Power Relations in the Urban Turkish Family," and Tansi Senyapili, "Economic Change and the Gecekondu Family," all in Kagitcibasi, *Sex Roles, Family and Community in Turkey*; and the essays in the volume edited by Abadan-Unat, *Women in Turkish Society*.

16. Kishwar and Vanita, "India: Widow Burning Revived."

17. Discussed in Siu, *Agents and Victims in South China*, pp. 289–290.

18. Lerner, *The Passing of Traditional Society*, esp. pp. 43–75.

19. Rousseau, *Discourse on the Origin and Foundations of Inequality*, p. 180.

20. For instance, many African women conducted trade and market relations for their families; in recent years, modernized cash economies geared toward men have replaced them and their economic role without giving them an alternative source of economic or social power. Clearly, women are quite rational to protest such erosion, even if they do defend tradition in the process. See, for example, Pellow, *Women in Accra*.

21. For a discussion of this problem see Bossen, "Women in Modernizing Societies."

22. For example, see Wallerstein, *The Modern World System*, or Cardoso and Faletto, *Dependency and Development in Latin America*. Also

see the discussions of the virtues and the problems of the developmental and dependency models in Khalaf, *Lebanon's Predicament*, pp.1–21, and Apter, *Rethinking Development*, pp. 23–32.

23. In addition to Marx's writings, see Bourdieu and Passeron, *Reproduction in Education, Society and Culture*; Bourdieu, *Outline of a Theory of Practice*, and *Distinction*. See also Giddens, *Central Problems in Social Theory*.

24. Unfortunately, this has often been the fate of subordinate groups even at the hands of those who profess to be in support of their interests. The fate of the peasantry under both socialist and capitalist societies offers a good example; see Moore, *The Social Origins of Dictatorship and Democracy*; and Scott, *Weapons of the Weak*.

25. For an interesting discussion of the class position of women, see Beneria and Roldan, *The Crossroads of Class and Gender*, especially pp.76–136; see also my discussion in chapter 6, part 2.

26. "But from the moment one man needed the help of another, as soon as they observed that it was useful for a single person to have provisions for two, equality disappeared, property was introduced, labor became necessary; and vast forests were changed into smiling fields which had to be watered with the sweat of men, and in which slavery and misery were soon seen to germinate and grow with the crops." Rousseau, *Discourse on the Origin and Foundations of Inequality*, pp. 151–152.

27. "Here is the ultimate stage of inequality, the extreme point which closes the circle. . . Here all individuals become equals again because they are nothing; and subjects no longer having any law except the will of the master, nor the master any other rule except his passions, the notions of good and the principles of justice vanish once again." Rousseau, *Discourse on the Origin and Foundations of Inequality*, p. 177. See also his argument in *A Discourse on the Arts and Sciences*.

28. Foucault, *Power/Knowledge*, p. 156.

29. Berman, *All That Is Solid Melts into Air*, p. 6.

30. See Graham-Brown, *Images of Women*, for a photographic history of this image of the veil.

31. See, for example Rosen, *Bargaining for Reality*.

32. Rogers, "Female Forms of Power and the Myth of Male Dominance."

33. See Gramsci, *Selections from the Prison Notebooks*, and also the discussions of hegemony by LaClau and Mouffe, *Hegemony and Socialist Strategy*, and Femia, "Hegemony and Consciousness in the Thought of Antonio Gramsci." The volume of essays edited by Sassoon, *Approaches to Gramsci*, contains essays on hegemony by Hobsbawm, Sassoon, and Buci-Glucksmann. See also Mouffe,"Hegemony and Ideology in Gramsci," in Mouffe, *Gramsci and Marxist Theory*.

34. Rousseau, *Discourse on the Origin and Foundations of Inequality*, p. 159. He continues: "Such was, or must have been, the origin of society and laws, which gave new fetters to the weak, and new forces to the rich, destroyed natural freedom for all time, established forever the law of property and inequality, changed a clever usurpation into an irrevocable right, and for the profit of a few ambitious men henceforth subjected the whole human race to work, servitude and misery." p. 160.

35. On the idea of political space, see Bourdieu, *Outline of a Theory of Practice*, or de Certeau, *The Practice of Everyday Life*.

36. Gramsci, *Selections from the Prison Notebooks*; see also the discussion of hegemonic politics during times of transition in LaClau and Mouffe, *Hegemony and Socialist Strategy*, especially chapter 3.

37. Foucault, *Power/Knowledge*, p. 98.

38. Bourdieu, "The Disenchantment of the World," p. 30.

2. LOWER-MIDDLE-CLASS WOMEN IN CAIRO

1. On the integration and differentiation of dominant and subordinate cultures, see Scott, "Protest and Profanation," for a discussion of great and little traditions, and see Ardener, *Perceiving Women*, for a discussion of dominant and muted cultures.

2. Shorter, "Cairo's Leap Forward," p. 5; statistics on Cairo's population are complicated by the question of the definition of the boundaries of "Greater Cairo," as the city continues its expansion outward. Estimates of Cairo's current population range from 10 to 14 million.

3. Waterbury, *Egypt*, pp. 125–127.

4. For a good description of the inconveniences and problems of a crowded Cairo, see Waterbury, *Egypt*, pp. 45–199.

5. For the classic description of the history, cultural development and social divisions of the city, see Abu-Lughod, *Cairo*.

6. Some recent ethnographic studies on different quarters of the city include: Hoodfar, "Survival Strategies in Low Income Neighborhoods of Cairo, Egypt"; Rugh, *Family in Contemporary Egypt*; Singerman, "Avenues of Participation"; Taher, "Social Identity and Class in a Cairo Neighborhood"; and Wikan, *Life Among the Poor in Cairo*.

7. For details on the housing crisis, see: Shorter, "Cairo's Leap Forward," pp. 24–35.

8. For a comparative example of the confusions of urban identity involved in the modernizing process in a Moroccan city, see Geertz, "Toutes Directions."

9. On the Nasser era and socialist reforms, see Waterbury, *The Egypt of Nasser and Sadat*; Abd al-Fadil, *The Political Economy of Nasserism*; Baker, *Egypt's Uncertain Revolution Under Nasser and Sadat*;

Hussein, *Class Conflict in Egypt*; Migdal, *Strong Societies and Weak States*; and Ansari, *Egypt*.

10. On Sadat's policies, see Waterbury, *The Egypt of Nasser and Sadat*, and "The 'Soft State' and the Open Door"; Baker, *Egypt's Uncertain Revolution under Nasser and Sadat*; Hinnebusch, *Egyptian Politics Under Sadat*; Ansari, *Egypt*; and Zaalouk, *Power, Class and Foreign Capital in Egypt*.

11. See Tucker and Stork, "In the Footsteps of Sadat"; Goldschmidt, *Modern Egypt*, pp. 163–168; Springborg, *Mubarak's Egypt*; Bianchi, *Unruly Corporatism*; and Tripp and Owen, eds., *Egypt Under Mubarak*.

12. For a description of these networks, see Singerman, "Avenues of Participation," and Rugh, "Coping with Poverty in a Cairo Community." For a comparative description of women's networks in Lebanon, see Joseph, "Working Class Women's Networks in a Sectarian State."

13. For a full description of the variety of dress in Cairo, see Rugh, *Reveal and Conceal*.

14. See Ibrahim, "Social Mobility and Income Distribution in Egypt," pp. 426–429, for this 1979 categorization scheme and the brief descriptions of the strata of Cairene society which follow.

15. Ibid., p. 425.

16. Ibid., p. 426. For full descriptions of lower-income life in Cairo, see Rugh, "Coping with Poverty in a Cairo Community"; Wikan, *Life Among the Poor in Cairo*; Atiya, *Khul-Khaal*, or Hoodfar, "Survival Strategies in Low Income Neighborhoods of Cairo, Egypt."

17. Ibrahim, "Social Mobility and Income Distribution in Egypt," pp. 426–427.

18. Ibid., p. 427.

19. Ibid., p. 427. For discussion of the divisions within the middle class, see Hatem, "Egypt's Middle Class in Crisis"; and Mohsen, "New Images, Old Reflections."

20. One reason she "does not need to work" is that their apartment is in a building partially owned by her father; this means that they are able to pay only a nominal rent. In a time when rent is the most expensive item in young families' budgets, this factor can add considerably to class security.

21. On the issue of class identity in Cairo, see Taher, "Social Identity and Class in a Cairo Neighborhood," and el-Messiri, *Ibn al-Balad*.

22. On the lower class family, see Rugh, *Family in Contemporary Egypt*.

23. For a study of the variation in Islamic ideals and behavior in a Malaysian village, see Scott, "Protest and Profanation."

24. See, for example, Lois Beck, "The Religious Lives of Muslim Women," or Mernissi, "Women, Saints and Sanctuaries."

25. This is beginning to change in some groups with the revival of

Islam and the stress on a place for women in this new version of the heritage. Some women now attend mosque meetings or Quran reading classes. See el Guindi, "Veiling Infitah with Muslim Ethic," and "Is There an Islamic Alternative"; and Hoffman, "An Islamic Activist."

26. See Morsy, "Sex Differences and Folk Illness in an Egyptian Village"; and Lewis, *Ecstatic Religion.*

27. See Ibrahim, "Anatomy of Egypt's Islamic Groups," and "Egypt's Islamic Activism in the 1980's"; Ayubi, "The Political Revival of Islam"; Dekmejian, *Islam in Revolution*; Dessouki, *Islamic Resurgence in the Arab World*; Marsot, "Religion or Opposition"; and el Guindi, "Is There an Islamic Alternative?"

28. This widespread feeling is especially interesting given that the lower-middle-class, particularly those members with recent rural backgrounds, seem to be the main supporters of militant fundamentalist groups. See, Ibrahim, "Anatomy of Egypt's Militant Islamic Groups," pp. 423–453.

29. For some possible revisions of the relations between men and women, see Nelson, "Public and Private Politics"; Rogers, "Female Forms of Power and the Myth of Male Dominance"; or Rosen, *Bargaining for Reality.* This question will be taken up in the last chapter.

30. See Arafa, *The Social Activities of the Egyptian Feminist Union.*

31. Nawal El Saadawi, "Introduction," in Toubia, *Women of the Arab World*, p. 2.

32. This problem in women's studies is paralleled in state-level studies of the developing world as well; see the discussion of the need for more work on the effect of peripheries on the center in Migdal, *Strong Societies and Weak States*, especially pp. xv–xviii.

3. WOMEN AT WORK OUTSIDE THE HOME

1. See, for instance, Tucker, *Women in Nineteenth Century Egypt*; or Pomeroy, *Women in Hellenistic Egypt.*

2. Ibrahim, "Social Change and the Industrial Experience," pp. 51–53.

3. For a detailed description, see Tucker, *Women in Nineteenth Century Egypt*, pp. 81–101.

4. For a discussion of the rise of feminist consciousness prior to the publication of *Tahrir al-marah* by Amin, see Badran, "Dual Liberation," pp. 20–24.

5. Marsot, "The Revolutionary Gentlewomen in Egypt," pp. 264–268.

6. Cited in Zurayk, "Women's Economic Participation" p. 24. Compare with a low of 2.2 percent in 1974 in Saudi Arabia and a high of 35.2 percent in 1975 in Turkey.

7. On the problems of data on women's work in the Middle East,

see Sullivan, "Women and Work in Egypt," and Zurayk, "Women's Economic Participation." See the latter for a discussion on improving data gathering and analysis techniques.

8. Sullivan, "Women and Work in Egypt," p. 18.

9. Youssef, "A Woman-Specific Strategy Statement," p. 17.

10. See Howard-Merriam, "Women, Education and the Professions in Egypt," pp. 256–270, and Papanek, "Class and Gender in Education–Employment Linkages," pp. 317–346.

11. On the lives of village women in Egypt, see Abaza, *The Changing Image of Women in Rural Egypt*; Khafagy, "Women and Labor Migration"; Morsy, "Sex Differences and Folk Illness in an Egyptian Village"; Taylor, "Egyptian Migration and Peasant Wives"; and Tucker, *Women in Nineteenth Century Egypt*, pp. 40–63.

12. Tucker, "Egyptian Women in the Workforce," p. 5.

13. In fact, with the drastic increases in male labor migration to Cairo and to other Arab countries, such work is probably increasingly performed by women as they become the *de facto* heads of households in many village communities. This labor, as mentioned earlier, is regarded as an extension of household work, and these women usually report themselves as "not working" on official surveys, due to the lack of actual cash wages received, the symbolic need to protect family honor and reputation, and the perception of women's ideal identity as housewife and mother.

14. Therefore, many of these women may actually be somewhat more restricted and therefore traditional in life-style, meaning that their daily labor is limited to working in the household, when they move to the center of modern life, the city, than they were in their native villages.

15. For descriptions of lower-class women's informal sector work in Cairo, see: Hoodfar, "Survival Strategies in Low Income Neighborhoods of Cairo, Egypt"; el-Messiri, "Self-Images of Traditional Urban Women in Cairo"; and Rugh, "Coping with Poverty in a Cairo Community," and "Women and Work."

16. Ibrahim, "Social Change and the Industrial Experience."

17. Sullivan, "Women and Work in Egypt," p. 9.

18. For accounts of life as a female factory worker, see Ibrahim, "Social Change and the Industrial Experience"; Hammam, "Women and Industrial Work in Egypt" and "Egypt's Working Women," and, for a historical perspective, Tucker, *Women in 19th Century Egypt*, pp. 84–91.

19. Kamphoefner, "What's the Use? The Household, Low-Income Women, and Literacy."

20. It has become more and more difficult for the government to provide these jobs, and waiting times for assignment have grown in

recent years to four to five years. See the discussion in Springborg, *Mubarak's Egypt*, pp. 137–140.

21. Sullivan, *Women in Egyptian Public Life.* For a comparative perspective on elite women, see Altorki, *Women in Saudi Arabia.*

22. On the crucial distinctions within the middle class, see Hatem, "Egypt's Middle Class in Crisis"; and Mohsen, "New Images, Old Reflections."

23. Similarly, the urban poor stress the qualities that make their lives different from both peasants and the urban middle classes. See el-Messiri, "Self Images of Traditional Urban Women in Cairo." El-Messiri cites the *bint al-balad* (daughter of the country or traditional urbanite) calling the *muwazzafa* (government employee) "conceited, superficial and neglectful of wifely duties." p. 532.

24. On the dialectic of identification and differentiation in class settings, see Newby, "The Deferential Dialectic."

25. For a discussion of the status of female government employees, see Adil Ibrahim, "Al-mar'a 'al-amala" *Al-Ahram al-Iqtisadi* (1984), 807:20–21.

26. Farghali, "Characteristics of the Female Labor Force in Cairo and Alexandria in 1976," p. 17.

27. For a deeper discussion of this problem of "need," see chapter 4.

28. The exchange rate in 1984 was about £E 1 to $1, but by 1988 it was £E .3 to $1. Thus the approximate equivalent in dollars in 1984 was $40 and by 1988, $26.

29. Single and married women have different forms of "family needs" of course; thus single women's salaries generally pay for the goods that will make a marriage and future home possible, while married women's pay funds the necessities and small luxuries of the household budget. These differences will be examined more closely in chapter 5.

30. This budget is based on the examples many women showed me of the written budgets they prepare and keep track of for their families. Most women seem very proud of this responsibility and keep strict accounts of the use of family funds.

31. One kilo of meat cost about £E 5 in 1984 and double that price by 1988.

32. On the variation from the ideal type which exists in traditional patterns of budget management in urban families, see Hoodfar, "Patterns of Household Budgeting and Financial Management in a Lower-Income Cairo Neighborhood."

33. A situation is arising where younger sisters, reaching the age of waiting for a job in the government queue, are now realizing that they may never find jobs this way. Their chances of securing a middle class husband, finding an affordable middle-class apartment, and generally maintaining middle-class status are significantly lower than chances

were for their older sisters, creating important class inequities within the family unit. This of course puts additional pressure on women who have obtained these jobs already.

34. Zamalek is an upper-middle-class, modernized, and Westernized part of the city, with many foreign residents. Helwan is a working-class area on the outskirts of Cairo with many factories, unpaved streets, limited facilities, and considerable construction of new apartment buildings. It is connected to Cairo by the metro system.

35. The indiscriminate use of medicines is very common even in the educated lower middle class. Private doctors are expensive, but lower-middle-class people feel clinics are only for the poor. Often, they will simply avoid going to seek help rather than pay the high costs of doctor's advice, trying folk remedies and self-prescribed medication, or using pharmacist's advice.

36. One of the major advantages of government work is the time at the office available for such tasks. Women working in factories, for instance, do not have this luxury, and therefore must do the work at home in even fewer hours.

37. Farghali, "Characteristics of the Female Labor Force in Cairo and Alexandria in 1976," p. 18.

38. On the problem of apathy in the bureaucracy, see Palmer, *The Egyptian Bureaucracy*, pp. 48–71.

39. See, for an argument against the public-private split in the Middle East, Nelson, "Public and Private Politics." For a more recent discussion, see Singerman, "Avenues of Participation."

40. For an interesting perspective on this molding process and the resulting loss to society, see Gilligan, *In a Different Voice*.

41. See, for example, the essays in Sargent, *Women and Revolution*.

42. On this argument, see the introduction to the interesting essays in Beechey, *Unequal Work*, pp. 1–16.

43. For a comparative perspective on this ambivalence and the lack of transition from economic influence to household power see Beneria, *The Crossroads of Class and Gender*, especially pp. 144–153.

4. WOMEN'S DILEMMA

1. On the wide range of usage of the term *ideology*, see Geertz, "Ideology as a Cultural System."

2. This view of ideology rests on discussions by Gramsci, in *Selections from the Prison Notebooks*; LaClau and Mouffe, in *Hegemony and Socialist Strategy*; Althusser, in "Ideology and Ideological State Apparatuses"; and Foucault, in *Power/Knowledge*.

3. See the discussion on Gramsci's reconceptualization of ideology in LaClau and Mouffe, *Hegemony and Socialist Strategy*, pp. 65–71, especially p. 67.

4. Ibid. p. 67.

5. See Graham-Brown, *Images of Women*; Alloula, *The Colonial Harem*; and Ahmed, "Western Ethnocentrism and Perceptions of the Harem."

6. It should be remembered that Egypt has a large Coptic minority as well, whose women face many of the same problems articulated in this study, but the language and symbols they use to understand and act on their dilemmas is different.

7. "The Quran on the Subject of Women," in Fernea and Bezirgan, *Middle Eastern Muslim Women Speak*, p. 13.

8. Ibid. p. 18.

9. See the discussion by Stowasser, "The Status of Women in Early Islam," pp. 14–25.

10. For an example of reinterpretation of the image of Eve, see Smith and Haddad, "Eve: Islamic Image of Woman."

11. See Hijab, *Womanpower*, pp. 29–35 for a full account of the family law story; also, al-Nowaihi, "Changing the Law on Personal Status in Egypt with a Liberal Interpretation of the Shari'a."

12. See Afshar, "The Legal, Social and Political Position of Women in Iran"; Ferdows, "Women and the Islamic Revolution"; and Yaganeh and Keddie, "Sexuality and Shi'i Social Protest in Iran."

13. Ferdows, "Women and the Islamic Revolution," pp. 288–290.

14. Ibid. p. 289.

15. Ibid. p. 290.

16. Ibid. p. 290. See also Yaganeh and Keddie, "Sexuality and Shi'i Social Protest in Iran," pp. 127–130.

17. See Yaganeh and Keddie, "Sexuality and Shi'i Social Protest in Iran" for elaboration of this point in the Iranian context.

18. On the interactions of the great and little tradition, see Scott, "Protest and Profanation."

19. On the image of women in different sectors of society in Cairo, see el-Messiri, *Ibn al-Balad*, and "Self-Images of Traditional Urban Women in Cairo"; Abdel Kader, "The Image of Women in Drama and Women's Programs on Egyptian TV"; Abu-Lughod and Amin, "Egyptian Marriage Advertisements"; Atiya, *Khul-Khaal*; Ibrahim, "Social Change and the Industrial Experience"; el Saadawi, *The Hidden Face of Eve*; al-Shamy, *Folktales of Egypt*; and Suleiman, "The Changing Attitudes Toward Women in Egypt."

20. The discussion that follows draws on the very interesting account of the Muslim view of sexuality and women in Sabbah, *Women in the Muslim Unconscious*. I also draw on observations from other works not specific to urban Egypt, including Dwyer, *Images and Self Images*; Abu-Lughod, *Veiled Sentiments*; Bauer, "Sexuality and the Moral 'Construction' of Women in an Islamic Society"; Fernea and Bezirgan, *Middle Eastern Muslim Women Speak*; Graham-Brown, *Images of Women*;

Mernissi, *Beyond the Veil*; and Mikhail, *Images of Arab Women*. Use of these sources from throughout the Middle East is not meant to imply that a universal image of women holds throughout the area, but observations from these works can combine to frame the generalized dominant image of the Muslim woman from which lower-middle-class Cairenes construct their own interpretive version, which I have presented in these pages.

21. See Musallam, *Sex and Society in Islam*, pp. 28, 31–34.

22. See the discussion on the "omnisexual woman" in Sabbah, *Women in the Muslim Unconscious*, pp. 34–35.

23. Arabic proverb.

24. See the discussion of the perception of appropriate male and female roles and women who work in lower class Cairo in el-Messiri, "Self-Images of Traditional Urban Women in Cairo," and in Rugh, "Women and Work."

25. On these difficulties, see Mohsen, "New Images, Old Reflections."

26. See Hoodfar, "Survival Strategies in a Low Income Neighborhood of Cairo, Egypt," p. 166; and Rugh, "Women and Work," pp. 281–287.

27. See the discussion of working conditions and morale in the government bureaucracy in Samir Izzat, "Sirk al-muwazzafin!" *Ruz al-Yusif* (1985), 61(2998):26–29.

28. For women, this is sometimes discussed as an advantage, since they save their energy and talents for use in the home rather than wasting them at the office. While this may be a short term advantage for some women, ultimately it degrades the status of the job of government office worker, contributing to the lowered prestige and income of these jobs.

29. On the economic situation, see al-Din, "Income Distribution and Basic Needs in Urban Egypt"; Waterbury, *Egypt*, and *The Egypt of Nasser and Sadat*, and "The 'Soft State' and the Open Door."

30. See the short story *The Shoes* by Iqbal Barakah, for a fictional illustration of this envy and conspicuous consumption, in Fernea, *Women and the Family in the Middle East*, pp. 289–292.

31. For a description of the rise of this new bourgeoisie in the aftermath of the *infitah* policies, see Zaalouk, *Power, Class and Foreign Capital in Egypt*.

32. For similar conclusions, see Wikan, "Living Conditions Among Cairo's Poor—A View from Below."

33. Controversy in the press over women's right to work become frequent in late 1986 and early 1987. For instance, overcrowding on the bus system is blamed on too many working women or an increase in crime is blamed on too many working women who neglect their children.

34. See chapter 6, part 2, for a discussion of this problem in more depth.

35. Bourdieu discusses a similar question regarding the competition between two competing economic ideologies in Algeria, one of work as traditional activity and one of work as capitalist productivity. See Bourdieu, "The Disenchantment of the World."

36. This deterministic explanation ignores the role of human agency, choice, and the uncertainties of political struggle. See chapter 6, part 2.

37. See Hatem, "Egypt's Middle Class in Crisis," and Hoffman-Ladd, "Polemics on the Modesty and Segregation of Women."

5. WOMEN'S SYMBOLIC ACTION

1. The term is Edward Said's, from his discussion of Western forms of knowledge and their power-laden manner of describing the East, in his book *Orientalism*.

2. Murphy, "Social Distance and the Veil," pp. 290–315, especially p. 290.

3. Of course, veiling and seclusion are not limited to the Middle East or even to Muslim cultures, and the excellent articles by Papanek, Sharma, and Pastner discuss the multiple uses of veiling and seclusion in the Asian context.

4. For example, see the photographs in Graham-Brown, *Images of Women*, or in Fernea and Fernea, "A Look Behind the Veil." For photos of dress in the Egyptian context, see Rugh, *Reveal and Conceal*.

5. Purdah in the Hindu context or footbinding and seclusion in the Chinese context are two prominent examples.

6. Fernea and Bezirgan, *Middle Eastern Muslim Women Speak*, p. 25. See also the translations of other verses regarding women on pp. 9–26. And see the discussion by Stowasser, "The Status of Women in Early Islam," p. 24.

7. Fernea and Bezirgan, *Middle Eastern Muslim Women Speak*, p. 20.

8. Stowasser, "The Status of Women in Early Islam," p. 24.

9. See Ramazani, "The Veil—Piety or Protest?"; and Stowasser, "The Status of Women in Early Islam," pp. 23–37.

10. Stowasser, "The Status of Women in Early Islam," pp. 33–34.

11. Beck and Keddie, *Women in the Muslim World*, p. 25; and Stowasser, "The Status of Women in Early Islam," p. 34.

12. For discussion of this point in various cultural contexts, see Murphy, "Social Distance and the Veil"; Sharma, "Women and their Affines"; or Abu-Lughod, *Veiled Sentiments*, pp. 159–67.

13. For an interesting discussion of the complexities of the meaning

of honor in one Middle Eastern context, see Abu-Lughod, *Veiled Sentiments*, pp. 78–117.

14. See, for a comparative example, Bauer, "Sexuality and the Moral 'Construction' of Women in an Islamic Society" on the gap between belief and behavior, and verbalization and action, among Iranian women.

15. For a comparative perspective on veiling, honor, and family relations, see Pastner, "A Social, Structural and Historical Analysis of Honor, Shame and Purdah"; and Schneider, "Of Vigilance and Virgins."

16. Such veiling in rural areas may be increasing in North Africa and elsewhere in the Middle East. For a discussion of increasing use of the veil in Algeria, see Tillion, *Le harem et les cousins*, chapter 9; or the discussion of this phenomenon throughout the Middle East by Beck and Keddie, *Women in the Muslim World*, pp. 8–9.

17. For an extreme version of this argument centering on women in Mediterranean communities, see Rogers, "Female Forms of Power and the Myth of Male Dominance."

18. See Betteridge, "To Veil or Not to Veil," and the other articles in Nashat, *Women and Revolution in Iran*.

19. For some examples, see Wikan, *Behind the Veil in Arabia*, pp. 88–109; or el-Messiri, "Self-Images of Traditional Urban Women in Cairo," p. 526.

20. The term is Papanek's, from her very interesting article, "Purdah: Separate Worlds and Symbolic Shelter."

21. See Shaarawi, *Harem Years*, pp. 7–10.

22. On early manifestations of the new veiling in Cairo, see the excellent article by el Guindi, "Veiling Infitah with Muslim Ethic." Also, see Williams, "A Return to the Veil in Egypt"; and Ibrahim, "Arab Social Change."

23. The specific history of the veil in rural Egypt or Bedouin communities is quite different from the story in Cairo. See, for instance, the discussion of veiling and honor in a Bedouin community in Egypt in Abu-Lughod, *Veiled Sentiments*.

24. Marsot, "The Revolutionary Gentlewomen in Egypt," p. 268.

25. On the variety of traditional dress, see Rugh, *Reveal and Conceal*.

26. Photo albums in people's homes often contain pictures taken a few years ago, showing female family members dressed in clothes that they would not wear today—generally pants, short skirts, sleeveless shirts, or bathing suits. I was often offered such clothes, which had been packed away, since I, being non-Muslim, could wear such things and they did not anticipate wearing them again. In fact, I was strongly encouraged to wear such clothes, as they were perceived as very attrac-

tive and feminine—unlike the boring and utilitarian longer skirts and modest shirts I wore while conducting this research.

27. For a full and very interesting discussion of the use of Islamic dress in this period, see el Guindi, "Veiling Infitah with Muslim Ethic," and "Is there an Islamic Alternative?"

28. El Guindi, "Is there an Islamic Alternative," especially p. 21, and "The Emerging Islamic Order"; see also the film made by Fernea and Gaunt, "A Veiled Revolution"; and the articles by Williams, "A Return to the Veil in Egypt," and Marsot, "Religion or Opposition."

29. See Betteridge, "To Veil or Not to Veil"; Nashat, "Women in the Ideology of the Islamic Republic," pp. 209–210; or Fischer, "In Defense of Ayesha."

30. See Marshall and Stokes, "Tradition and the Veil," or Marshall, "Culture Crisis, Islamic Revival and the Reactivation of Patriarchy," pp. 4–10.

31. "Afghan Refugee Women Suffering From Isolation Under Islamic Custom," *New York Times* (March 3, 1988).

32. Zaki Nagib Mahmud, "Redda fi 'alim al-moda'," *al-Ahram* (April 9, 1984).

33. "Li al-katib al-sakhir min al-higab," and Ahmed Musa Salim, "Al-redda an al-higab li katib yanqusuhu al-sawab," both in *al-Akhbar* (May 11, 1984).

34. It is interesting to note that wearing the *higab* seems to be decreasing now among women in the university setting and the higher ranks of the middle class, where it originated.

35. These were generally older working women, and had a different experience and set of expectations about the change of working outside the home. They worked hard to get their positions, as leaders in women's move into the government offices, and they complain that younger women take for granted the gains they struggled over for. This, of course, is very similar to the complaints many feminists in America voice over their daughters' values and behavior.

36. This includes several of the women who claimed they would never wear such clothes; their situation will be discussed further in chapter 6, part 2.

37. Several women I met who wore the *higab* explained that they too wanted to dress in this more intense version of veiled dress; however, they said they were not allowed to work in government offices wearing gloves or with their faces covered, as the government "needed to see people's faces, so that spies could be identified."

38. Or, it might be added, Coptic Christian women. Christian women also work in these offices and their minority position is emphasized as more and more women adopt covering clothes.

39. However, some women are participating in creating a new, alternative Islam, although their numbers are perhaps small; see el Guindi, "Is There an Islamic Alternative?" or Hoffman, "An Islamic Activist."

40. This use of the *higab* as a marriage strategy for some women is also cited in Mohsen, "New Images, Old Reflections," p. 69.

41. This answer contrasts with that given by older women who do not work outside the home; they generally professed indifference or a lack of comprehension as to why veiling was such a controversial matter, coupled with a general feeling that it was probably best for their daughters. Its irrelevance to the immediacies of their own life made veiling a matter of small import to them; they continue to wear the traditional dress they have always worn.

42. See Marshall and Stokes, "Tradition and the Veil"; el Guindi, "Is There an Islamic Alternative?"; Yeganeh and Keddie, "Sexuality and Shi'i Social Protest in Iran"; and Afshar, "The Legal, Social and Political Position of Women in Iran."

43. Both men and women said the expense of getting married is becoming almost impossible; they claimed it required nearly £E 10,000 for a young couple to celebrate a marriage and set up a suitable lower-middle-class apartment. Compare with the estimates of £E 6000–15,000 on marriage expenses by among lower-class families during the same period in Cairo. Singerman, "Avenues of Participation," p. 18.

44. On the competition for marriage partners between lower-middle-class and upper-middle-class women, see Mohsen, "New Images, Old Reflections," pp. 67–68.

45. The number of veiled women grew considerably from 1984 to 1988, but among single women it remains a less popular choice. Single women who do veil tend to wear more token concessions to covered dress, with attractive silky scarves draped loosely over the head for example. As one woman commented, "Well, I can't cover too much, after all I want to get married some day!" Among single women, veiling does not seem to be a compelling choice, although the pressures on all women are now growing stronger. On this development, see the discussion in chapter 6, part 2.

46. Foucault, *The History of Sexuality* and *Power/Knowledge*, pp. 55–62, and 90–91.

6. THE NEW VEILING AS ACCOMMODATING PROTEST

1. On Gramsci's conception of hegemony, see Gramsci, *Selections from the Prison Notebooks*; Femia, "Hegemony and Consciousness in the Thought of Antonio Gramsci"; LaClau and Mouffe, *Hegemony and Socialist Strategy*; Sassoon, *Approaches to Gramsci*; and Mouffe, *Gramsci and Marxist Theory*.

2. This idea of a dominant ideology and the creation of a false consciousness among subordinates is discussed in Abercrombie, Hill, and Turner, *The Dominant Ideology Thesis*.

3. On hegemonic relations as relations of struggle, see LaClau and Mouffe, *Hegemony and Socialist Strategy*, especially pp. 134–145.

4. Willis, *Learning to Labour*.

5. See Scott, "Protest and Profanation," "Hegemony and the Peasantry," and *Weapons of the Weak*, pp. 314–350.

6. Gramsci, *Selections from the Prison Notebooks*, and *Selections from the Cultural Writings*.

7. See Connerton, *How Societies Remember*, for a discussion of the newly developed styles of dress worn in Paris during and immediately after the French Revolution, pp. 10–11.

8. For example, see Afshar, "The Legal, Social and Political Position of Women in Iran"; Ferdows, "Women and the Islamic Revolution"; Yeganeh and Keddie, "Sexuality and Shi'i Social Protest in Iran"; and Betteridge, "To Veil or Not to Veil."

9. See el Guindi, "Veiling Infitah with Muslim Ethic," "Is There an Islamic Alternative?" and "Veiled Activism."

10. Cloward and Piven, "Hidden Protest."

11. Ibid. Especially pp. 655–660.

12. Lewis, *Ecstatic Religion*, especially chapter 3. Also see Morsy, "Sex Differences and Folk Illness in an Egyptian Village," in Beck and Keddie, *Women in the Muslim World*, pp. 599–616.

13. See the discussion of routine resistance in Scott, *Weapons of the Weak*, pp. 255–278.

14. See the interesting consideration of women's part in political activity in the Middle East in *Middle East Report* 138(1986), especially the article by Judith Tucker, "Insurrectionary Women" pp. 9–13, which concludes with the idea that women use the "strategy—passive resistance—and the weapon—the taunt—of the weak." p. 13. Also see Suad Joseph's comment in her article, "Women and Politics in the Middle East," p. 3–7 in the same issue, that women's political participation is often "found in gender-linked social spaces." p. 6.

15. From Beck and Keddie, *Women in the Muslim World*, p. 19.

16. Piven and Cloward, *Poor People's Movements* especially chapter 1, "The Structuring of Protest."

17. De Certeau, "On the Oppositional Practices of Everyday Life."

18. De Certeau, *The Practice of Everyday Life*, especially pp. 29–42 and 91–130.

19. On the political uses of memory, see de Certeau, "On the Oppositional Practices of Everyday Life," p. 41.

20. This form of accommodation is paralleled in Western offices where women don suits and ties to gain acceptance.

21. The realm of power will shift away from the state and legal

repression to the area of creating power, as in the formation of desire, see Foucault, *The History of Sexuality*, especially pp. 89–91 and *Power/Knowledge*, especially pp. 78–108.

7. ACCOMMODATING PROTEST AND THE REPRODUCTION OF INEQUALITY

1. Foucault, *The History of Sexuality*, p. 96.

2. For a discussion of the problems of formulating an alternative working-class consciousness, see Parkin, *Class Inequality and Political Order*, especially pp. 79–102.

3. Gramsci, *Selections from the Prison Notebooks*, especially pp. 419–425. See also Alberto Cirese, "Gramsci's Observations on Folklore," in Sassoon, *Approaches to Gramsci*, pp. 212–247.

4. Gramsci's own account of hegemony is much richer than that of many who have narrowed it to an idea of passive consent; he discusses hegemony, for example, in both its active and passive guises. See the article by Buci-Glucksman, "Hegemony and Consent," pp. 116–126, in Sassoon, *Approaches to Gramsci*, for an account of the range of ways in which the hegemonic goal can be accomplished. Also see the discussion of his idea of contradictory consciousness below.

5. For similar appraisals of subordinate actors' ability to assess and act on their situation when possible, looking at the working class, peasants and blacks respectively, see Moore, *Injustice*; Scott, *Weapons of the Weak*; and Genovese *Roll, Jordan, Roll*.

6. See the interesting essay by Hartmann, "The Unhappy Marriage of Marxism and Feminism," in Sargent, *Women and Revolution*, pp. 1–41.

7. See the essays in the volume edited by Sargent, *Women and Revolution*.

8. See the argument for historical, rather than solely theoretical, perspective on the interplay of class and gender, in Beneria and Roldan, *The Crossroads of Class and Gender*, p. 10. Their study is a detailed account of the intersection of class and gender among lower-class women in Mexico City. Also, see the discussion on competing economic ideologies and class pressures in Algeria, which is suggestive for understanding class and gender competition, in Bourdieu, "The Disenchantment of the World."

9. This fact is enhanced by women's different positions in the life cycle, when different forms and degrees of power are available to individual women; their support of the current system may vary considerably over their lifetime. The problems of a mother-in-law are well known by young wives, and even though living in the extended household is becoming more rare, women still complain frequently about

the restrictions and complications mothers-in-law inject into their family life.

10. In this way women's position can be likened to the position of many participants in service industries, or low-level managers, or secretaries, who hold what Wright has termed "contradictory class positions" which lead them to act and to hold attitudes at times derived from an upper-class, and at times from a lower-class perspective. See Wright, *Class, Crisis, and the State*, especially pp. 61–83.

11. See Marysa Navarro, "The Personal Is Political: Las Madres de Plaza de Mayo," in Eckstein, *Power and Popular Protest*, pp. 241–258.

12. The discussion of hegemonic interaction as the politics of articulation and discourse by LaClau and Mouffe in *Hegemony and Socialist Strategy* is especially useful. This idea of constrained discussion within the limits of an overarching ideology forms the framework for much of Foucault's work on power as circulations within a discourse as well; see *Power/Knowledge*.

13. On the struggles to create identity, I have found the following works particularly insightful: Foucault, "The Ethic of Care for the Self as a Practice of Freedom"; and Berman, *The Politics of Authenticity* and *All That Is Solid Melts into Air*.

14. Bourdieu, *Outline of a Theory of Practice*; see also the discussion of Bourdieu in de Certeau, *The Practice of Everyday Life*, especially pp. 56–60.

15. Even after meeting me, these media images remained overwhelmingly powerful for women. Often, I was told that I was a very unusual Western woman (which they ascribed to my identity as partly Arab); their evidence was that I did not dress or act in the ways American women are portrayed on television. Despite my efforts to describe typical American women and distinguish them from media exaggerations, women remained unconvinced.

16. See Ahmed, "Early Feminist Movements in Turkey and Egypt," in Hussain, *Muslim Women*, pp. 121–122.

17. Rosen argues that women speak from and bargain from an alternative reality, but I think Gramsci's formulation of "contradictory consciousness" addresses the problem that this alternative reality does not seem to evolve into a true alternative which can confront the existing reality except at a minimal level of manipulation. See Rosen, *Bargaining for Reality* and Gramsci, *Selections from the Prison Notebooks*, especially pp. 325–334.

18. De Certeau, *The Practice of Everyday Life*, p. 18.

19. For a full study of tradition and change, see Shils, *Tradition*; see also Hobsbawm and Ranger, *The Invention of Tradition* for a collection of essays on the theme of the revival of and creation of "tradition."

20. Not all fundamentalist leaders are male, of course, and in general they present a range of views on women's possible opportunities

and role. For a detailed account, see Hoffman-Ladd, "Polemics on the Modesty and Segregation of Women in Contemporary Egypt," Hoffman, "An Islamic Activist." Also see Zuhur, "Image Formation and Flexibility."

21. Ibid. p. 23.

22. De Certeau, "On the Oppositional Practices of Everyday Life," p. 41.

23. De Certeau, *The Practice of Everyday Life*, pp. 29–42.

24. Ibid. p. xvii.

25. Ibid. p. 106.

26. Ibid. p. xix.

27. Ibid., p. 37.

28. Janeway, *The Powers of the Weak*, especially pp. 157–233.

29. Havel, *The Power of the Powerless*, especially pp. 23–96.

30. Scott, *Weapons of the Weak*.

31. Berman, *All That Is Solid Melts into Air*, especially pp. 219–228.

32. Ibid., p. 193.

33. Ibid., p. 226.

34. Dostoyevsky, from the *Notes from the Underground*, quoted in Berman, *All That Is Solid Melts into Air*, p. 226.

35. De Certeau, *The Practice of Everyday Life*, p. xix.

36. De Certeau, *The Practice of Everyday Life.* p. xix.

37. For example, see Cloward and Piven, "Hidden Protest," for the argument that women tend to pursue individual, self-destructive, deviant behavior, or simply endure oppression, rather than actively protest.

38. Gramsci, *Selections from the Prison Notebooks*. For an argument for this view of Gramsci's hegemony, and the struggle to create a new hegemony, see Mouffe, "Hegemony and Ideology in Gramsci," in Mouffe, *Gramsci and Marxist Theory*, especially pp. 185–198. See also the discussion of antagonisms and hegemony in chapter 3 of LaClau and Mouffe, *Hegemony and Socialist Strategy*, pp. 93–148.

39. See Gramsci's reflections on the modern Prince in *Selections from the Prison Notebooks*, pp. 125–205.

40. Gramsci, *Selections from the Prison Notebooks*, especially pp. 326–27, and 333. See also the discussion in Femia, "Hegemony and Consciousness."

41. "Backstage" is Goffman's term from his work on the political implications of backstage behavior and relations in public. See *Relations in Public*. Also see the article by Newby, "The Deferential Dialectic."

42. On "backstage behavior," see Goffman, *The Presentation of Self in Everyday Life*, especially pp. 106–140. On the myth of male dominance, see Rogers, "Female Forms of Power and the Myth of Male Dominance."

43. Unfortunately, feminist groups in Cairo, like similar organizations in the West, do little to meet the needs of women at this socio-economic level, focusing instead on the problems of upper and upper-middle-class professional women. Lower-middle-class women are not isolated from each other, but their meetings with other women have no organized programs linked to feminist goals. Thus, there is no organizational outlet to increase women's sense of ability to alter the foundation of social relations.

BIBLIOGRAPHY

Abadan-Unat, Nermin. *Women in Turkish Society.* Leiden: E. J. Brill, 1981.

Abaza, Mona. "The Changing Image of Women in Rural Egypt." *Cairo Papers in Social Science* (1987) 10:3.

Abd al-Fadil, Mahmoud. *The Political Economy of Nasserism: A Study in Employment and Income Distribution Policies in Urban Egypt, 1952–1972.* New York: Cambridge University Press, 1980.

Abd al-Khalek, Gouda and Robert Tignor. *The Political Economy of Income Distribution in Egypt.* New York: Holmes and Meier, 1982.

Abdalla, Ahmed. *The Student Movement and National Politics in Egypt.* London: Saqi Books, 1985.

Abd al-Rahman, Awatif, Elma Lititia Anani, and Alkaly Miriama Kheitu. "Women and the Mass Media in Africa: Case Studies from Sierra Leone, the Niger and Egypt." United Nations Economic Commission for Africa, 1981.

Abdel Kader, Soha. "The Image of Women in Drama and Women's Programs on Egyptian T.V." Ph.D dissertation, Cairo University, 1982.

Abercrombie, Nicholas, Stephan Hill, and Bryan Turner, eds. *The Dominant Ideology Thesis.* London: Allen and Unwin, 1980.

Abu-Lughod, Janet and Lucy Amin. "Egyptian Marriage Advertisements: Microcosm of a Changing Society." *Marriage and Family Living* (1961), 23(2):127–137.

Abu-Lughod, Janet. *Cairo: 1001 Years of the City Victorious*. Princeton: Princeton University Press, 1971.

Abu-Lughod, Janet. "Migrant Adjustment to City Life: The Egyptian Case." In George Gmelch and Walter Zenner, eds., *Urban Life: Readings in Urban Anthropology*, pp. 71–90. New York: St. Martin's Press, 1980.

Abu-Lughod, Lila. *Veiled Sentiments*. Berkeley: University of California Press, 1986.

Abu-Lughod, Lila. "The Romance of Resistance: Tracing the Transformations of Power through Bedouin Women," *American Ethnologist* (1990), 17(1):41–56.

Afshar, Haleh. "Muslim Women and the Burden of Ideology." *Women's Studies International Forum* (1984), 7(4): 247–250.

Afshar, Haleh. "The Legal, Social, and Political Position of Women in Iran." *International Journal of the Sociology of Law* (1985), 13:47–60.

Ahmed, Leila. "Western Ethnocentrism and Perceptions of the Harem." *Feminist Studies* (1982), 8(3):521–34.

Ahmed, Leila. "Early Feminist Movements in Turkey and Egypt." In Freda Hussain, ed., *Muslim Women*, pp. 111–126, New York: St. Martin's Press, 1984.

al-Ahram.

Al-Ahram al-Iqtisadi

al-Akhbar.

Alloula, Malek. *The Colonial Harem*. Minneapolis: University of Minnesota Press, 1986.

Althusser, Louis. "Ideology and Ideological State Apparatuses." In *Lenin and Philosophy*, pp. 127–186, New York: Monthly Review Press, 1971.

Althusser, Louis. *For Marx*. London: New Left Books, 1977.

Altman, Israel. "Islamic Movements in Egypt." *The Jerusalem Quarterly* (1979), 10:87–105.

Altorki, Soraya. *Women in Saudi Arabia: Ideology and Behavior Among the Elite*. New York: Columbia University Press, 1986.

Altorki, Soraya and Camillia Fawzi El-Solh, eds. *Arab Women in the Field: Studying Your Own Society*. Syracuse, New York: Syracuse University Press, 1988.

Ansari, Hamied. *Egypt: The Stalled Society*. Albany: State University of New York Press, 1986.

Antoun, Richard. "On the Modesty of Women in Arab Muslim Villages: A Study in the Accommodation of Traditions." *American Anthropologist* (1968), 70(4):671–698.

Apter, David. *The Politics of Modernization*. Chicago: University of Chicago Press: 1965.

Apter, David. *Rethinking Development*. Beverly Hills: Sage, 1987.

Arafa, Bahiga. *The Social Activities of the Egyptian Feminist Union*. Cairo: Elias Modern Press, 1954.

Ardener, Shirley, ed. *Perceiving Women*. New York: John Wiley, 1975.

Aswad, Barbara. "Key and Peripheral Roles of Noble Women in a Middle East Plains Village." *Anthropological Quarterly* (1967), 40(3):139–152.

Atiya, Nayra. *Khul-Khaal: Five Egyptian Women Tell Their Stories*. Syracuse, New York: Syracuse University Press, 1982.

Aulas, Marie-Christine. "Sadat's Egypt: A Balance Sheet." *MERIP Reports* (1982), 107:6–18.

Ayubi, Nazik. "The Political Revival of Islam: The Case of Egypt." *International Journal of Middle East Studies* (1980), 12:481–499.

Azari, Farah, ed. *Women of Iran: The Conflict with Fundamentalist Islam*. London: Ithaca Press, 1983.

Badran, Margot. "Dual Liberation: Feminism and Nationalism in Egypt, 1870s-1925." *Feminist Issues* (1988), 8(1):15–34.

Baker, Raymond. *Egypt's Uncertain Revolution Under Nasser and Sadat*. Cambridge: Harvard University Press, 1978.

Baron, Beth. "Unveiling in Early Twentieth-Century Egypt: Practical and Symbolic Considerations." *Middle Eastern Studies* (1989), 25(3):370–386.

Bauer, Janet. "Sexuality and the Moral 'Construction' of Women in an Islamic Society." *Anthropological Quarterly* (1985), 58(3):120–130.

Beck, Lois and Nikki Keddie, eds. *Women in the Muslim World*. Cambridge: Harvard University Press, 1978.

Beck, Lois. "The Religious Lives of Muslim Women." In Jane I. Smith, ed., *Women in Contemporary Muslim Societies*, pp. 27–57. Lewisburg: Bucknell University Press, 1980.

Beechey, Veronica. *Unequal Work*. London: Verso, 1987.

Beneria, Lourdes and Martha Roldan. *The Crossroads of Class and Gender: Industrial Homework, Subcontracting and Household Dynamics in Mexico City*. Chicago: University of Chicago Press, 1987.

Berger, Peter and Thomas Luckmann. *The Social Construction of Reality*. New York: Anchor Books, 1967.

Berman, Marshall. *The Politics of Authenticity*. New York: Atheneum, 1980.

Berman, Marshall. *All That Is Solid Melts into Air*. New York: Penguin Books, 1988.

Betteridge, Anne. "To Veil or not to Veil: A Matter of Protest or Policy." In Guity Nashat, ed., *Women and Revolution in Iran*, pp. 109–129, Boulder, Colorado: Westview, 1983.

Bianchi, Robert. *Unruly Corporatism: Associational Life in Twentieth-Century Egypt*. New York: Oxford University Press, 1989.

189

Boserup, Ester. *Women's Role in Economic Development.* London: Allen and Unwin, 1970.

Bossen, Laurel. "Women in Modernizing Societies." *American Ethnologist* (1975), 2(4):587–602.

Boudon, Raymond. *The Unintended Consequences of Social Action.* London: MacMillan, 1982.

Bourdieu, Pierre. *The Algerians.* Boston: Beacon, 1962.

Bourdieu, Pierre. *Outline of a Theory of Practice.* New York: Cambridge University Press, 1977.

Bourdieu, Pierre, and Jean-Claude Passeron. *Reproduction in Education, Society and Culture.* London: Sage, 1977.

Bourdieu, Pierre. "The Disenchantment of the World," In *Algeria 1960,* pp. 1–94. New York: Cambridge University Press, 1979.

Bourdieu, Pierre. *Distinction: A Social Critique of the Judgement of Taste.* Cambridge: Harvard University Press, 1984.

Bourque, Susan and Donna Divine. *Women Living Change.* Philadelphia: Temple University Press, 1985.

Cardoso, F. H. and Enzo Faletto. *Dependency and Development in Latin America.* Berkeley: University of California Press, 1979.

Clifford, James and George Marcus, eds. *Writing Culture: the Poetics and Politics of Ethnography.* Berkeley: University of California Press, 986.

Cloward, Richard and Frances Fox Piven. "Hidden Protest: the Channeling of Female Innovation and Resistance." *Signs* (1979); 4(4):651–669.

Cole, Juan. "Feminism, Class, and Islam in Turn of the Century Egypt." *International Journal of Middle East Studies* (1981), 13:387–407.

Connerton, Paul. *How Societies Remember.* New York: Cambridge University Press, 1989.

Davis, Susan. *Patience and Power: Women's Lives in a Moroccan Village.* Cambridge: Schenkman.

De Certeau, Michel. "Actions culturelles et strategie politique: sortir du cercle." *Revue Nouvelle* (1974), 351–360.

de Certeau, Michel. "On the Oppositional Practices of Everyday Life." *Social Text* (1980), 3:3–43.

de Certeau, Michel. *The Practice of Everyday Life.* Berkeley: University of California Press, 1984.

Dekmejian, R. Hrair. *Islam in Revolution.* Syracuse, New York: Syracuse University Press, 1985.

Dessouki, Ali E. Hilal. *Islamic Resurgence in the Arab World.* New York: Praeger, 1982.

al-Din, Amr Mohie. "Income Distribution and Basic Needs in Urban Egypt." *Cairo Papers in the Social Sciences* (1982), 5(3).

Dreyfus, Hubert and Paul Rabinow. *Michel Foucault: Beyond Structuralism and Hermeneutics.* Chicago: University of Chicago Press, 1982.

Dwyer, Daisy. *Images and Self Images: Male and Female in Morocco.* New York: Columbia University Press, 1978.

Eckstein, Susan, ed. *Power and Popular Protest: Latin American Social Movements.* Berkeley: University of California Press, 1989.

"Egyptian Women: Past, Present and Future." Arab Republic of Egypt: Ministry of Information, 1985.

Elliott, Carolyn. "Theories of Development: An Assessment." *Signs* (1977), 3(1):1–8.

Elson, Diane and Ruth Pearson. "The Latest Phase of the Internationalization of Capital and Its Implications for Women in the Third World." Unpublished Discussion Paper, IDS, University of Sussex, England.

Engels, Frederick. *The Origin of Family, Private Property and the State,* Eleanor Leacock, ed., New York: International Publishers, 1972.

Esposito, John, ed. *Islam and Development.* Syracuse, New York: Syracuse University Press, 1980.

Esposito, John. *Women in Muslim Family Law.* Syracuse, New York: Syracuse University Press, 1982.

Fahmy, Hoda Youssef. "Changing Women in a Changing Society: A Study of Emergent Consciousness of Young Women in the City of Akhmim in Upper Egypt." Unpublished Master's Thesis, American University in Cairo, 1978.

Fakhouri, Hani. *Kafr El-Elow: An Egyptian Village in Transition.* New York: Holt, Rinehart and Winston, 1972.

Fanon, Frantz. *The Wretched of the Earth.* New York: Grove Press, 1963.

Farghali, Fathi. "Characteristics of the Female Labor Force in Cairo and Alexandria in 1976." Unpublished General Diploma Paper, Cairo Demographic Center, 1981.

Farghali, Fathi. "Female Labor Force Participation in Greater Cairo." Cairo Demographic Center Monograph Series 11, 1982 Seminar.

Femia, Joseph. "Hegemony and Consciousness in the Thought of Antonio Gramsci." *Political Studies* (1975), 23(1):29–48.

Ferdows, Adele. "Women and the Islamic Revolution." *International Journal of Middle East Studies* (1983), 15(2):283–298.

Fernea, Elizabeth. *Guests of the Sheik.* New York: Doubleday, 1965.

Fernea, Elizabeth Warnock and Basima Qattan Bezirgan, eds. *Middle Eastern Muslim Women Speak.* Austin: University of Texas Press, 1977.

Fernea, Elizabeth and Robert Fernea. "A Look Behind the Veil." *Human Nature* (1979), 2:68–77.

Fernea, Elizabeth and Marilyn Gaunt. "A Veiled Revolution." Film, 1982.

Fernea, Elizabeth and Marilyn Gaunt. "The Price of Change." Film, 1982.

Fernea, Elizabeth Warnock, ed. *Women and the Family in the Middle East: New Voices of Change.* Austin: University of Texas Press, 1985.

191

Firth, Raymond. *Symbols: Public and Private.* Ithaca: Cornell University Press, 1973.

Fischer, Michael. "In Defense of Ayesha: women in Iran." *New Society* (1978), 44:537–538.

Flores, Alexander. "Egypt: A New Secularism?" *Middle East Report* (1988), 153:27–30.

Foucault, Michel. *Power/Knowledge.* New York: Pantheon, 1972.

Foucault, Michel. *The History of Sexuality.* New York: Vintage, 1980.

Foucault, Michel. "The Ethic of Care for the Self as a Practice of Freedom." In James Bernauer and David Rasmussen, eds., *The Final Foucault*, pp. 1–20, Cambridge: MIT Press, 1987.

Gaventa, John. *Power and Powerlessness: Quiescence and Rebellion in an Appalachian Valley.* Chicago: University of Illinois Press, 1980.

Geertz, Clifford. "Ideology as a Cultural System," In *The Interpretation of Cultures*, pp. 193–234, New York: Basic Books, 1973.

Geertz, Clifford. *Works and Lives: the Anthropologist as Author.* Stanford, California: Stanford University Press, 1988.

Geertz, Clifford. "Toutes Directions: Reading the Signs in an Urban Sprawl." *International Journal of Middle East Studies* (1989), 21:291–306.

Genovese, Eugene. *Roll, Jordan, Roll: The World the Slaves Made.* New York: Vintage, 1976.

Ghoussoub, Mai. "Feminism—or the Eternal Masculine—in the Arab World." *New Left Review* (1987), 161:3–19.

Giddens, Anthony. *Central Problems in Social Theory: Action, Structure and Contradiction in Social Analysis.* Berkeley: University of California Press, 1979.

Gilligan, Carol. *In a Different Voice.* Cambridge: Harvard University Press, 1982.

Goffman, Erving. *The Presentation of Self in Everyday Life.* New York: Anchor, 1959.

Goffman, Erving. *Interaction Ritual.* New York: Anchor, 1967.

Goffman, Erving. *Relations in Public.* New York: Harper Colophon Books, 1971.

Goldschmidt, Arthur. *Modern Egypt: the Formation of a Nation-State.* Boulder, Colorado: Westview, 1988.

Gordon, David. *Women of Algeria: An Essay on Change.* Cambridge: Harvard University Press, 1968.

Graham-Brown, Sarah. *Images of Women.* New York: Columbia University Press, 1988.

Gramsci, Antonio. *Selections from the Prison Notebooks.* Quinton Hoare and Geoffrey Nowell Smith, eds. New York: International Publishers, 1971.

Gramsci, Antonio. *Selections from Cultural Writings.* David Forgacs and

Geoffrey Nowell-Smith. eds. Cambridge: Harvard University Press, 1985.

Gramsci, Antonio. *An Antonio Gramsci Reader.* David Forgacs, ed. New York: Schocken Books, 1988.

Gran, Judith. "Impact of the World Market on Egyptian Women." *MERIP* (1977), 58:3–7.

El Guindi, Fadwa. "Veiling Infitah with Muslim Ethic: Egypt's Contemporary Islamic Movement." *Social Problems* (1981), 28(4):465–487.

El Guindi, Fadwa. "Is There An Islamic Alternative? the Case of Egypt's Contemporary Islamic Movement." *International Insight* (1981), 1(6):19–25.

El Guindi, Fadwa. "The Emerging Islamic Order: The Case of Egypt's Contemporary Islamic Movement." *Journal of Arab Affairs* (1982), 1(2):245–263.

El Guindi, Fadwa. "Veiled Activism: Egyptian Women in the Contemporary Islamic Movement." *Femmmes de la Mediterranee, Peuples Mediteraneens* (1983), 22,23:79–89.

El Guindi, Fadwa. "The Mood in Egypt: Summer Heat or Revolution in the Air?" *Middle East Insight* (1986), 4:30–39.

Halpern, Manfred. *The Politics of Social Change in the Middle East and North Africa.* Princeton: Princeton University Press, 1963.

Hamman, Mona. "Egypt's Working Women: Textile Workers of Chubra el-Kheima," *MERIP Reports* (1979), 82: 3–7.

Hammam, Mona. "Women and Industrial Work in Egypt: The Chubra el-Kheima Case." *Arabic Studies Quarterly* (1980), 2(1):50–69.

Hatem, Mervat. "The Politics of Sexuality and Gender In Segregated Patriarchal Systems: The Case of Eighteenth- and Nineteenth-Century Egypt." *Feminist Studies* (1986), 12(2):251–274.

Hatem, Mervat. "The Alliance Between Nationalism and Patriarchy in Muslim Personal Status Laws: The Case of Modern Egypt." *Feminist Issues* (1986), 6(1):19–43.

Hatem, Mervat. "Egypt's Middle Class in Crisis: the Sexual Division of Labor." *Middle East Journal* (1988), 42(3):407–422.

Havel, Vaclav. *The Power of the Powerless.* Armonk, New York: M.E. Sharpe, 1985.

Hawwa'.

Hibbon, Sally, ed. *Politics, Ideology and the State.* London: Lawrence and Wishart, 1978.

Hijab, Nadia. *Womanpower: The Arab Debate on Women at Work.* New York: Cambridge University Press, 1988.

Hinnebusch, Raymond. *Egyptian Politics Under Sadat.* New York: Cambridge University Press, 1985.

Hobsbawm, Eric and Terence Ranger, eds. *The Invention of Tradition.* New York: Cambridge University Press, 1983.

193

Hoffman, John. *The Gramscian Challenge: Coercion and Consent in Marxist Political Theory.* New York: Basil Blackwell, 1984.

Hoffman, Valerie. "An Islamic Activist: Zaynab al-Ghazali." In Elizabeth Fernea, ed., *Women and the Family in the Middle East*, pp. 233–255, Austin: University of Texas Press, 1985.

Hoffman-Ladd, Valerie. "Polemics on the Modesty and Segregation of Women in Contemporary Egypt." *International Journal of Middle East Studies* (1987), 19(1):23–50.

Hoodfar, Homa. "Survival Strategies in Low-Income Neighborhoods of Cairo, Egypt." Ph.D dissertation, University of Kent, 1988.

Hoodfar, Homa. "Patterns of Household Budgeting and Financial Management in a Lower-Income Cairo Neighborhood." In Daisy Dwyer and Judith Bruce, eds., *A Home Divided*, pp.120–143. Stanford, California: Stanford University Press, 1988.

Hoodfar, Homa. "Return to the Veil: Personal Strategy to 'Public' Participation in Egypt." Unpublished paper, 1989.

Hopwood, Derek. *Egypt: Politics and Society, 1945–84.* London: Allen and Unwin, 1985.

Howard-Merriam, Kathleen. "Women, Education and the Professions in Egypt." *Comparative Education Review* (1979), 23:256–270.

Hussain, Freda, ed. *Muslim Women.* New York: St. Martin's Press, 1984.

Hussein, Mahmoud. *Class Conflict in Egypt.* New York: Monthly Review Press, 1973.

Ibrahim, Barbara. "Social Change and the Industrial Experience: Women as Production Workers in Urban Egypt." Ph.D dissertation, Indiana University, 1980.

Ibrahim, Saad Eddin and Nicholas Hopkins, eds. *Arab Society in Transition.* Cairo: American University in Cairo Press, 1977.

Ibrahim, Saad Eddin. "Anatomy of Egypt's Militant Islamic Groups." *International Journal of Middle East Studies* (1980), 124):423–453.

Ibrahim, Saad Eddin. "An Islamic Alternative in Egypt: The Muslim Brotherhood and Sadat." *Arab Studies Quarterly* (1982), 4(1,2):75–93.

Ibrahim, Saad Eddin. "Arab Social Change: Six Profiles." *Jerusalem Quarterly* (1982), 23:13–24.

Ibrahim, Saad Eddin. "Social Mobility and Income Distribution in Egypt, 1952–1977." In Gouda Abdel Khalek and Robert Tignor, eds., *The Political Economy of Income Distribution in Egypt*, pp.375–434. New York: Holmes and Meier, 1982.

Ibrahim, Saad Eddin. "Egypt's Islamic Activism in the 1980s." *Third World Quarterly* (April 1988), 10(2): 632–657.

Janeway, Elizabeth. *Powers of the Weak.* New York: Knopf, 1980.

Jenson, Jane, Elisabeth Hagen and Ceallaigh Reddy, eds. *Feminization of the Labor Force.* New York: Oxford University Press, 1988.

Joseph, Suad. "Working-Class Women's Networks in a Sectarian State: A Political Paradox." *American Ethnologist* (1983), 10(1):1–22.

Joseph, Suad. "Women and Politics in the Middle East." *Middle East Report* (1986), 138:3–9.

Kagitcibasi, Cigdem, ed. *Sex Roles, Family and Community in Turkey.* Bloomington, Indiana: Indiana University Turkish Studies, 1982.

Kamphoefner, K.R. " 'What's the Use!' The Household, Low-Income Women, and Literacy." Unpublished Paper, 1988.

Khafagy, Fatma. "Women and Labor Migration." *MERIP Reports* (1984), 124:17–21.

Kishwar, Madhu and Ruth Vanita. "India: Widow Burning Revived." *Off Our Backs* (1988), 18(12–13).

Khalaf, Samir. *Lebanon's Predicament.* New York: Columbia University Press, 1987.

Knauss, Peter. *The Persistence of Patriarchy.* New York: Praeger, 1987.

LaClau, Ernesto and Chantal Mouffe. *Hegemony and Socialist Strategy: Towards a Radical Democratic Politics.* London: Verso, 1985.

Lerner, Daniel. *The Passing of Traditional Society: Modernizing the Middle East.* New York: Free Press, 1958.

Lewis, I. M. *Ecstatic Religion.* Baltimore: Penguin Books, 1971.

Loza, Sarah. "Work and Family in Egypt." Unpublished Paper. Cairo: April, 1988.

Mabro, Robert and Samir Radwan. *The Industrialization of Egypt: 1939–1973.* London: Clarendon, 1976.

MacLeod, Arlene Elowe. "Accommodating Protest: Working Women and the New Veiling in Cairo," Ph.D Dissertation, Yale University, 1987.

Maher, Vanessa. *Women and Property in Morocco.* Cambridge: Cambridge University Press, 1974.

Makhlouf, Carla. *Changing Veils: Women and Modernization in North Yemen.* Austin: University of Texas Press, 1979.

Mann, Michael. *Consciousness and Action Among the Western Working Class.* New York: MacMillan, 1973.

Margolis, Diane. "Considering Women's Experience: A Reformulation of Power Theory." *Theory and Society* (1989), 18:387–416.

Margulies, Ronnie and Ergin Yildizoglu. "The Political Uses of Islam in Turkey." *Middle East Report* (1988), 153:12–17.

Marshall, Susan and Randall Stokes. "Tradition and the Veil: Female Status in Tunisia and Algeria." *Journal of Modern African Studies* 9(1981), 19(4): 625–647.

Marshall, Susan. "Paradoxes of Change: Culture Crisis, Islamic Revival, and the Reactivation of Patriarchy." *Journal of Asian and African Studies* (1984), 19(1 and 2):1–17.

Marsot, Afaf Lutfi al-Sayyid. "The Revolutionary Gentlewomen in Egypt." In Lois Beck and Nikki Keddie, eds., *Women in the Muslim World*, pp. 261–277, Cambridge: Harvard University Press, 1978.

Marsot, Afaf Lutfi al-Sayyid. "Religion or Opposition? Urban Protest Movements in Egypt." *International Journal of Middle East Studies* (1984), 16:541–552.

Marsot, Afaf Lutfi al-Sayyid. *A Short History of Modern Egypt.* New York: Cambridge University Press, 1985.

Marx, Karl. *Capital.* trans. David Fernbach. New York: Vintage, 1981.

Mernissi, Fatima. *Beyond the Veil.* New York: John Wiley, 1975.

Mernissi, Fatima. "Women, Saints and Sanctuaries." *Signs* (1977), 3(1):101–112.

Mernissi, Fatima. "Zhor's World: A Moroccan Domestic Worker Speaks Out." *Feminist Issues* (1982), 2(1): 3–31.

Mernissi, Fatima. "Women and the Impact of Capitalist Development in Morocco." Parts 1 & 2. *Feminist Issues* (1982), 2(2):69–104, and (1983), 3(1):61–112.

Mernissi, Fatima. *Le Maroc raconte par ses femmes.* Rabat: Societe Marocaine des Editeurs Reunis, 1984.

Mernissi, Fatima, ed. *Femmes partagées: famille-travail.* Casablanca: Editions Le Fennec, 1988.

El-Messiri, Sawsan. *Ibn al-Balad: A Concept of Egyptian Identity.* Leiden: E. J. Brill, 1978.

El-Messiri, Sawsan. "Self-Images of Traditional Urban Women in Cairo." In Lois Beck and Nikki Keddie, eds., *Women in the Muslim World*, pp. 522–540, Cambridge: Harvard University Press, 1978.

Migdal, Joel. *Strong Societies and Weak States: State Society Relations and State Capabilities in the Third World.* Princeton: Princeton University Press, 1988.

Mikhail, Mona. *Images of Arab Women.* Washington, D.C.: Three Continents Press, 1979.

Minai, Naila. *Women in Islam.* New York: Seaview Books, 1981.

Minces, Juliette. *The House of Obedience.* London: Zed Press, 1982.

Mohsen, Safia. "The Egyptian Woman: Between Modernity and Tradition." In Carolyn Mathiasson, ed., *Many Sisters*, pp. 37–58. New York: Free Press, 1974.

Mohsen, Safia. "New Images, Old Reflections: Working Middle Class Women in Egypt." In Elizabeth Fernea, ed. *Women and the Family in the Middle East*, pp. 56–71. Austin: University of Texas Press, 1985.

Molyneux, Maxine. "Mobilization Without Emancipation: Women's Interests, the State and Revolution in Nicaragua." *Feminist Studies* (1985), 11(2):227–254.

Moore, Barrington, Jr. *Social Origins of Dictatorship and Democracy.* Boston: Beacon Press, 1966.

Moore, Barrington, Jr. *Injustice: The Social Bases of Obediance and Revolt.* White Plains, New York: M.E. Sharpe, 1978.

Morsy, Soheir. "Sex Differences and Folk Illness in an Egyptian Village." In Lois Beck and Nikki Keddie, eds., *Women in the Muslim World,* pp. 599–617. Cambridge: Harvard University Press, 1978.

Mouffe, Chantal, ed. *Gramsci and Marxist Theory.* Boston: Routledge and Kegan Paul, 1979.

Murphy, Robert. "Social Distance and the Veil." In Louise Sweet, ed., *Peoples and Cultures of the Middle East,* pp. 290–315. New York: Natural History Press, 1970.

Musallam, B. F. *Sex and Society in Islam: Birth Control Before the Nineteenth Century.* New York: Cambridge University Press, 1983.

Nadim, Nawal. "Family Relationships in a Harah in Cairo." In Saad Eddin Ibrahim and Nicholas Hopkins, eds., *Arab Society in Transition,* pp. 107–20. Cairo: American University in Cairo Press, 1977.

Nashat, Guity, ed. *Women and Revolution in Iran.* Boulder, Colorado: Westview, 1983.

Nelson, Cynthia. "Changing Roles of Men and Women: Illustrations from Egypt." *Anthropological Quarterly* (1968) 41(2):57–78.

Nelson, Cynthia. "Public and Private Politics: Women in the Middle Eastern World." *American Ethnologist* (1974), 1(3):551–563.

Newby, Howard. "The Deferential Dialectic." *Comparative Studies in Society and History* (1975), 17(2):139–164.

Al-Nowaihi, Mohammed. "Changing the Law on Personal Status in Egypt Within a Liberal Interpretation of the Shari'a." *Middle East Review* (1979), 9(4):40–49.

Ortner, Sherry and Harriet Whitehead, eds. *Sexual Meanings.* New York: Cambridge University Press, 1981.

Orwell, George. *The Road to Wigan Pier.* London: Left Book Club, 1937.

Palmer, Monte, Ali Leila, and El Sayed Yassin. *The Egyptian Bureaucracy.* Syracuse, New York: Syracuse University Press, 1988.

Papanek, Hannah. "Purdah: Separate Worlds and Symbolic Shelter." *Comparative Studies in Society and History* (1973), 15(3):289–325.

Papanek, Hannah. "Class and Gender in Education-Employment Linkages." *Comparative Education Review* 29 (1985): 317–346.

Parkin, Frank. *Class Inequality and Political Order.* New York: Praeger, 1971.

Pastner, Carroll McC. "A Social, Structural and Historical Analysis of Honor, Shame and Purdah." *Anthropological Quarterly* (1972), 45(4):248–262.

Pellow, Deborah. *Women in Accra: Options for Autonomy.* Algonac, Michigan: Reference Publications, 1977.

Peristiany, J. G. *Honor and Shame: The Values of Mediterranean Society.* Chicago: University of Chicago Press, 1966.

197

Perlman, Janice. "Rio's Favelas and the Myth of Marginality." *Politics and Society* (1975), 5(2): 131–161.

Perlmutter, Amos. "Egypt and the Myth of the New Middle Class: A Comparative Analysis." *Comparative Studies in Society and History* (1967), 10(2):46–65.

Phillipp, Thomas. "Feminism and Nationalist Politics in Egypt." In Lois Beck and Nikki Keddie, eds. *Women in the Muslim World*, pp. 277–294. Cambridge: Harvard University Press, 1978.

Piven, Frances Fox. "The Social Structuring of Political Protest." *Politics and Society* (1976), 6:297–326.

Piven, Frances Fox, and Richard Cloward. *Poor People's Movements: Why They Succeed, How They Fail.* New York: Vintage, 1977.

Piven, Frances Fox. "Women and the State: Ideology, Power, and the Welfare State." In Alice Rossi, ed., *Gender and the Life Course*, pp. 265–287. New York: Aldine, 1985.

Pomeroy, Sarah. *Women in Hellenistic Egypt.* New York: Schocken Books, 1984.

Rabinow, Paul. *Symbolic Domination.* Chicago: University of Chicago Press, 1975.

Rabinow, Paul and William Sullivan. *Interpretive Social Science: A Reader.* Berkeley: University of California Press, 1979.

Ramazani, Nesta. "The Veil—Piety or Protest?" *Journal of South Asian and Middle Eastern Studies* (1983), 7(2):20–36.

Ricoeur, Paul. "The Model of the Text: Meaningful Action Considered as a Text." *Social Research* (1971), 38: 529–562.

Ridd, Rosemary and Helen Callaway, eds. *Women and Conflict: Portraits of Struggle in Times of Crisis.* New York: New York University Press, 1987.

Rogers, Susan Carol. "Female Forms of Power and the Myth of Male Dominance: A Model of Male/Female Interaction in Peasant Society." *American Ethnologist* (1975): 2(4):727–756.

Rosaldo, Michelle Zimbalist and Louise Lamphere, eds. *Woman, Culture and Society.* Stanford, California: Stanford University Press, 1974.

Rosen, Lawrence. *Bargaining for Reality: The Construction of Social Relations in a Muslim Community.* Chicago: University of Chicago Press, 1984.

Rousseau, Jean-Jacques. *The First and Second Discourses.* Roger Masters, ed., New York: St. Martin's Press, 1964.

Rugh, Andrea. "Coping with Poverty in a Cairo Community." *Cairo Papers in the Social Sciences* (1979), 2(1).

Rugh, Andrea. *Family in Contemporary Egypt.* Syracuse, New York: Syracuse University Press, 1984.

Rugh, Andrea. "Women and Work: Strategies and Choices In a Lower-Class Quarter of Cairo." In Elizabeth Fernea, ed., *Women and the*

Family in the Middle East, pp. 273–289. Austin: University of Texas Press, 1985.

Rugh, Andrea. *Reveal and Conceal: Dress in Contemporary Egypt.* Syracuse, New York: Syracuse University Press, 1986.

Ruz al-Yusif.

al-Saadawi, Nawal. *The Hidden Face of Eve.* Boston: Beacon Press, 1980.

Sabbah, Fatna A. *Woman in the Muslim Unconscious.* Mary Jo Lakeland, trans., Elmsford, New York: Pergamon Press, 1984.

Said, Edward. *Orientalism.* New York: Pantheon, 1978.

Saifullah-Khan, Verity. "Purdah in the British Situation." In Diana Leonard Barker and Sheila Allen, eds., *Dependence and Exploitation in Work and Marriage.* New York: Longman, 1976.

Sallach, David L. "Class Domination and Ideological Hegemony." *Sociological Quarterly* (1974), 15(1):38–51.

Sallam, Azza Mohamed Ahmed. "The Return to the Veil Among Undergraduate Females at Minya University, Egypt." Ph.D dissertation, Perdue University, 1980.

Sargent, Lydia, ed. *Women and Revolution.* Boston: South End Press, 1981.

Sassoon, Anne Showstack, ed. *Approaches to Gramsci.* London: Writers and Readers, 1982.

Schneider, Jane. "Of Vigilance and Virgins: Honor, Shame and Access to Resources in Mediterranean Societies." *Ethnology* (1971), 10(1): 1–24.

Scott, James C. *The Moral Economy of the Peasant: Rebellion and Subsistence in Southeast Asia.* New Haven: Yale University Press, 1976.

Scott, James C. "Hegemony and the Peasantry." *Politics and Society* (1977), 7(3):267–296.

Scott, James C. "Protest and Profanation: Agrarian Revolt and the Little Tradition." *Theory and Society* (1977), 4(1 and 2):1–38 and 211–246.

Scott, James C. *Weapons of the Weak: Everyday Forms of Peasant Resistance.* New Haven: Yale University Press, 1985.

Sen, Gita and Caren Grown. *Development, Crises, and Alternative Visions.* New York: Monthly Review Press, 1987.

Shaaban, Bouthaina. *Both Right and Left Handed: Arab Women Talk About Their Lives.* London: The Women's Press, 1988.

Shaarawi, Huda. *Harem Years: Memoirs of an Egyptian Feminist.* Margot Badran, trans. and ed., New York: the Feminist Press, 1987.

Shahin, Zeinab Mohammad. "Conformists, Manipulators and Rebels: Problems of Self-Conception among Women in a Changing Society." Unpublished Master's Thesis, American University in Cairo, 1975.

al-Shamy, Hasan M., ed. *Folktales of Egypt*. Chicago: University of Chicago Press, 1980.

Sharabi, Hisham. *Neopatriarchy: A Theory of Distorted Change in Arab Society*. New York: Oxford University Press, 1988.

Sharma, Ursula. "Women and their Affines: the Veil as a Symbol of Separation." *Man* (1978), 13(2):218–233.

Shils, Edward. *Tradition*. Chicago: University of Chicago Press, 1981.

Shorter, Frederic. "Cairo's Leap Forward: People, Households and Dwelling Space." *Cairo Papers in Social Science*, forthcoming.

Simmel, Georg. *On Women, Sexuality and Love*. Guy Oakes, trans., New Haven: Yale University Press, 1984.

Singerman, Diane. "Avenues of Participation: Family and Politics in Popular Quarters of Cairo." Unpublished paper presented at the annual meeting of the Middle East Studies Association, 1986.

Siu, Helen. *Agents and Victims in South China*. New Haven: Yale University Press, 1989.

Smith, Jane, ed. *Women in Contemporary Muslim Societies*. Lewisburg, Pennsylvania: Bucknell University Press, 1980.

Smith, Jane and Yvonne Haddad. "Eve: Islamic Image of Woman." *Women's Studies International Forum* (1982), 5(2):135–144.

Smock, Audrey and Nadia Youssef. "Egypt." In Janet Giele and Audrey Smock, eds., *Women: Roles and Status in Eight Countries*, pp. 35–79. New York: John Wiley, 1977.

al-Sokkari, Myrette Ahmed. "Basic Needs, Inflation and the Poor in Egypt." *Cairo Papers in the Social Sciences* (1984), 7(2).

Springborg, Robert. *Mubarak's Egypt: Fragmentation of the Political Order*. Boulder, Colorado: Westview, 1989.

Stino, Laila. "The Working Wife: Attitudes, Perceptions and Role Expectations of Five Male Cairenes." Unpublished Master's Thesis, American University in Cairo, 1976.

Stowasser, Barbara. "The Status of Women in Early Islam." In Freda Hussain, ed., *Muslim Women*, pp. 11–43. New York: St. Martin's Press, 1984.

Suleiman, Michael. "Changing Attitudes Toward Women in Egypt: the Role of Fiction in Women's Magazines." *Middle Eastern Studies* (1978), 14(3):352–371.

Sullivan, Earl. "Women and Work in Egypt." *Cairo Papers in Social Science* (1981), 4(4).

Sullivan, Earl. *Women in Egyptian Public Life*. Syracuse, New York: Syracuse University Press, 1986.

Tabari, Azar. "The Enigma of the Veiled Iranian Woman." *MERIP Reports* (1982), 103:22–27.

Taher, Nadia Adel. "Social Identity and Class in a Cairo Neighborhood." *Cairo Papers in Social Science* (1986), 9(4).

Taylor, Elizabeth. "Egyptian Migration and Peasant Wives." *MERIP Reports* (1984), 124:3–10.

Thompson, E. P. *The Making of the English Working Class.* New York: Vintage, 1966.

Thompson, E. P. *The Poverty of Theory and other Essays.* New York: Monthly Review Press, 1978.

Thompson, John B. *Studies in the Theory of Ideology.* Cambridge: Polity Press, 1984.

Tillion, Germaine. *Le harem et les cousins.* Paris: Editions du Seuil, 1966.

Toubia, Nahid, ed. *Women of the Arab World.* New Jersey: Zed Press, 1988.

Tripp, Charles and Roger Owen, eds. *Egypt Under Mubarak.* New York: Routledge, 1989.

Tucker, Judith. "Egyptian Women in the Workforce: A Historical Survey." *MERIP Reports* (1976), 50: 3–9.

Tucker, Judith. *Women in Nineteenth Century Egypt.* New York: Cambridge University Press, 1985.

Tucker, Judith. "Insurrectionary Women: Women and the State in 19th Century Egypt." *Middle East Report* (1986), 138:9–14.

Tucker, Judith and Joe Stork. "In the Footsteps of Sadat," *MERIP Reports* (1982), 107:3–6.

Utas, Bo, ed. *Women in Islamic Societies.* New York: Olive Branch Press, 1983.

Wajcman, Judy. *Women in Control: Dilemmas of a Workers' Co-operative.* Milton Keynes: Open University Press, 1983.

Walby, Sylvia. *Patriarchy at Work.* Minneapolis: University of Minnesota Press, 1986.

Wallerstein, Immanuel. *The Modern World System.* New York: Academic Press, 1974, 1980.

Waltz, Susan. "Another View of Feminine Networks: Tunisian Women and the Development of Political Efficacy." *International Journal of Middle East Studies* (1990), 22(1): 21–36.

Waterbury, John. *Egypt: Burdens of the Past, Options for the Future.* Hanover, New Hampshire: American Universities Field Staff, 1976.

Waterbury, John. *The Egypt of Nasser and Sadat: The Political Economy of Two Regimes.* Princeton: Princeton University Press, 1983.

Waterbury, John. "The 'Soft State' and the Open Door: Egypt's Experience with Economic Liberalization, 1974–1984." *Comparative Politics* (1985), 18(1):65–85.

Webster, Sheila. "Harim and Hijab: Seclusive and Exclusive Aspects of Traditional Muslim Dwelling and Dress." *Women's Studies International Forum* (1984),7(4):251–257.

Wikan, Unni. *Life Among the Poor in Cairo.* London: Tavistock, 1980.

Wikan, Unni. *Behind the Veil in Arabia*. Baltimore: Johns Hopkins University Press, 1982.

Wikan, Unni. "Living Conditions among Cairo's Poor—a View from Below." *Middle East Journal* (1985) 39(1):7–26.

Williams, John Alden. "A Return to the Veil in Egypt." *Middle East Review* (1979), 11(3):49–54.

Willis, Paul. *Learning to Labour*. Westmead: Saxon House, 1977.

Wilson, Boydena R. "Glimpses of Muslim Urban Women in Classical Islam." In Barbara Harris and JoAnn McNamara, eds., *Women and the Structure of Society*, pp. 5–12. North Carolina: Duke University Press, 1984.

Wright, Erik Olin. *Class, Crisis, and the State*. London: New Left Books, 1978.

Yaganeh, Nahid and Nikki Keddie. "Sexuality and Shi'i Social Protest in Iran." In Juan Cole and Nikki Keddie, eds., *Shi'ism and Social Protest*. New Haven: Yale University Press, 1986.

Young, Kate, Carol Wolkowitz, and Roslyn McCullagh. *Of Marriage and the Market*. London: CSE Books, 1981.

Youssef, Nadia. *Women and Work in Developing Societies*. Berkeley: University of California Press, 1974.

Youssef, Nadia. "Egypt: From Seclusion to Limited Participation." In Janet Zollinger Giele and Audrey Chapman Smock, eds., *Women: Roles and Status in Eight Countries*, pp. 35–79. New York: John Wiley, 1977.

Youssef, Nadia. "A Woman-Specific Strategy Statement: The Case of Egypt." AID Bureau of Program and Policy Coordination Report, Cairo, 1980.

Zaalouk, Malak. *Power, Class and Foreign Capital in Egypt: The Rise of the New Bourgeoisie*. New Jersey: Zed Books, 1989.

Zenie-Ziegler, Wedad. *In Search of Shadows: Conversations with Egyptian Women*. New Jersey: Zed Books, 1988.

Zolberg, Aristede. "Moments of Madness." *Politics and Society* (1972), 2(2):183–209.

Zuhur, Sherifa. "Image Formation and Flexibility: Islamic Oppositionist Views on Women in Egypt." Unpublished Paper presented at the Middle East Studies Association, 1988.

Zurayk, Huda. "Women's Economic Participation." In Frederic Shorter and Huda Zurayk, eds., *Population Factors in Development Planning in the Middle East*, pp.3–58. New York: the Population Council,1985.

Zurayk, Huda. "Dawr al-mar'a fi al-tanmiya al-igtima'iyya al-iqtisadiyya fi al-buldan al-'arabiyya." *Al Mustaqbal al Arabi* (1988), 109:78–113.

INDEX